Isaac Bashevis Singer and the Eternal Past

Isaac Bashevis Singer and the Eternal Past

"One imagines one possesses and in reality one
is possessed. . . ."
———André Gide, *The Immoralist*

Irving H. Buchen

New York • New York University Press
London • University of London Press Limited
1968

Acknowledgments

Quotations from Joel Blocker's and Richard Elman's "Interview with I. B. Singer." Originally published November, 1963, *Commentary*. Reprinted from *Commentary*, by permission; copyright © 1963 by the American Jewish Committee.

Quotations from Emil Fackenheim's "Judaism and the Meaning of Life." Originally published in April, 1965, *Commentary* and reissued in *Quest for Past and Future*, Indiana University Press (1968). Reprinted here with special permission of *Commentary* and Indiana University Press.

Quotations from Michael Fixler's "The Redeemers: Themes in the Fiction of Isaac Bashevis Singer." Originally published in the Spring, 1964, *Kenyon Review*. Copyright © 1964 by Kenyon College. Reprinted by permission of the publisher and author.

Quotations from Cecil Hemley's "Isaac Bashevis Singer" in *Dimensions of Midnight: Poetry and Prose*, copyright 1945 by Cecil Hemley and copyright 1966 by Elaine Gottlieb Hemley. Reprinted here by special permission of Ohio University Press.

Quotations from Abraham Heschel's *Between God and Man*, copyright 1959 by Abraham Heschel. Reprinted here by special permission of Harper and Row.

Quotations from Milton Hindus' "Isaac Bashevis Singer" in *Jewish Heritage Reader*, ed. Morris Adler, copyright 1965 by Milton Hindus. Reprinted here by special permission of Taplinger Publishing Company.

Quotations from Irving Howe's and Eliezer Greenberg's "Introduction" to *A Treasury of Yiddish Stories,* copyright 1954 by Irving Howe and Eliezer Greenberg. Reprinted here by special permission of The Viking Press.

Quotations from Ted Highes's "The Genius of Isaac Bashevis Singer." Reprinted with permission from *The New York Review of Books.* Copyright © 1965 The New York Review.

Quotations from Dan Jacobson's "The Problem of Isaac Bashevis Singer." Originally published in the February, 1965, *Commentary.* Reprinted from *Commentary,* by permission; copyright © 1965 by the American Jewish Committee.

Quotations from Gershon G. Scholem's *Major Trends in Jewish Mysticism,* copyright © 1946, 1954 by Schocken Books, Inc., and from Gershon G. Scholem's *On the Kabballah and Its Symbolism,* copyright © 1965 Schocken Books, Inc. Reprinted here with special permission of Schocken Books, Inc.

Quotations from Leo Schwarz's *Mutations of Jewish Values in Contemporary Fiction.* The B. G. Rudolph Lectures in Judaic Studies, Syracuse University, 1966. Reprinted here with special permission of Syracuse University.

Quotations from Isaac Bashevis Singer's "Introduction" to I. J. Singer's *Yoshe Kalb,* copyright 1966 by Isaac Bashevis Singer. Reprinted here by special permission of Harper and Row.

Quotations from Isaac Bashevis Singer's "Realism and Truth." Reprinted from *Reconstructionist,* Vol. XXVIII, No. 9, June 4, 1965, with permission of the publishers.

Quotations from Isaac Bashevis Singer's "What's In It for Me," copyright © 1965, by Harper's Magazine, Inc. Reprinted here from the October, 1965, issue of Harper's Magazine by permission of the author.

Quotations from the novels and short stories of Isaac Bashevis Singer, various copyrights by Isaac Bashevis Singer. Reprinted here by special permission of Farrar, Straus & Giroux and the author.

for
DAUCHU

Preface

I decided to examine the works of Isaac Bashevis Singer in translation because Isaac Bashevis Singer decided to exist in translation:

> I am very happy about my books being in English. In English my audience is a very real one. . . . I always take the business of being translated very seriously . . . because when I read some of the Yiddish writers in English, especially Sholem Aleichem, I knew how bad translation could be. . . . For years I worked together with the translators of *The Family Moskat*. . . . Since that time I have taken part in the translation of every one of my books. . . . good translation is possible, but it involves hard work for the writer, the translator, and the editor. . . . To me the translation becomes as dear as the original.[1]

All languages, like the people who use them, are unique and often what makes them distinctive is precisely

what cannot be translated. Yiddish, too, has its own linguistic tyrannies.[2] But over and above these special quali-
ties, which after all every language possesses in its own
way, there is the overriding difference—Yiddish being the
language of the diaspora. As such, Yiddish has built into
it the psychology of the ghetto; it is an inside language
meant for insiders. To select a representative example:
when Saul Bellow translated "Gimpel the Fool" he understandably rendered the word "heder" as "school." But
what was lost in translation was not mere coloring or
nuance but a commitment of an exiled people. For a
"heder" was the only school of the ghetto. There, one
studied the Torah, the talmudic and other commentaries
on the Bible, and Jewish history. There an exiled people
prepared itself for the additional and paradoxical burden
of being chosen. For Singer the single word "heder" therefore rapidly binds a way of learning with a way of living.
Gimpel may be a simpleton but he is not an ignoramus;
foolishness may be forgiven but ignorance of Jewish traditions never. Thus, not surprisingly, when Gimpel, who
is familiar with the Talmud, wishes to put forth an independent view, he characteristically anticipates and silences all opposition by striking the verbal pose of
the rabbinic sages and by asking, " 'Where is it written . . . ?' "

But the translations of Singer are special, even official. They are sanctioned because Singer works with the
translator. As a result, the fidelity to Yiddish is mirrored
by a fidelity to English. The tyrannies of both languages
meet in an informed if not perfect reciprocity. Often,
the collaboration took an unexpected form. For many
years, Singer's principal editor was Cecil Hemley, himself a short-story writer and poet. Now Hemley did not
know Yiddish, although Hemley and Singer, for example,

are listed as the translators of *The Slave*. What took place was this: Singer translated into English from the point of view of Yiddish; Hemley then complemented the process by responding and editing from the point of view of English. The result was not a perfect translation—none exists—and it is not even a meaningful ideal. Rather, what finally emerged was something as strong, alive, and dear; or as Singer puts it, "I edit and supervise all that is translated. As a result, it is like a second original." [3] By involving himself in the rites of passage, he is able to insure not only its artistic independence in another language, but also its artistic integrity—a "second original." Specifically, Singer describes the beneficial process of give-and-take by noting that whereas Yiddish permits and even encourages repetition and overstatement, English resists such excesses. As a result, the translations "are in many ways more direct, more to the point." As for the lack of adequate equivalents, Singer responds by putting his trust in the new life of his new original: "Of course, you struggle over a word. The Yiddish 'fresser' does not mean exactly the same thing as 'glutton' in English. But then because so many things don't mean the same, the adjustment takes care of itself."

When asked if he were satisfied with the results of such collaboration, Singer replied, "If it's not 100 per cent, it is 90 per cent." [4] The remark is not mere compromise; indeed, it perhaps embodies a realistic ideal which informs Singer's style and thought. To Singer all existence and art are at best 90 per cent—perhaps, paradoxically at their best that way. Those who seek 100 per cent whether in art, religion, politics, or translation produce a whole which ironically is less than the sum of the parts. In all things, gaps—of 10 per cent—exist. They are necessary evils—eliminated they create greater evils. Close

the gaps and man is blurred into God or God into man;
utopian politics abrogate messianic finality and morality;
and existence becomes everything or nothing. Eliminate
gulfs and one also leaves no room for demons and for
responsive readers. In other words, by preserving gaps,
Singer has created the conditions which insure the autonomous life not only of his translations, but also of his
demons. In the process, he has produced a literature
whose power is largely manifested and confirmed by in-
viting the reader's act of completion. This book is therefore written for those who read Singer as literature,
whether in translation or in the original or in both, and
who, in finding Singer's gaps significant and vital, agree
with Cecil Hemley: "even the English will do." [5]

Parts of this book first appeared in journals whose
editors deserve separate acknowledgement: Benjamin
Weintrob of the *Chicago Jewish Forum;* James Korges
of *Critique: Studies in Modern Fiction;* and Ernest J.
Lovell of *Texas Studies in Language and Literature.* Help
and encouragement were provided by many, especially
Professors Gay Wilson Allen, Oscar Cargill, Milton
Hindus, J. Hillis Miller, and Earl Wasserman. A Summer
Grant in 1967 from the American Council of Learned
Societies helped to bring the work to completion. A Re-
search Grant from Fairleigh Dickinson University con-
siderably eased the task of finalizing the manuscript.

Mr. Robert Giroux, Singer's scrupulous editor, and
Miss Lila Karpf, Director of Subsidiary Rights, for Farrar, Straus and Giroux were also most helpful. Mr. Giroux
read the last third of the first chapter and suggested cor-
rections of fact and phrasing. Miss Karpf arranged for
me to have access to short stories prior to the publication
of *The Séance and Other Stories* (1968). Mr. Singer him-

self was generous of his time. I did not set out to write
Singer's official biography. But because I was anxious to
be accurate, and because Mr. Singer was equally concerned with correcting many errors about his life and
works that have appeared in print, he agreed to answer
my many questions and to examine and approve the entire first chapter.

Madison, New Jersey
1968   5728

Notes

1. Joel Blocker and Richard Elman, "An Interview with Isaac
   Bashevis Singer," *Commentary*, XXXVI (November, 1963), 370.
2. One of the most informed and sophisticated treatments of Yiddish as a literary language is that of Irving Howe and Eliezer
   Greenberg in the "Introduction" to *A Treasury of Yiddish
   Stories* (New York, 1954). Especially valuable is the discussion
   of Yiddish as containing inherent problems of form: "Yiddish
   is breezy in tone, richly idiomatic in flavor, free in its literary
   possibilities. This very freedom, of course, is also a severe burden: many a Yiddish writer suffers from an absence of inherited
   modes and forms" (28). What problems the Yiddish writer faced
   are further described by Howe and Greenberg. The Yiddish
   writer

   > had to discover, if he could, why Yiddish seemed to lend
   > itself so naturally to intimate speech and to resist so stub-
   > bornly more formal address; why it collaborated with the
   > lyric poet so willingly and with the epic so grudgingly;
   > why it took to the picaresque narrative of a Cervantes but
   > not to the psychological webbing of a Henry James; why
   > it frequently reached the loving empathy of a Turgenev
   > but so seldom the metaphysical rhetoric of a Melville. Just
   > as the Yiddish writer had the task of reweaving the fabric
   > of national consciousness, so he had to improvise, to con-
   > quer and create, his own language. (32)

3. Conversations with I. B. Singer. I have spent many hours talking and listening to Singer. I always have found his conversation of a piece with his writing: scrupulous, direct, and surprising. The ground rules, though unspoken and unnegotiated, were always respected: he was the writer and I was the critic; he would not do my work and I could not do his. In this connection, when an interviewer asked Singer to "explain" aspects of his work, he replied, " 'I'm not able to give you a real explanation. Let the critics do that' " ("A Conversation with Isaac Bashevis Singer," *The Eternal Light,* NBC-TV [November 6, 1966], reproduced by The Jewish Theological Society of America with NBC, T–138, 10). Wherever Singer's comments appear in this study and do not carry a specific reference to a published work, they are remarks garnered in actual conversation.

4. Rochelle Girson, "Interview with I. B. Singer," *Saturday Review* (June 16, 1962), p. 19. Singer is not alone in creating second originals. Sholem Aleichem translated many of his own pieces; so did Sholem Asch. Indeed, Asch presented his *Three Cities* in three originals: Yiddish, Hebrew, and English. And then, of course, Nabokov translates his own works without a collaborator.

5. "Isaac Bashevis Singer," in *Dimensions of Midnight: Poetry and Prose* (Athens, Ohio, 1966), p. 225. At the time of his untimely death, Hemley was director of Ohio University Press which published the above volume posthumously. The English version of *In My Father's Court* (1966), which originally appeared in Yiddish in 1956, is dedicated to Hemley.

Hereafter, where more than one date appears for a work, as for example *In My Father's Court* (1956; 1966), the first date refers to the Yiddish original, the second to the translation. For a discussion of the complexities involved in the publication of Singer's works, see the latter half of the first chapter on his life and works. For a chronological listing, see the Bibliography.

Contents

The Child is Father of the Man. . . .
——William Wordsworth, "Ode:
Intimations of Immortality from
Recollections of Early Childhood"

I.

Life and Works

In her sixteenth year, Bathsheba Zylberman, the daughter of the Bilgoray Rabbi, received two marriage proposals.[1] One was from the son of a wealthy family in Lublin; the other from a poor Hasidic rabbi, Pinchos-Mendel, from nearby Tomaszov. To Bathsheba the choice rested on one consideration alone: which one was the better scholar? Her father, who frowned upon Hasidic mysticism, reluctantly admitted the one from Tomaszov. For Bathsheba that settled the matter. The wedding took place in the *shtetl* or small village of Bilgoray located in south eastern Poland near the Austrian border. The year was 1889 or, according to the Jewish calendar, 5649. The time chosen was shortly after Shavuot or Pentecost, which commemorates the giving of the Ten Commandments.[2] And thus it was that two distinguished, although very different, rabbinical families were joined and that the rational strains of Bathsheba merged with the mystical yearnings of Pinchos-Mendel Singer. And the inclinations of both parents passed on to their second son, Isaac, who later when he came to write adopted the name of Bashevis to honor his mother's half of the legacy.[3]

Although Pinchos-Mendel already was a rabbi, he did not have official sanction. At this time in Poland, as earlier and later and elsewhere, rabbis achieved such status by passing an examination in Russian and by paying a courtesy call on the local governor. To prepare the young man for these requirements, and also to make up for his lack of income during this period, it was customary for the young couple to spend a boarding period at the home of the wife's parents. But when, eight years later, that period was up, Pinchos-Mendel announced that he would not take the official examination and instead would seek a rabbinate where he could be an unofficial rabbi.

The family of the Bilgoray Rabbi was shocked. Bathsheba's mother, fearful that her daughter would starve, urged her to get a divorce. But two children already had been born: Hinde Esther and Israel Joshua. Moreover, Pinchos-Mendel surprised everyone by securing a rabbinate in the small village of Leoncin, located a few miles outside of Warsaw. In 1897 the family of four journeyed nearly two hundred miles by train and wagon to Leoncin and lived there for ten years. On July 14, 1904, Isaac Bashevis Singer was born, and two years later his younger brother Moishe. Most biographical accounts list Singer's birthplace as Radzymin, but although that is where his birth is officially recorded, the town of Leoncin, about which Israel Joshua wrote in *Of a World That Is No More* (1946), is the correct birthplace. Nevertheless, Radzymin has special importance, for it served as a future though short-lived home of the Singers.

In Radzymin a new rabbinical dynasty had been founded many years earlier by Rabbi Yekele who was

known as a wonder-working rabbi. He issued charmed
coins and pieces of amber to cure barrenness and illness.
It was said that his incantations had the power to revive
even those near death. Although there was no outstanding
heritage or following associated with this new dynasty,
Rabbi Yekele opened a *yeshivah*. The grandson of Rabbi
Yekele gave the post of director to Pinchos-Mendel and in
the summer of 1907 the family now of six journeyed from
Leoncin to Radzymin.

At the age of three Singer learned his *aleph-beth* or
"abc's." He also began to perplex his father with questions: Where is the end of the world? Why do birds fly
and worms crawl? Where is God? What does He look like?
(Singer confesses he is still asking the same questions.)
Among Orthodox Jews it is customary to celebrate the
beginning of school with a party and to put a drop of
honey on the first page of the *aleph-beth* to signify that
learning is sweet. But life was anything but sweet for
Rabbi Pinchos-Mendel in Radzymin. Although Rabbi
Yekele's grandson had promised a good living, no salary
was even mentioned. A few rubles were doled out now
and then, and the family was in great need. Things went
from bad to worse and, after about a year in Radzymin,
the family suddenly moved to Warsaw in 1908 and arrived with its few possessions at No. 10 Krochmalna
Street.

Accustomed to small, backward villages, the Singers
found Warsaw a marvel. Big and powerful boats floated
on the Vistula River; trolleys ran swiftly over cobblestone
streets. An enormous monument of King Zygmunt, poised
above four stone mermaids, reached for the sky. The elegant Saxony Gardens, where handsomely dressed couples
strolled in the afternoon, was surrounded by tall apartment buildings laced with ironwork balconies. Gaslights

linked the dark streets and burnished the hand-wrought railings that enclosed lovely homes and courtyards. But for all Singer knew, he might just as well have been back in Radzymin, for Krochmalna Street was in the Jewish quarter and was essentially a *shtetl* within a large city.

The upstairs flat at No. 10 was comparatively primitive. Light and heat were provided not by gas but by kerosine and coal which had to be lugged in heavy containers. There were no toilet facilities within the flat. Everyone in the building shared an outhouse in the courtyard. And it was dark and filthy; rats and mice were always there. Many children suffered from constipation and later from nervous disorders due to such outhouses. The apartment itself was barely furnished. No pictures adorned the walls nor statues the mantel. They were considered idolatrous and in violation of the second commandment against graven images. The body itself was looked upon as a mere appendage of the soul. Indeed, the "world"—the secular world of Warsaw—was regarded as *tref* (unclean). Nearly fifty years later, Singer, in his memoirs, acknowledged his father's suspicions: "Many years were to pass before I began to understand how much sense there was in this attitude" (68).

In Warsaw, Pinchos-Mendel was the unofficial rabbi of Krochmalna Street and earned what living he could by serving, for a fee, as a judge of a *Beth-Din* or ecclesiastical court. The tragicomic people and problems that passed through Singer's house and into his memory and memoirs often put Rabbi Pinchos-Mendel to severe tests. But because the *Beth-Din* was based on the notion that there can be no justice without godliness and because his father was strong in his faith, Rabbi Pinchos-Mendel kept both justice and God alive on Krochmalna Street. As Singer notes, "Out of my father's mouth spoke the Torah, and all under-

stood that every word was just. I was often witness to how
my father, with his simple words, routed pettiness, vain
ambition, foolish resentment, and conceit" (71). But the
enemy of discord was within no less than without, and
Pinchos-Mendel could not settle the disputes within his
own family as well as he did those of strangers.

Israel Joshua, who favored his mother's rationalism,
became increasingly sceptical of his father's mysticism.
Singer's sister, Hinde Esther, was convinced that her
mother did not love her. Actually, it was not a problem of
love but of incompatibility. Hinde Esther had inherited
her father's Hasidic exultation which clashed with her
mother's commonsensical attitude. Often hysterical, Hinde
Esther frequently had mild epileptic fits and seemed at
times to be possessed by a dybbuk; Singer's portrait of
Rechele in *Satan in Goray* may be based in part on his
sister. Unlike his older brother or sister, who favored one
parent or the other, Singer took after both. Indeed, the
ease with which he moves in his work from the synagogue
to the brothel, from heavenly seraphim to satanic imps,
may largely have its roots in the confluence of parental
legacies. But it is important to stress that Singer does not
fuse the mystical and rational. Rather, he brings them together in a durable and responsive antithesis, which results in a vision that is simultaneously responsive to and
sceptical of everything celestial and terrestrial, freakish
and familiar. However, when it came to his writing itself,
Singer's father, not his mother, provided the model.

Although Rabbi Pinchos-Mendel was a writer of
religious commentaries, he nevertheless shared with all
writers the need to see his work in print. Indeed, at one
time, although the family was hard-pressed, he took a
considerable portion of a gift of money to have part of an
unpublished manuscript set in type. Hinde Esther also

appeared to have some literary talent and her letters at least evidenced a strong command of language. Israel Joshua suddenly experienced a great desire to draw and already was engaged in reading what he called "literature." Singer, too, became infected with the family scribbling habit and often could hardly wait for the Sabbath, when no work is permitted, to be over so that he could resume his sketches. Assuming that his son would follow in his footsteps and be an author of religious works, Pinchos-Mendel gave him advice which, I believe, Singer followed in his literary religious works: " 'Be straightforward in your reasoning, and avoid casuistry. None of the great scholars tortured the text. True, they dug deep, but they never made mountains out of molehills' " (171).[5]

In his tenth year, Singer received his first secular book from his older brother. It was Dostoevsky's *Crime and Punishment* in Yiddish. Although he found it heavy going, he recalls being drawn to the loneliness and reasoned madness of Raskolnikov; Singer himself feared at the time that there was so much going on in his own head that he would soon go mad. The book had a lasting influence. Singer's later fascination with the criminal in *The Magician of Lublin, The Manor,* and in many short stories is undoubtedly related to the influence of Dostoevsky. Moreover, in both Singer and Dostoevsky criminality enjoys a curious partnership with saintliness and ultimately works the psychological up to the religious. Above all, the influence of Dostoevsky cemented the crucial influence of Israel Joshua who was to become Singer's supreme mentor. Indeed, Singer's "taste for heresy" was whetted by his older brother's increasing emancipation. As in many Jewish homes, the kitchen was the arena for discussion and debate. Singer listened while his brother attacked the unworldly Asiatic Jews of the Jewish quarter and *shtetlach* who submitted to all kinds of indignities and squalor when, through socialism and Zionism, a brave new world could be theirs. But Pinchos-Mendel countered that the Turks and Arabs were not about to welcome the Jews to Palestine with open arms; nor would the czar turn his lands over to the poor. Such things could come about only through war and the killing of the innocent. Israel Joshua sought support in the Yiddish writers like I. J. Peretz, living in Warsaw at that time, who agitated for reform. Singer recalls his father's reply:

> My father used to say that secular writers like Peretz were leading the Jews to heresy. He said everything they wrote was against God. Even though Peretz wrote in a religious vein, my father called his writing "sweetened poison," but poison nevertheless. And from his point of view he was right. Everybody who read such books sooner or later became a worldly man and forsook the traditions. In my family, of course, my brother had gone first, and I went after him. For my parents, this was a tragedy.[6]

The first act of that tragedy dramatically began when Israel Joshua moved out of the house. He was twenty-one, the year was 1914, and his new residence was an artist's studio.

But a son is still a son and making sure that he eats regularly transcends political and religious differences. Often, Bathsheba would entrust packages of food to Singer to be brought to his brother. The first time Singer visited his brother's bohemian studio, he was shocked. Hanging on the walls were not only paintings, but paintings of nudes. Young Jewish girls smoked and talked freely with painters and sculptors who no longer wore, as Singer still did, earlocks and skull caps. It was like another world;

Singer listened entranced to the discussions of art, politics, and the eternal favorite, the Jewish question. From the liberal and often libertine atmosphere of his older brother's studio, Singer would go to the study house, the transition evidently posing no problem or contradiction. On the contrary, as Singer states, "Even in my stories it is just one step from the study house to sexuality and back again" (240). In this connection, it is perhaps significant that when Singer first read *Crime and Punishment* it reminded him of the mystical writings of the Cabala.

In the summer of 1914 Israel Joshua was conscripted into the Russian Army. But before Warsaw fell, he had deserted and was hiding in Warsaw. When the Germans entered, he no longer had to hide and began his literary career by writing stories for a newly established Orthodox newspaper. In the same year—1917—that Singer at the age of thirteen technically became a man from the Jewish point of view by being a *bar-mitzvah*, a son of the commandments, the Russian Revolution occurred and Czar Nicholas, under house arrest, amused himself by chopping wood. The winds of change affecting Singer's own life and coming of age were part of the larger forces altering the face and fate of European Jewry, and in his work Singer regularly focuses on just such coincidences of personal and communal history.

In the summer of 1917 Israel Joshua bribed a German official and obtained a visa for his mother to visit Bilgoray. It had been many years since she left her native village. Moreover, she had had a dream in which she saw her father's face aglow with the radiance of one who has left this earth. No arguments could convince her that her father was still alive. Indeed, Singer claims that he was inclined toward the occult through his mother's dreams.

Singer accompanied his mother to Bilgoray in 1917 and stayed there for four years, until he was about eighteen. It was a crucial experience for the young Singer because he was not just visiting the home of his grandfather, whom he had never known, but journeying back in time to a Jewish past. Bilgoray, which was removed from the railroad and in turn had been insulated from worldly influence by the Bilgoray Rabbi and later by his son, had remained unaltered since the middle ages. Speaking of the town, Singer himself has said "it was pretty much the same as it must have been during the time of Chmielnicki [seventeenth-century Cossack leader]. . . . I could have written *The Family Moskat* (which takes place in Warsaw) without having lived in Bilgoray, but I could never have written *Satan in Goray* or some of my other stories without having been there." [7]

The indebtedness can be indicated with greater precision. Bilgoray in the novel becomes the substitute for the actual, nearby town of Goray. Singer's Aunt Rochele, who believed in magic, amulets, and ghosts, undoubtedly served together with Singer's sister as the composite for Rechele (same linguistic approximation). The Bilgoray Rabbi appears as the Orthodox patriarch, Rabbi Benish. In addition, while in Bilgoray, Singer supplemented his regular studies of the Talmud by dipping into the forbidden mystical writings of the Cabala and thus became saturated in that special apocalyptic and messianic world that imparts to *Satan in Goray* its urgent fervor and fever. Above all, the visit to Bilgoray demonstrated to the young Singer that the past is not past and that ghosts can exist and even thrive in the twentieth century. For the first time he experienced the reality of a transmigrated soul: "In this world of old Jewishness I found a spiritual treasure trove. I had a chance to see our past as it really was. Time seemed to flow backward. I lived Jewish history" (290).

But just as many of Singer's characters are caught between two worlds and generations, so he himself, for all his movement back to the past and to old traditions, was also moving forward toward the future and to emancipation. Singer began to study Hebrew grammar thoroughly and wrote his first Hebrew poem when he was fourteen. He read the Hebrew works of Bialik, Czerniochowsky, Jacob Cohen, and Schneyur; and for a period of years he wrote poems and stories exclusively in Hebrew and even published a few in a Hebrew newspaper. Eventually, he turned away from Hebrew for reasons which, in light of the translations of his own works, may be somewhat ironic. Because he used a great deal of dialogue and because his characters spoke Yiddish, he constantly was engaged in translating their conversations into Hebrew. Finally, he asked himself, "What am I, a writer or a translator? And I came to the conclusion that I must write in Yiddish because it was . . . the language of the people I wanted to write about." [8]

Increasingly, Singer experienced dislocation. The first urgings of sex scattered his dreams and sleep. He walked around with a brooding air and wore the mantle of melancholy with quiet extravagance. He quickly transformed two worldly contemporaries, Notte Shverdsharf and Meir Hadas, into disciples with his Byronic notion that the noblest thing a man could do was to kill himself. Notte and Meir agreed, but tempered their fatalism with involvement in Zionist, Bundist, Bolshevik, and other groups. Singer characteristically insisted on total gloom and resisted all communal tampering with his singularity. But he did continue his self-education in secular matters.

He was helped by the library and conversation of Todros, the worldly local watchmaker; just as in *The Family Moskat,* Jekuthiel, the watchmaker, serves as midwife to Asa Heshel's birth into the modern world of philosophy and science.[9] Singer's further readings of non-Jewish materials, curiously enough, was aided by the United States. Shortly after the war, Americans sent sacks of white flour and Yiddish translations of European authors to Polish villages. Through this unofficial, cultural lend-lease, Singer for the first time read Reisen, Strindberg, Turgenev, Tolstoy, Maupassant, and Chekhov. But perhaps the author who provided the major dislocation and deflected Singer from Orthodoxy was Spinoza, whom Singer first came to know indirectly through Hillel Zeitlin's *The Problem of Good And Evil* and Stupnicki's commentaries. In short, what was taking place in the heart and mind of the adolescent Singer was nothing less than a Jewish version of the eternal "Battle of the Books," a conflict power fully recreated in *The Family Moskat* and *The Manor.*

Because the visit to Bilgoray was such a crucial and even pivotal experience, it might be meaningful at this point to pause in the story of Singer's life in order to assess its relation to his works. Singer's adolescence is a study in strain. He walks a tightrope between two ages and worlds; he is on the way to becoming both a modern man and a transmigrated soul. While he pores and puzzles over Spinoza he unknowingly hums an old Hasidic melody. He reads Dostoevsky and studies the Cabala until the two begin to counterpoint and coincide with each other. Determined to pursue free inquiry, he resists the Orthodox surrender of eternal questions to God's jurisdiction. And yet he is aware even at this point that although the secular philosophers are intoxicating and profound, they neither provide answers to the eternal questions nor offer peace or clarity. In other words, the dualistic legacy of his parents finds confirmation and extension in the literary and philosophical crosscurrents that now beset the young Singer. They also beset Singer the writer.

Singer's works tend to resist classification. They are simultaneously supernatural and rational, strange and familiar. To be sure, his works often lean toward one or the other pole and thus support the notion that they are basically of two types: the demonic and the historical. But that initial clarity has to be hedged, for what ties both types together is not mode but scale. Singer is preoccupied with excess—with those who seek 100 per cent. Controlled and counseled by contraries, he constitutionally resists extremes. In the demonic novels and short stories, the excesses are cosmic and messianic and emerge out of man's relation with God. In the historical works, the excesses are individual and communal and grow out of man's relation with his fellowman. But far from being mutually exclusive, the modes are transmutations of each other. Thus, in the historical works the demonic appears as the sceptical; in the demonic pieces the historical is heightened to the messianic. What eases Singer's transmigrations from one mode and world to another is his notion that between the holy and the unclean, between the supernatural and human, there exists a secret partnership. As he notes in his memoirs, "The heder, too often described as a place where innocent children suffered at the hands of a sloppy, ill-tempered teacher, was not quite that. What was wrong with society was wrong with the heder" (219). In many ways, Singer's sceptical attitude towards the world was prepared for by his sceptical attitude toward a religion which disdained that world. In short, the visit to Bilgoray made tension the center of Singer's power. According to him, that is also the key to all significant literature: "what

both of these books have, *Sherlock Holmes* and Dostoevski, is the tension. . . . You feel tense in them. You are
never bored, as happens sometimes with modern books,
where they give you everything except the feeling of tension, of really being interested." [10] To be sure, before Singer explores the tension of excess in his works, he
experiences it in his own life and in the lives of those
around him.

Singer's activities, friendships, reading, and poses
while in Bilgoray caused considerable embarrassment to
his mother and her family. But the crowning blow came
when Singer agreed to his friend Notte's request to teach
a beginner's class in Hebrew to the worldly boys and girls
of the town. To his mother's family, the first official act
of the grandson of the Bilgoray Rabbi was to besmirch
his holy name. The fact is, however, that what was happening to Singer was happening to Bilgoray itself. The dislocations of the war had brought to this small village Jewish
families who were worldly and even sophisticated, a
situation recreated in *The Manor*. Then, too, the young
men who had served in the army were brought in contact
with secular and competitive ways and values, and returned, like Asa Heshel in *The Family Moskat,* restless
and wrenched. To be sure, Singer, absorbed in Bilgoray
the essential raw materials of his later works, but it was
more an unconscious assimilation than one actively sought
and valued. Indeed, he became increasingly impatient
with his ignorance and the provincialism of life in small
towns. He yearned to go to Warsaw to study. At just about
that time, in 1920, Singer's father accepted a post as rabbi
in a small town not too far away from Bilgoray. Hinde
Esther was already married and in London, where she
went to live after the Germans invaded Belgium. Israel
Joshua was earning what living he could as a Yiddish

journalist in Kiev. Singer refused to go with his mother,
father, and younger brother Moishe to another *shtetl* in
Galicia. A compromise was effected: Singer could return
to Warsaw but he had to attend a seminary and continue
his rabbinical studies. Thus, in 1921 he enrolled at the
Tachkemoni Rabbinal Seminary in Warsaw.

He remained there only about a year. Singer himself
has called it one of the "worst times of my life." He never
had enough to eat; often, he was close to starvation. Like
a vagabond, he seldom slept in the same place twice. Nor
did his studies make his stark existence any easier to bear.
At the seminary he found "a lot of the things they taught
there I knew already. My knowledge of secular works was
backward, but in religious matters I knew a great deal." [11]
It is significant that during this time Singer read and was
drawn to Knut Hamsun, for Hamsun, especially in his
earlier novel *Hunger* (1890), gave powerful expression to
the same grinding poverty that Singer was enduring and
was to suffer for nearly twenty years. Recently, Singer
wrote an introduction to a newly translated edition of
Hunger and his comments, although primarily literary,
are also burdened with biographical weight:

> European writers know that he is the father of the
> modern school of literature in his every aspect—his
> subjectiveness, his use of flashbacks, his lyricism. The
> whole modern school of fiction in the twentieth cen-
> tury stems from Hamsun, just as Russian literature
> in the nineteenth century "came out of Gogol's great-
> coat." . . . Hamsun belonged to that select group of
> writers who not only interested a reader but virtu-
> ally hypnotized him. [12]

Singer quit the seminary and returned to Bilgoray,
earning what meager living he could by giving Hebrew

lessons. But by 1923 he was again back in Warsaw. His family had by then settled in Galicia, and Singer, who remained in Warsaw until he came to the United States in 1935, was never to see his mother and father or his brother Moishe again.

Back in Warsaw in 1923, Singer became a proofreader for *Literarishe Bletter,* a Yiddish literary magazine, and benefited by working, as he puts it, in the "kitchen of literature." He remained on the staff almost to the time he left for America. His salary was six dollars a week, which was not bad for that time, except that he never was paid regularly; one week he would receive a dollar and a half, the next week two. Fortunately, his brother, who by then was married and had returned from Russia to Poland, helped him with occasional meals and clothes. Singer also became a translator of pulp novels into Yiddish for newspapers. But he also translated a number of serious works. He rendered Knut Hamsun's *Pan* and *Victoria* into Yiddish in the late twenties. He also translated Stefan Zweig's *Roman Rolland* and later Thomas Mann's *The Magic Mountain.* Asked what he did with the passages of French in Mann's novel, Singer replied that "since it was bad French I had to translate it into bad Yiddish. You don't have to make a great effort to write bad Yiddish." [18] In addition, he translated two of Erich Remarque's novels, *All Quiet on the Western Front* and *The Way Back,* the latter appearing as late as 1931. Even in America he worked as a translator; his Yiddish version of Leon Glaser's *From Moscow to Jerusalem* appeared in 1938.

Proofreader and translator, Singer was also slowly developing as a writer in his own right. To be sure, it was difficult initially; in the early twenties he still was experimenting with Hebrew. Then, when he turned to Yiddish, he was dissatisfied with his early efforts and tore them all up. Significantly, perhaps, his first work to be published was a short story. It was entitled "Women" and appeared in *Literarishe Bletter*. In 1927 "Grandchildren" and "The Village Gravedigger" were published in *Warshawer Shriften*. In the same year, Singer's brother published his first novel, *Blood Harvest*. Subsequent to that novel, Israel Joshua became more and more disenchanted with writing in Yiddish. Indeed, according to Singer, his older brother created a sensation in the late twenties by sending a letter to several Yiddish newspapers in which he said, among other things, that writing in Yiddish was a humiliating experience for a writer. He thought for a while about turning to Hebrew, but Hebrew was not then a living language, as it is today. There were no Hebrew words for ordinary modern objects. Then, too, the Hebraists alive and active in Warsaw in the twenties were a small group and more interested in matters of philology than literature. After a subsequent brief flirtation with French and German, Israel Joshua returned to Yiddish and correspondingly to Jewish materials. He wrote *Yoshe Kalb* (Yasha the Loon) in 1932. It was an enormous success in Warsaw as well as in America.[14]

The success of *Yoshe Kalb* is significant because the impotence Israel Joshua suffered prior to its composition is also a central experience in both Singer's own life and works. If excess is Singer's principal theme, impotence is the form it takes. In *Satan in Goray*, Itche Mates fails his wife and community. Cut off from his Jewish past, Asa Heshel is without power in Warsaw. Above all, what Israel Joshua went through is undoubtedly reflected in *The Magician of Lublin*: there, as in Israel Joshua's life, turning away from Yiddish or Jewish materials almost leads to the impotence of conversion. Indeed, when Israel Joshua finally settled back into slavery and wrote *Yoshe Kalb*, he recovered not only his ability as a writer, but his very life: Singer notes, "I saw then what the right theme can do for a writer. My brother revived not only spiritually but also physically. He began to look better; his blue eyes glowed with new interest and expectation." [15]

Yoshe Kalb also established Israel Joshua's international reputation and resulted in his going to America. Israel Joshua had sent the manuscript of the novel to Abraham Cahan, then the editor of the Jewish Daily Forward. Cahan was ecstatic about it and promptly arranged for its serial publication in the Forward. The novel also attracted the attention of the Yiddish Art Theater, and Maurice Schwartz immediately began negotiating for its dramatic adaptation. The play was, with the exception of The Dybbuk, the greatest success of the Yiddish theater and led to Israel Joshua being invited to America. When he arrived, he was lionized and taken up by members of the Forward and Yiddish theatrical circles.

While his older brother was in New York, reaping the success of writing again in Yiddish and about Jewish materials, Singer was composing his first novel. In between his proofreading and translating, he was putting together a story of communal satanic possession set in the seventeenth century. All during 1933, he worked on the manuscript of Satan in Goray which ultimately established his unique and powerful demonic style. The novel was accepted for serial publication by Globus and appeared in 1934. In 1935 the Warsaw Yiddish P.E.N. Club published Satan in Goray in book form. The novel, which I consider Singer's best, was reprinted in Yiddish in the United States in 1943 and translated into Hebrew in Tel Aviv in 1953. The English translation by Jacob Sloan appeared in 1955.

The year 1935 was crucial for other reasons. The poison of Hitler was already beginning to spread. Singer's older brother had left for America in 1934 to work for the *Forward* and Singer said, "Without him, I was a limp man without a crutch." To understand why he already considered himself a cripple requires some comment about his first marriage. In the late twenties Singer was living with a young Communist, Runia. He explained, "We were never married by a rabbi. She was my wife. We were very progressive in those days." A son, Israel, was born at the end of 1929. Singer relates the balance of the story:

> She was a communist and the only place for her was the new "holy land"—Russia. All I knew was that the Stalinists attacked my brother, his novel *Yasha Kalb* [sic], the *Forward,* as the only obstacles in the way of world revolution. And so Runia took my son and went off to that new haven which turned out to be a butcher shop. Two years later, she was exiled. She went to Turkey and then to Palestine where her mother was living. There she and my son stayed. I did not see my son again until twenty years later.

Asa Heshel's heated discussions with the young Communist Barbara in *The Family Moskat,* as well as similar conversations recorded in *The Manor,* undoubtedly reflect those Singer had with his first wife. Moreover, his concern for his son appears in his autobiographical short story "The Son" as well as in the attempts by Jacob in *The Slave* to rescue his son from the Poles of Pilitz. In short, by 1935, with his older brother in America, his wife and son in Russia, his parents in Galicia, the lack of financial success of *Satan in Goray,* the prospect of the Nazis—Singer had no reason to stay when his brother urged him to come to the United States.

In 1935 Singer arrived in New York and lived for a time in the Williamsburgh section of Brooklyn. Although

he was reunited with his brother and his brother's family
and he secured a free-lance position with the *Forward*, he
once again tasted the reality of being a ghost in an alien
country: "I came from Poland in 1935, and my first im-
pression was here that Yiddish literature was of no avail;
it's dead. This is what people told me and I felt so myself.
And suddenly, I felt that I was in a cemetery." [16] For
nearly ten years, Singer was an underground man; his
shadow seemed to have more life than he had:

> When I came to this country I lived through a terri-
> ble disappointment. I felt then—more than I believe
> now—that Yiddish had no future in this country. In
> Poland, Yiddish was very much alive when I left.
> When I came here it seemed to me that Yiddish
> was finished: it was very depressing. The result was
> that for five or six or maybe seven years I couldn't
> write a word. Not only didn't I publish anything
> in those years, but writing became so difficult a chore
> that my grammar was affected. I couldn't write a
> single worthwhile sentence. I became like a man
> who was a great lover and is suddenly impotent,
> knowing at the same time that ultimately he will re-
> gain his power. I shouldn't even have tried to write
> anything, but I did try again and again, without suc-
> cess. The novel I tried to write I eventually threw
> away. In later years when I looked at it I was startled
> to find that it was the work of an illiterate man—and
> this was after I had written *Satan in Goray* and knew
> Yiddish fairly well. It was a real case of amnesia.
> One has to get a very great blow to act in such a
> way. But after a while I got over it, just like the
> lover whom I spoke of. [17]

What brought this great collapse about? Many things,
not the least of which was Singer's feeling that as a Yiddish

writer he was without a future. Although the *Forward* and other Yiddish newspapers and magazines existed, there was the foreboding sense that Yiddish was a dying if not a dead language. Many years later, Singer would quip that there is no better language in which to write about ghosts than a dead language. But in the late thirties the situation was more grim, for it must be recalled that as Hitler advanced into Poland, including the town where his parents and his younger brother Moishe were living, Yiddish was being killed off in the gas chambers. More and more, Singer found himself without roots. In the late thirties, his wife and son five thousand miles away, his own family in danger of extermination, he experienced psychological incarceration. Sealed off from a future, tied to a present which was a living hell, Singer contemplated suicide and was visited by the ghosts of the past.

In 1937 Singer met his present wife, Alma. She was then married and had a son and daughter. In 1939 she was divorced and in 1940 married Singer. Born in Munich and well-educated, especially for a Jewish woman in those days, Alma Singer had to work as a saleswoman in order to supplement the meager living Singer made as a free lancer on the *Forward*. They moved into an apartment on Ocean Avenue in Brooklyn. Singer recalls, "It was the nicest apartment I ever had. It looked out over trees. Best of all, it was empty of furniture; and there is nothing nicer than an apartment that is empty of furniture." Singer, who later came to love parakeets, adds that he did not have any birds then: "I couldn't support birds." Little by little, he began to write again. Long works fell apart in his hands, but he was able to make some progress with short stories. The first story that promised to flourish began: "I am the Primeval Snake, the Evil One, Satan. The cabala refers to me as Samael and the Jews sometimes call me merely, 'that one.' " Having given "The Destruction of Kreshev" a sharp start, Satan without fanfare then goes about establishing his power and reality: "It is well-known that I love to arrange strange marriages. . . ." The story goes on to detail the sexual perversions of Lise, the daughter of Reb Bunim, and concludes, like *Satan in Goray* and "The Gentleman from Cracow," with the community being possessed by Satan. It is one of Singer's characteristic gothic parables and ends with the suicide of Lise. This story, along with the "Diary of One Not Born," "Zeidlus the Pope," and "Two Corpses Go Dancing," supplemented the reissue of *Satan in Goray and Other Tales* in Yiddish in 1943. One thousand copies were printed by Farlag Matones; royalties amounted to ninety dollars.

Although Singer was beginning to write again in the early forties and to emerge from his amnesia, he encountered resistance from his editor at the *Forward*:

When I came to this country, I wrote then, even as I write today, many ghost stories about spirits and so on, and in the Yiddish circles, this kind of writing was strange. I remember my editor telling me, "Why do you write about things the readers have already forgotten? These things might have been valid two hundred years ago, but not today." But you know writers—young writers—are sometimes very stubborn. I kept on writing in the same way and didn't listen to my editor. In many cases, he fought me, tried to convince me what he wanted me to be, a social writer, to write about the situation of tailors in New York, how badly they live and how they fight for their existence. Somehow, these things did not appeal to me.[18]

Rambling around alone in his apartment on Ocean Avenue, he experienced the alienation of being apart not only from America and the English language but also from Europe and the transplanted Yiddishists of New York.

Curiously, what finally wrenched Singer free of literary impotence was a tragic loss; if he received a "great blow" by coming here, it evidently required an equally great blow to make him accept life in general and the reality of the literary life of the past. In 1944, one year after the republication of *Satan in Goray*, Singer's older brother and mentor, Israel Joshua Singer, died at the age of fifty-one. Singer said, "It was the greatest misfortune of my entire life. There was only one consolation—whatever would happen later would never be as bad as this." There is no question that it was a great loss. However, in light of Singer's later career it evidently was also a great release. His conscious devotion to his brother is not at issue here; nor is Israel Joshua Singer's generosity or his ability. What, nevertheless, is clear is that Singer's preoccupation in his works with the supplanting of Esau by Jacob and his equally strong determination to persist in his demonic bent and to appear in translation, suggest the possibility that Singer was working in the shadow, not the light, of his older brother. To be sure, the good influences were there, and without I. J. Singer, Singer probably would have remained in Warsaw and, like Asa Heshel of *The Family Moskat*, perished in the Warsaw ghetto. Still, a strong brother and his influence may obscure more than it nourishes. Besides, by coming into his own literary birthright, Singer has been able to pay his brother the most lasting tribute.

In any case, one year after his brother's death Singer began serious work on his first long family chronicle, *The Family Moskat*. It appeared in serial form from 1945 to

1948 in the *Forward*. It was published in book form in
Yiddish by Morris S. Sklarsky in 1950 in two volumes. In
the same year, it was awarded the Louis Lamed Prize. In
1950 the novel was translated into English by A. H. Gross.
Since *The Family Moskat* was the first novel of Singer's to
be published in English, it provides the occasion for examining his relations with publishers, translators, and
audiences in the United States.

Financially, Singer has not fared well from the sale
of his books in Yiddish. In all, he has published four books
in Yiddish in the United States. As noted, *Satan in Goray
and Other Stories,* which appeared in 1943, earned only
$90 in royalties. For *The Family Moskat* (1950) he re-
ceived $250. *In My Father's Court* (1956) brought $300,
and *Gimpel the Fool and Other Stories* (1963), $400. Sin-
ger's first publisher in English was Alfred A. Knopf who
brought out *The Family Moskat* in 1950. (It was reissued
in 1965 by Farrar, Straus and Giroux, Singer's present
publishers.) A selection of the Book Find Club, *The
Family Moskat* sold 35,000 copies. Royalties, however,
amounted to only $2,000 because the translator's fees were
deducted from the author's total.

The Family Moskat represented a turning point in
Singer's career for a number of reasons. He had never sold
that many books before. It was his first major presentation
before a new American audience. It was his first translated
work; and on this last point hangs, perhaps, the most important difference. Unfortunately, A. H. Gross died before
he could complete the translation. His daughter Nancy
Gross along with Maurice Samuel and Lyon Mearson
undertook the balance of the translation as well as the
problems of editing. But for the first time Singer became
actively involved as well; and he admits that much of what
he knows of English was gained in the intensity of this

collective enterprise. Above all, from that point to the present, he has involved himself in the translations of all his works.

In 1954 Singer had the good fortune of making the acquaintance of Cecil Hemley and his wife Elaine Gottlieb. Hemley at that time was editor of Noonday Press and enormously taken with his work, especially his short stories. Hemley, together with the editor Dwight W. Webb and associate editor Elizabeth Pollet, sought to make Singer better known in translation. They helped to place his work in quality magazines. "Gimpel the Fool," translated by Saul Bellow, appeared in *Partisan Review* in 1953 and aroused considerable attention. "From the Diary of One Not Born" appeared in a subsequent issue of the same journal. *Midstream* published "The Wife Killer"; *Commentary,* "The Gentleman from Cracow" and "Fire"; *New World Writing,* "The Mirror." In 1955, the excellent translation of Jacob Sloan presented *Satan in Goray* before English readers for the first time. At the age of fifty-one Singer found himself hailed as a new figure in the literary world. Above all, Hemley and Webb of Noonday Press conceived the idea of publishing his first collection of short stories in translation in 1957.

Gimpel the Fool and Other Stories contained twelve stories. Only one, "The Old Man," which appeared in Warsaw in 1933, was not written in the United States. Clearly, the years of impotency were over. Equally important, the critics confirmed Singer's power: Irving Howe called him a genius and later went on to write the first serious article on his work; *The Times Literary Supplement* described the title story as the greatest *schlemiel* tale in literature; Milton Hindus struck the right double note by referring to Singer as one of the most brilliant Yiddish and one of the most important contemporary writers in

America. In recognition of Singer's achievement to date, the American Academy and National Institute of Arts and Letters awarded Singer a grant in 1959. The Noonday Press, born in mid-century, provided a writer obsessed with the past a future.

In 1959 Singer wrote and had serialized in the *Forward*, *The Magician of Lublin*. (The French edition, which appeared in 1965, was named the best foreign novel of the year.) A translation by Elaine Gottlieb, Hemley's wife, and Joseph Singer, the son of Israel Joshua Singer, was published by Noonday in 1960. In the same year Noonday Press merged with Farrar, Straus and Giroux. Roger Straus, Paula Diamond, then director of subsidiary rights, and her assistant Lila Karpf, who is now in charge of subsidiary rights, became Singer's literary agents. In 1961 *The Spinoza of Market Street* appeared. Singer's publishers succeeded in placing Singer's stories in practically every major magazine, ranging from the *Saturday Evening Post* to the *Chicago Review*, from *Playboy* to *Encounter*.

In 1961 *The Slave* was composed and serialized in the *Forward*. Hemley and Singer worked on the translation together and it appeared in 1962. The book was selling very well, and one day Roger Straus called Singer and told him that he thought *The Slave* would be a best seller. Singer recalls the experience:

> He was excited but I was fearful. I will become a best seller and have no peace. So I prayed to God —for in my own way I am a religious man—and asked Him not to give me a best seller. God listened and said to Himself: "All these years this poor man has been praying and asking for this and for that. But never have I granted one of his requests. But this one I will grant."

In the same philosophical or playful vein, commenting on his not being wealthy, he remarked, "We already have too many rich writers, many of them poor writers." [19]

In 1963 his third collection of stories, *Short Friday and Other Stories,* appeared; and the next year Singer was honored by being elected to the National Institute of Arts and Letters, the only American member of the Institute to write in another language. At about the same time, Singer began his lecturing career on college campuses. His academic success, perhaps, led David Boroff to designate him "the in-writer" of 1965 among college intellectuals, more so than even Saul Bellow and Bernard Malamud.[20] Indeed, in 1966, the same year that the English version of *In My Father's Court* appeared, Singer was writer-in-residence at Oberlin, and in the spring of 1967 at the University of California. He has just spent the spring of 1968 as visiting professor of literature at the University of Wisconsin.

Singer's most recent novel is *The Manor.* The original manuscript numbered about 2,000 pages. Singer cut drastically, hoping he would be able to bring it out in one volume. The first volume has appeared but he is so unhappy about all that has been taken out he and his publishers have revised their original plan to bring out the second novel in the fall of 1968. Instead, Singer will restore a great deal of the flesh that had been removed, and the work will be published in two volumes, probably in the fall of 1969. The first will be amplified and called *The Manor;* the second, *The Estate.* On the differences between working on a long novel and a short story, Singer remarked: "I follow Tolstoy in construction of a large novel. When you write a chronicle, you are building a warehouse. When you write a short story or a short novel, you are building a home. A lot has to go in a warehouse. In a short work you can concentrate on quality. In a large novel, you give only essentials. In short stories, you elaborate." Equally interesting is Singer's attitude toward serialization. He is the only major writer whose works still regularly appear in serial form prior to publication. Although *The Magician of Lublin* and *The Slave* were completed before they ran in the *Forward* in installments, that was not the case with *The Family Moskat, The Manor,* and two untranslated longer novels, *Shadows by the Hudson* (1957) and *A Ship to America* (1958). But Singer, far from being troubled by having to write an installment each week, finds serialization "a delight. You have to work. You can't come up with any excuses. The printer is waiting for you. It is true that your control cannot be perfect —but that's not really possible anyway in a novel, only in a short story. Besides, you can't write a novel of a thousand pages without serialization. It's too frightening."

What is Singer like today? He appears to be genuinely surprised by his success. He reacts with astonishment when a parallel between his life and that of his characters is pointed out to him. He hardly reads any contemporary authors, although he is always promising his audiences that he will someday read Bellow, Malamud, and Joseph Heller so that he may better answer their questions. He keeps up with the latest experiments on psychic research and ESP, although he readily admits that there are more fakers than genuine spiritualists in the field. When he misplaces or loses his glasses, he blames it on imps who delight in frustrating his ability to read and to write. He is full of plans. His fourth collection of short stories is scheduled for the fall of 1968: *The Séance and Other Stories.* He is amplifying *The Manor* and working on *The Estate.* He then hopes to translate *Shadows by the Hudson* and *A Ship to America,* both of which deal with American settings and characters. Having lived in America for more

than thirty years, he now feels ready to write about this
country, as if an entire new life has opened before him.
Having been kept alive so long by the illusion of the past,
he, perhaps, now has created a basis for preserving the
illusion of the future:

> There was a famous philosopher, Vaihinger, who
> wrote a book called *The Philosophy "As If,"* in
> which he showed that we all behave "as if." The "as
> if" is so much a part of our life that it really isn't
> artificial. After all, what could be more artificial than
> marriage? . . . Every man assumes he will go on liv-
> ing. He behaves *as if* he will never die. So I wouldn't
> call my attitude artificial. It's very natural and
> healthy. We have to go on living and writing.[21]

Or, perhaps, the entire matter of Singer's future is more
meaningfully presented in his response to a question about
his subsequent plans. He replied, "My future is my past."

Notes

1. The sources of information for this chapter are numerous. First
and basic, Singer happily has provided in *In My Father's Court*
(1956; 1966) a great deal of biographical material, although it
is scattered throughout the book and often chronologically out
of order. I have drawn heavily on these passages. Then, because
the memoirs only take Singer up to about his eighteenth year
and there is considerable misinformation about Singer's subsequent years, he was good enough to provide me with additional
information and to read this chapter. The interview with Singer
conducted by Joel Blocker and Richard Elman is an extremely
valuable source of biographical and other information, although
again the reminiscences are scattered and in need of chronological reconstruction ("An Interview with Isaac Bashevis Singer,"
Commentary, XXXVI [November, 1963], 364–69). I also found
the impressions of Richard Elman interesting, although fre-

quently merely confirmatory since many are based on statements made in the *Commentary* interview ("The Spinoza of Canal Street," *Holiday*, 38 [August, 1965], 83–87). A candid accounting of Singer's financial and editorial arrangements with various publishers appears in his article "What's In It for Me," *Harper's* [October, 1965], 172–73. Singer's introduction to the reissue of Israel Joshua Singer's *Yoshe Kalb* (New York: Harper and Row, 1965) contains a revealing discussion of the intramural fights between the right wing Yiddishists and Stalinists in the 1920's in Poland. Finally, additional information was provided in a television interview on November 6, 1966: *The Eternal Light:* "A Conversation with Isaac Bashevis Singer" (printed by NBC and The Jewish Theological Society of America, T–138, 1–14).

2. I have supplied here equivalents from the Jewish calendar as well as chronological references to Jewish festivals for two reasons: first, to be faithful to the special atmosphere of Singer's upbringing; and second, to indicate that he, like Dante, employs a religious calendar as well as the biblical events it commemorates as an organizing framework for many of his works, especially for *The Slave* and *The Manor*.

3. All of Singer's Yiddish works that have appeared in book form bear the name of Isaac Bashevis. His translated works bear the name of Isaac Bashevis Singer. His journalism, most of which he minimizes and which has appeared in the *Jewish Daily Forward*, appears under the name of Isaac Warshawsky (the man from Warsaw). To be sure, almost all his novels and many of his short stories first appeared in the *Forward;* indeed, he is probably the only living major writer whose works regularly have appeared in serial form. But here again it is only when he is pleased with the work that he uses the name of Isaac Bashevis or Isaac Bashevis Singer.

4. Israel Joshua, whose first novel was *Blood Harvest* (1927), was eleven years Singer's senior. *Yoshe Kalb* (1932) was translated into English and appeared the next year under the unfortunate title of *The Sinner*. His most famous work, and deservedly so, is the masterful *The Brothers Askenazi* (1935) which, along with his later *The Family Carnovsky* (1943), influenced Singer in the writing of his own family chronicles. He died in New York in 1944. In addition to *Yoshe Kalb,* Harper and Row plans to reissue *The River Breaks Up* (1938) and *East of Eden* (1939).

5. A further tie to his father: Singer to this day still writes, as did his older brother, in marbleized paper-covered composition books with single lines—the same books his father used for his

religious commentaries (see Singer's "Introduction" to *Yoshe Kalb* [New York, 1965], pp. vii–viii).

6. Blocker and Elman, "A Conversation with Isaac Bashevis Singer," *Commentary*, XXXVI (November, 1963), 368–69.

7. *Ibid.*, p. 368.

8. *Ibid.*

9. Is it, perhaps, more than biographical fidelity that leads Singer to retain the watchmaker in *The Family Moskat?* Saturated in philosophy, he surely is aware that the French Mechanistic philosophers employed the metaphor of the watchmaker to describe the Prime Mover and that their aim was to free many from superstition and achieve enlightenment.

10. "A Conversation with Isaac Bashevis Singer," *The Eternal Light*, p. 4.

11. Blocker and Elman, p. 367.

12. "Introduction" to Knut Hamsun's *Hunger* (New York, 1967).

13. Blocker and Elman, p. 370.

14. See Singer's "Introduction" to *Yoshe Kalb* (New York, 1966), pp. v–vi.

15. *Ibid.*

16. "A Conversation . . . ," p. 5.

17. Blocker and Elman, p. 369.

18. "A Conversation . . . ," p. 6.

19. Isaac Bashevis Singer, "What's in It for Me," *Harper's* (October, 1965), p. 173. Much of the publishing information noted in the last few pages comes from this article. Curiously and yet properly, when an author begins to write, the story of his life increasingly becomes the story of his works.

20. "The College Intellectual, 1965 Model," *New York Times Magazine* (December 6, 1964), pp. 36–37, 134–37.

21. Blocker and Elman, p. 365.

*The thing that has been, it is that
which shall be, and that which is done
is that which shall be done, and there
is no new thing under the sun.*

————Ecclesiastes 1:9

2.

The Family Moskat
and Jewish Saga

The Family Moskat (1950), Singer's first novel to be published in America and in English, although written second, is a family saga.[1] In the tradition of George Eliot, Tolstoy, Galsworthy, Thomas Mann, Jules Romains, and Roger Martin du Gard,[2] Singer's novel runs to over six hundred pages in the shortened, revised English edition of 1950 and reissue of 1965. It spans the first four decades of this century, weaves together the families of the Moskats, Bermans, Katzenellenbogens, and presents a cavalcade of nearly one hundred Polish, Russian, Austrian, and German characters. The novel is sprawling and depressingly encyclopedic, and thus shares with all fictional chronicles two faults common to the *genre*.[3] First, a scope so comprehensive that the mode tends to lose the privacy of fiction and become history. Second, a *dramatis personae* so numerous and variegated that the traditional novelistic focus on the individual is blurred. Nevertheless, both defects, though serious, perhaps would not be viewed with as much alarm by a Jewish writer as by a non-Jewish writer. In other words, *The Family Moskat* provides the occasion not only for an easy entrance to Singer's fictional world, but also for examining the special situation and difference of the Jewish writer. In Singer's case, at least, the latter concern is an inextricable part of the former.

I

The traditional Jewish artist is hemmed in by restrictions. The Second Commandment forbids graven images. In addition, the God of the Old Testament jealously guards His mystery and repeatedly rejects the consolation of incarnation. His "manifestations" eschew the actual and are limited to the verbal.[4] Obedient for many centuries to such injunctions and conditions, the traditional Jewish artist channeled all his creative impulses into sanctioned religious areas. Nor did he necessarily suffer for all that. David, after all, is an outstanding poet, and early and later ritualistic and architectural art is distinguished. Then, too, Mohammed's famous characterization of the Jews as the People of the Book should be multiplied to the People of the Books, for in addition to the Bible or Torah, there are the many commentaries on the Old Testament which are storehouses of tales and stories. In fact, it was possible in the commentaries to harmonize art and religion. The desire to tell a story served the religious end of concretizing or illuminating a moral or biblical explanation. And if that story begot other tales, they also provided additional moral ballast. The important point, however, is that when Jewish writers, under the impetus of the Jewish Enlightenment and other later movements,[5] began to venture timidly outside the traditional areas (and writing in Yiddish was in itself a compromise), they evidenced a decided preference for the tale or moral parable. As a result, the Yiddish short story is a special artistic creation.

Like its ancestral original in the commentaries, the Yiddish short story is not a self-contained, separative creation. Rather, it is a small unit of a larger continuum. The tales of Mendele Mocher Sforim, I. L. Peretz, and Sholom Aleichem—the classical Yiddish trio—are tied together by the regular reappearance of characters and situations, and are informed and shaped by the common physical and emotional geography of the *shtetl*. The stories in the commentaries are played out against the backdrop of the Torah; the tales of Yiddish writers reverberate against the background of the Family of Israel. Peretz, in fact, saw his artistic mission as forging *die goldene Keit* of Jewish continuity. Long before Faulkner created his mythical county, Yiddish writers fashioned a comprehensive, variegated fictional world, complete with its own recurrent cast of characters, situations of tension, and historically saturated geography. In consequence, Yiddish short stories essentially are abbreviated family sagas. In other words, in Yiddish literary tradition the long family chronicle does not signify a break from the short story but is an outgrowth of it.[6] Indeed, the tales of Mendele, Peretz, and Sholom Aleichem strung together present the same saga of collective destiny as does the typical family epic. Singer is partial to this pattern because he is a master of both forms.[7] Moreover, what his works reveal is that the bond that binds both modes together in a macrocosmic-microcosmic relationship is history.

As noted earlier, the tendency toward history is regarded as one of the defects of the family saga. But though it does contribute to diffusion, the Jewish writer, far from being disturbed by the prospect of history intruding into fiction, cherishes history as the heart of fiction. To the Jew history is the meeting ground between God and man. It has to be, for whereas in Greek mythology man plays no part in the genealogy of the Gods, the "history" of God in Judaism cannot exist apart from the history of the people Israel. Or to put it another way, because the Jewish God rejected tangibility, He is an unfinished God—a God not of finality but of duration. He thus has burdened the Jew with history—with the arena for fulfilling the original impulses of creation. Moreover, because to the Jews the Messiah has not yet come, history is the medium between God's messianic promise and man's communal efforts to realize that promise. In short, history represents the convenant in continuum. It is the Jewish incarnation. The artistic aim of the family chronicle or its concentrated counterpart, the short story, is to align the timely with the timeless and thereby employ current history as a stepping stone to biblical or eternal history. Accepting these burdens, Singer has sought in *The Family Moskat* to present a Jewish saga which is simultaneously modern and ancient. His tale is essentially a creation story fleshed with modern events. Belief is its genesis and anarchy its terminus. The ancient-modern saga moves from Eden to the Tower of Babel to the Deluge. The following summary of Singer's novel is presented in both general and specific terms to suggest the mythical nature of the historical pattern.

The Family Moskat typically spans three generations. The first is led by a primal sire, an original, an Adam— Meshulam Moskat. He embodies the clarity and piety perhaps naïvely associated with the past. Like Forsythe and Buddenbrooks, he is a dominant and dominating figure who appears to be the founder not only of the family and family business, but also of the human race. His power and virility appear in the wealth he acquires and the number of children he sires. Often, like his biblical prototypes, he has children by more than one woman. *The Family Moskat* begins with Meshulam taking a third wife.

Moskat's children, by their sheer numbers and vocational variety, represent the second generation. Appropriately, they introduce the principle of divergence. In them, the traditional monad begins to crack open, revealing the rich and pluralistic possibilities outside the familial code, *shtetl,* or business. Excited by the new vistas and yet uncertain what to do with such freedom, the second generation heralds a terrible beauty about to be born. Their divergences from tradition create conflicts, especially between father and son, the most intimate and perennial version of the gulf between generations. Although at this point there is considerable discord in the familial Eden, it is not yet unmanageable or total. But when the third generation appears and begins to take on a radical shape, the initial image of clarity and homogeneity gives way to prismatic fragmentation.

The primal sire is now dead and hardly remembered by the new generation. Meshulam's own children are old, often infirm and self-indulgent. Family reunions are awkward and embarrassing occasions for nonrecognitions and misunderstandings. Secret vows are made never to attend one of these affairs again.[8] For the first time grandsons are engaged in professions which, according to the older standards, would be regarded as worldly or scandalous. The granddaughters reenact the drama of Nora in *A Doll's House.* This latest generation no longer lives in the same neighborhood but is scattered all over Poland, even the world. The members speak different languages, have forgotten Yiddish or never learned it, and confront each other at family affairs like the assemblage around the Tower of Babel. They conceive of themselves as individuals whose quest for personal identity is not involved in

familial or Jewish identity. In short, they are citizens of
the modern world experiencing the freedom of a new
exile.

The following passage from the novel nicely sums
up the full arc:

> Old Meshulam Moskat had been a king among Jews;
> and, with all their faults, his sons had managed to
> stay Jews. But the grandchildren had completely
> alienated themselves from the old ways. (551)

In the same vein but with a revealing biblical analogy,
Pinnie, one of Meshulam's last surviving sons, surveys the
enormous family at a gathering:

> Pinnie gazed at them and shrugged his shoulders. A
> miracle of God! He had hardly realized that old
> Meshulam had left behind such a multitude. But
> still it was not the same as in the old days. Then,
> when the family gathered at the old man's for the
> Channukah holiday or Purim, they were all cut from
> the same cloth. But now Pinnie compared them in
> his mind to the animals and fowl of Noah's ark.
> There was such a bewildering variety of types. . . .
> (566–67)

Finally, Leah, having divorced her religious husband and
married Meshulam's overseer, having been to America and
back, reflects on her personal version of the familial arc:
" 'Ah, what a strange brood she had given birth to; a rabbi,
an apostate, a teacher in college, a Wall Street lawyer!' "
(572). In short, in Singer's familial pattern, variety and
secularity become historical synonyms.

To the traditional Jewish writer who is saturated in
the Bible as history, the family saga presents the oppor-

tunity to present history as a kind of Bible.[9] The ease with
which biblical parallels are evoked is matched only by the
facility with which other ethnic and national ideologies
can be accommodated. For the Jewish ideal, one can substitute the Puritan tradition, Midwestern pastorialism, the
Southern code, and even the American dream. Perhaps,
the Negro movement and the state of Israel may in time
also confirm the full and accurate run of the familial arc.
Indeed, it would not be farfetched to claim that every
family saga, no matter what communal or particular ideological burden it bears, ultimately presents the precarious
journey of belief into the modern world. The Jews at the
beginning of *The Family Moskat* are recognizable as Jews.
Those at the end of the novel are merely individuals who
happen to be Jewish. To the former, God is an object of
daily and familiar devotion. To the latter, God is as alien
to them as they have become to the concept of being
chosen. In short, *The Family Moskat* is a Jewish novel in
the process of becoming a modern novel. The historical
assimilation is matched by an artistic assimilation. In ancient times, the Deluge came; in modern times, and Singer
terminates his saga there, the Nazi holocaust.

II

Just as the prospect of the family saga becoming history does not disturb the Jewish writer (although the
events it records may), so the deemphasis of the individual
—the other major defect of the form—is not in itself a
cause for alarm. Indeed, from the traditional point of
view the concept of individuality divorced from community is suspect. It has to be, for the Messianic promise is
not an individualistic but a collective commitment. In fact,
the emergence of separative individuality along with ro-

mantic love and secular learning are the perennial three signs both of the breakup of the Jewish community and of the frustration of messianic promise.[10] The presence of all three at the end of Singer's novel brings about a comprehensive correlation in which the separation from God is accompanied and often preceded by the separation from the family and the community.

Characteristically, Singer's presentation of the dilemma of individuality appears in the more revealing dilemma of marriage, for to Singer Jewish reality is defined as the reality of relationships. Marriage thus serves as the most congenially artistic means of examining and judging the Jewish *shtetl*. Indeed, because in Singer's world the breakdown of marriage often involves the rejection of Jewishness, both losses become emblematic of the larger disintegration of the community. The particular source of marital discord in Singer's works is mismatching. The short story, "Big and Little," as its title suggests, completely revolves about an oddly yoked couple. In *The Family Moskat*, Abram Shapiro compares his marriage to a "square peg in a round hole" (51). Nyunie sums up his domestic lot in less revealing sexual terms: " 'Not a wife— a plague' " (180). In one of Singer's short stories, the Devil confesses that one of his most successful stratagems is to mismatch people in marriage. And in a revealing slip of the tongue, Abram Shapiro speaks of marrying Asa Heshel and Hadassah " 'According to the law of Moses and Ishmael—I mean Israel' " (51). Indeed, Abram Shapiro's slip echoes one of Singer's most merciless and perverse treatments of mismatching. In "The Gentleman from Cracow," the satanic benefactor consecrates or desecrates his own marriage with Hodle, the town witch, with the following inverted ritual:

> The groom held out a triangular ring and, instead
> of saying, "With this ring be thou consecrated to
> me according to the laws of Moses and Israel," he
> said, "With this ring, be thou desecrated to me ac-
> cording to the blasphemy of Korah and Ishmael."
> (39)

Prior to this black mass and marriage, all the other un-
married inhabitants of Frampol are coupled in the frenzy
of a *Walpurgis Nacht*. Twelve-year-old boys are mated
with spinsters, midgets with giants, beauties with cripples.
To be sure, "The Gentleman from Cracow" is set in a
distant time, in a superstitious and unworldly village, and
is beset by a full-fledged devil. But those differences are
not peculiar to Frampol, for the same dislocations occur
in the more "modern" setting of *The Family Moskat*.

Throughout the entire novel there is not a single love
relationship that lasts or bears any resemblance to its glow-
ing origins. Couples claw at each other, castrate each other,
are unfaithful, remain together to practice the special art
of intimate sadism, divorce each other, and implant their
sour hostilities in their children. What all these botched
and blemished marriages lead to is intermarriage which
at least in Singer's world is the ultimate mismatch (420).
With that final act the individual divorces himself not only
from the family, but also from God. Indeed, the image of
Jewish tradition in tatters at the end of the novel finds
its counterpart in the marital debris and carnage scattered
throughout the novel. So total and unrelieved is the discordant portrait of marriage that by the end of the novel
marriage appears to represent Singer's metaphor not only
of the dilemma of individuality, but also the dilemma of
mortality.

To be sure, in a few other works, notably *The Slave*

and "Short Friday," a metaphor of immortality is generated. Significantly, love crowns belief. The communication
between husband and wife, both sexual and spiritual, becomes communion. In fact, in such lovely relationships,
marriage is the threshold of religion, for in Singer's world
a man's relationship with his wife disciplines and determines his relationship with God. But *The Family Moskat*
features discord, not harmony; the bond between love and
belief is not sustained but broken. To ask the question
"Why does love go wrong?" is simultaneously to ask "Why
is belief lost?" Perhaps the character who provides the fullest answers to both questions is Asa Heshel.[11]

III

When Asa Heshel Bannet, the grandson of the revered
Rabbi Dan Katzenellenbogen of Tereshpol Minor, arrives
in Warsaw almost the first sight that greets him is that of
a cripple: "A legless man rolled on a small wooden plat-
form. He stretched out his hand toward Asa Heshel." In
Asa Heshel's pocket there is a worn copy of Spinoza's
Ethics. Spinoza maintains one should not feel pity for the
infirm. But the legless man cries out for help and Asa
Heshel, in his first disagreement with the great philosopher, gives the cripple a copper coin (22). Walking on,
Asa Heshel encounters a ragpicker "with a dirty white
beard and a sack on his shoulder, and hears his rasping
voice, 'What'll you sell? What'll you sell? . . . I buy pots
and pans, old shoes, old hats, rags, rags.' " Asa Heshel, ever
the philosopher, thinks to himself: "The ragpicker must
have a deeper meaning. . . . What he really meant was:
'Rags, that's all that's left of our striving' " (23).

After Asa Heshel has been in Warsaw for a while and
after he has met Hadassah and tasted the despair of those

who are star-crossed lovers, he looks out of his window
one night and sees:

> Down below in the courtyard a beggar woman bent
> over a box, a sack on her shoulders, poking with a
> hook among the refuse. She pulled out a couple of
> rags, and stuffed them into the sack. She lifted a
> shrunken, worn face toward the upper windows and
> sang out in a thin voice: "I buy bones, I buy rags.
> Bones, bones." (99)

Asa Heshel had been glancing at the heavens and meditating on Spinoza, but the sight of this human scavenger
drives all lofty thoughts and philosophy away. He concludes: "Once . . . she too was young, and the ox whose
bones she now sought to buy was a calf leaping about in
the meadows. Time makes refuse of all things. No philosophy could alter that." Finally, one night while Asa
Heshel and Hadassah are aimlessly walking the cold, dark
streets they pass a slaughterhouse:

> Porters with hoses were swishing water on the stone
> floor. Slaughterers stood near bloodfilled granite vats,
> slitting the necks of ducks, geese, and hens. Fowls
> cackled deafeningly. The wings of a rooster, its
> throat just slit, fluttered violently. . . . A little fur-
> ther on, in the fish market, stood tubs, barrels,
> troughs. In the stale-smelling water, carp, pike and
> tench swam about. Beggars sang in quavering voices,
> cripples stretched out stumps of arms. (158)

The Family Moskat opens with and is carried along
by images, which in their cacophony of decay, disfigure-
ment, and death, bring about a grisly fusion of man, matter, and animals. The living live off the dead, and what

they cannot use then becomes refuse for the subterranean world of cripples who haunt urban streets and assault the peace of the heavens and the sensibilities of philosophers. Fusing Swift and Dickens, Singer presents garbage as the excrement of the city. But then turning that excremental vision to communal ends, he indicates that the fragmented marriages find their objective correlative in the slaughtered animals and the army of the crippled living-dead. The entire novel is orchestrated as a collective elegy. Its main theme is not life but death, or rather the extent and intrusion of death in life. Its real setting is not the asphalt jungle but the concrete cemetery: "Beginning with the two cemetery plots that, years before, Reb Mushalam had bought . . . an entire path of graves had developed" (549). Its final result is such a sour devaluation of the present that it leads to the pessimistic proverb: "Family prestige is in the cemetery" (532).[12]

The point of all this is to dramatize with unflinching ugliness the entire prospect of transience. Does nothing last? Not youth, beauty, love, marriage? And if not, is Asa Heshel without justification in echoing Ivan Karamazov's cry, " 'Everything is permitted!' "? The moral anarchy and nihilism that spew out of the disgust with life, or rather with the collusion of life and death, is Singer's way of dramatizing the issue of God. In more fashionable terms, it has been called the issue of absurdity. But that term is neither fashionable nor new to Singer and other Yiddish writers. Indeed, the Yiddish theater might be called the first theater of the absurd. The particular absurdity in *The Family Moskat* is provided by Spinoza who, like a specter of insane lucidity, reigns over this entire grisly scene of human debris with serene impotence. In more comprehensive terms, absurdity to Singer is man's second fall: the first involves the loss of paradise; the second the loss of purpose. There are thus two dramas in *The Family Moskat*. The first is set in Asa Heshel's birthplace, Tereshpol Minor, a small, isolated town where time has stood still for generations and where tradition has remained more or less intact. The second takes place in modern Warsaw where Asa Heshel arrives, significantly, at the turn of the century. In journeying from Tereshpol Minor to Warsaw, Asa Heshel travels from the past to the present. In the process, he acts out not only the eternal drama of the loss of paradise, but also the modern drama of the loss of purpose.

IV

In Singer's world purity is as illusory as permanence; even in Eden there was a serpent. Thus, although Asa Heshel's heritage is distinguished, it is not without hints of discord. His paternal grandfather, Reb Bannet, "never touched food before sunset, mortified his flesh with cold baths, and in the winter rolled his body in the snow" (25). Reb Bannet's asceticism was coupled with a fervent study of the mystical Cabala, a dangerous partnership in Singer's works and to some extent in Jewish history. His maternal grandfather, Rabbi Katzenellenbogen,[13] traced his lineage back to King David and had a chart to prove it. Plagued by the presence of mystical hasteners of the Messiah, Rabbi Katzenellenbogen also lives a hellish domestic life. His daughter, Finkel, Asa Heshel's mother, was deserted by her husband. The Rabbi's two sons, Zaddock and Levi, are "empty heads and dawdlers" who live at their father's house and at his expense. Rabbi Katzenellenbogen, in despair about what to do with his children and finding that old age does not free him from worldly temptations, falls into melancholy.[14]

As a child, Asa Heshel was considered a prodigy; "At
five he was studying Talmud, at six he began the Talmudic
commentaries, at eight the teacher had no more to give
him" (26–27). His future seemed brilliant, especially if
he pursued a middle course between the extremes represented by his two grandfathers. But excesses often beget
a counter excess; Asa Heshel begins his deflective turn by
moving outside traditional channels and reading the works
of the heretic Solomon Maimon.[15] He then takes up with
Jekuthiel, the local watchmaker and atheist, at whose
house he has access to the literary works of Klopstock,
Goethe, Schiller, and Heine; and to the philosophies of
Spinoza, Kant, and Hegel. The intellectual walls of the
ghetto begin to crumble and ironically or symbolically
Asa Heshel is weaned from the People of the Book by
books.

Initially, Asa Heshel cannot read enough. But after
the first heady excitement wears off, he finds that the eternal questions and doubts still persist. From his orthodox
grandfather he receives no final answers; from the philosophers he receives an over-abundance of answers. Convinced that the truth is still to be found, Asa Heshel
castigizes his own ignorance and plunges deeper. Soon he
decides he must go to Warsaw and pursue his studies in
a more systematic manner at a university. His movement
from the country to the city adds further reinforcement
to the modernity of Asa Heshel's archetypal journey.

In Warsaw, pursuing abortive secular studies, Asa
Heshel is presented by Singer with the psychology of a
schizophrenic. Torn between his religious and modern
selves, he is a curious mixture of the "small town Yeshivah
student and the cosmopolitan" (78). His talk is at once
playful, even frivolous, and yet heavily laden with philosophical and talmudic quotations (207). Hadassah, his mis-

tress, makes the following entry in her diary: "Asa Heshel is so restless. He said that the modern Jew is not a human being. He's so full of contradictions" (424). Many different characters in the novel separately confirm that his face is a "mixture of youth and age," a mixture he passes on to his son (416, 419). Adele, Asa Heshel's wife, soon after their marriage writes to her mother:

> From what he tells me about his family it's quite clear that they're a bunch of religious primitives. Their way of life is just as though they were still in the Middle Ages. Even Asa Heshel himself is a mixture of barbarousness and modernity. That's why it's often so hard to understand him. (210)

The value of Adele's view is its prejudice. Because she considers herself "enlightened" and cut off from primitive practices, she is unable to understand Asa Heshel's dilemma of serving as a receptacle for the ghosts of the past. Asa Heshel is a study of strain, especially Jewish strain. In Singer's world the pull of the past is the pull of God. The pull of the present and of the future is the pull of the modern world. God is uncompromising, tyrannical, and patient. The modern gods and world are relativistic, pluralistic, and anxious. The impulse of the soul is constancy; God cherishes and is jealous of such fidelity. The impulse of the body is variety; the Devil is legion and applauds endless striving. God has yet to send the Messiah; the modern religionists of humanity seek utopian realization within their lifetime. The traditional hero of the Old Testament wrestles with his adversary Satan; the Faustian hero of the modern world makes a pact with the Devil.

Ironically, perhaps, it is Adele who finally presents the key to Asa Heshel's dislocation. Shortly before the end of the novel and before the invasion of Poland by the

Nazis, Asa Heshel, who has decided to stay behind in Warsaw, comes to say farewell to Adele and his son who are
fleeing. She looks at his face and notes the same mixture
of youth and age still straining his contenance. She tries
to puzzle out what tortures him so:

> Was it the failure to have had a career? Did his heart
> long for someone? She was on the point of asking
> him, but suddenly she knew; he was not a worldly
> man by his very essence. He was one of those who
> must serve God or die. He had forsaken God, and
> because of this he was dead—a living body with a
> dead soul. She was astonished that this simple truth
> had eluded her until now. (582)

The tragedy of Asa Heshel is the tragedy of misplaced
devotion. Asa Heshel yearns for God and for justice but
comes to the conclusion that the two are irreconcilable. To
him, God becomes an obstacle not a means to life. Turning away, he tries to expend and to exchange his love for
the divine for the love of the human and the world. He
alternately tries to make every experience final, like love,
or temporary, like sex. When separately both fail, he attempts to fuse the two with the heat of blasphemy. On
the holiest night of the year, Yom Kippur, the Day of
Atonement, on which all judgments for the year will be
finally recorded, Asa Heshel commits adultery. But it does
not work. His thoughts give him no peace: "Generations
of rabbis, saints, rabbinical wives had purified themselves
in order that he might be born. And here he was spend-
ing the night of Yom Kippur with another man's wife"
(316). Moreover, God does not answer Asa Heshel's equally
blasphemous desire to be punished.[16] Instead, the ironic
frustration Asa Heshel experiences is the final failure of
the absurd hero. His desire to free himself from God and

to achieve Faustian and Promethean independence results in his perpetual inability to die.

Frittering away his great capacity for love on a series of quick, short-lived relationships, Asa Heshel frustrates his deepest desire to spend his life for something that will outlast it. He also incapacitates himself for forming any lasting relationship and thus becomes part of that grisly fusion of man, matter, and animals. And yet Asa Heshel does form one relationship, and it is a significant one. He decides to remain behind in the Warsaw ghetto. His reasons are not completely clear to himself but he feels that he has at last laid his despair to rest. Besides, he prophetically remarks, " 'I have a feeling that all of humanity is caught in a trap. No going forward and no going back. We Jews will be the first victims' " (527).

In the history of Asa Heshel, Singer has attempted to record the history of the Jew in exile. The central burden Asa Heshel bears is that of belief in a world and time increasingly alien to such devotion. Because the Jew exists on the periphery of society and history, he first encounters the onslaught of disbelief which, in biblical fashion, is then followed by man's persecution of his brother. In a state of spiritual exhaustion, Asa Heshel chooses to remain in Warsaw, an act that for all its passivity and even weakness represents his desire still to remain a Jew.

Notes

1. *The Family Moskat* first appeared in serialized form in the *Forward* from 1945 to 1948. The original Yiddish edition in 1950 was in two volumes. A revised, shorter English translation was published in 1950; out of print, it was reissued in 1965. Although *Satan in Goray* (1935) was composed and printed before this family chronicle, I have altered the chronological order of treat-

ment for a number of reasons. First, *The Family Moskat* is in many ways autobiographical and thus enjoys an intimacy with the story of Singer's life that appeared in the preceding chapter. Second, Singer's family saga rapidly and nicely reveals the way in which his religious and demonic concerns are inevitably involved in history. Finally, because his most recent novel *The Manor* is also a family chronicle, the examination of *The Family Moskat* first prepares the way for what will be treated last.

2. In this connection, one should also recall the influence of Singer's brother, I. J. Singer, especially through *The Brothers Ashkenazi* (1935) and *The Family Carnovsky* (1943). In addition, the epic poem, *Pan Tadeusz* (1834), of Adam Mickiewicz (1798–1855) may be an important touchstone for at least two reasons. First, the poem is cited in *The Family Moskat* (53). Second, Mickiewicz's work, which traces Polish society in Lithuania during the time of Napoleon's campaign against Moscow in 1811–1812, presents the same memorializing of a society that is about to be destroyed or pass away as does Singer in his saga.

3. The family chronicle is not unusual in this respect. Indeed, every major novelistic form contains the seeds of its structural undoing. And in at least two instances, aside from that of the family saga, Singer is proof of such built-in defects. For example, *The Magician of Lublin* is a picaresque novel. The essential problem with this form is that it has to end; and terminus is the very antithesis of the form. Singer's attempted solution, like that of Cervantes and Twain, is lame; it consists of a weak letter from Emilia to Yasha. Then, there is the matter of the gothic tale. The form moves character toward caricature and narration toward parable. To reestablish versimilitude, Singer makes the same mistake that Faulkner did in *Sanctuary* and that, perhaps, Melville did in *Billy Budd:* he attempts to provide objective documentation for miraculous happenings. In this case, as in many others, Singer should have been more responsive to the attitude expressed in the first line of one of his recent stories: " 'No, one needn't be insane to get a crazy idea into one's head' " ("The Boudoir," *Vogue* [April, 1966], p. 148).

4. The ancient Hebrew mind in contrast to that of the Greek seems to have been more impressed by time than space. As a correlation, the Greek language was richer in nouns and adjectives that describe attributes primarily in space, whereas the Hebrew language was more insistent on verbs that record the attributes of duration. In ancient Hebrew there is no special word for painting.

The reason for these many contrasts is not hard to find.

The Jewish God has no face or form whereas the Greek gods were tangible and multiple. With respect to art, man is never termed a creator in Judaism but at best a maker. Isaiah notes that creation neither can be contained nor imprisoned by any image made by man (29:16). For a fuller discussion of the entire subject, see Boaz Cohen, "Art in Jewish Law," *Judaism*, 3 (Spring, 1954), 165–76.

5. Under the influence of all the many movements we associate with the birth of the modern world, Judaism spawned a number of diverse and often divisive factions. Although clearly this is not the place to retell that story, which has been more amply and skillfully related by Heinrich Graetz in his multivolume *History of the Jews* (Philadelphia, 1941), two basic trends can be noted.

The first approaches Judaism essentially as a religion, the second as an ethnic nationality. Within the first there were the strongly opposing forces of Orthodoxy and Reform Judaism with mystical neo-Hasidism having little to do with either. Yiddishism, Bundism, and Zionism, all treated in *The Family Moskat* and examined in Chapter III of this study, constitute the central developments of the second group.

6. Milton Hindus, in his thorough and penetrating survey of Singer's fiction (*Jewish Heritage Reader* [New York, 1965]), quite rightly challenges the general contention that the genius of Yiddish literature lies primarily or exclusively in the field of the short story. Hindus cites Linetski's autobiographical *Polish Boy*, and some of the works of Mendele, Sholem Asch, and the Singer brothers, as proof of Yiddish ability in longer forms. Hindus's corrective is valuable but perhaps what also should be stressed is that through history the modes become not alternatives but versions of each other. Indeed, *Satan in Goray*, which is really a novella, is written in the style of the Hebrew *pinkassim*, a kind of community chronicle, and thus nicely concentrates what the family chronicle elaborates. Then, what should be remembered is the Hasidic emphasis on storytelling which, in its recounting of the deeds of saints, not only initially existed side by side with traditional commentaries, but also ultimately took on an equal value with those commentaries (see Gershom Scholem, *Trends of Jewish Mysticism* [New York, 1946], p. 349). Finally, that the short story could present, if not the fullness at least the suggestive outline of the familial saga, appears in Peretz's "The Four Generations" and Singer's own "The Little Shoemakers." In the latter, Singer traces many generations of Orthodox Jews who bear biblical names—from Poland to America, from the seventeenth to the twentieth centuries.

7. Obviously, Singer is not alone here. Charles Angoff, who has

written many short stories, still is at work on a multiple family novel. Dan Jacobson, the South African-born Jewish writer, who is noted for his short stories, including "The Zulu and the Zayda," recently published a family novel, *The Beginners* (1966). Significantly the names of some of his characters are David, Rachel, Sarah, and Joel.

8. A rapid, pathetic, and familiar example of the gulf between generations and countries appears in the thoughts of the American-born Mendy who has come to Warsaw with his family:

> He had been eager for his trip to Europe, but now he was fed up. He was tired of everything—the family, the hotels, the filth, the monstrous food, this constant talking and listening in Yiddish. He longed to be back in New York. . . . He was bored by them all—those queer uncles and aunts, who, even though he stood a head taller than any of them, kept on pinching his cheeks as though he were a baby. He made up his mind that when he got back to New York he'd never look at those greenhorns again. He'd never come to Europe again, except mainly to England. (452)

The subtitle of Thomas Mann's *Buddenbrooks* is *The Decay of a Family.*

9. A recent example of the Jewish writer's perennial quest for an eternal background is Bernard Malamud's novel, *The Fixer* (1966). Malamud explains his aim: "I did not want simply to novelize the actual case of a persecuted Jew. My problem was to disinvent history and invent mythology with the object of portraying timeless injustice" (quoted in *New York Times Book Review* [September 4, 1966], p. 8).

10. See Irving Howe's masterful presentation not only of this phase of Jewish history, but also the entire secular messianic offshoots of traditional Orthodoxy in his "Introduction" to *A Treasury of Yiddish Stories,* edited by Irving Howe and Eliezer Greenberg (New York, 1954), pp. 1–71.

11. As Singer's explicitly autobiographical memoir *In My Father's Court* (1966) reveals, *The Family Moskat* is clearly Singer's fictionalized autobiography. In particular, Asa Heshel's traditional background and his modern rootlessness undoubtedly reflect those of Singer himself or of his older brother (closer in age to Asa Heshel), or a combination of both.

12. Singer's notion of death-in-life appears in ultimate form in his story "Jachid and Jechidad," which describes how two sinful angels are sentenced to death by being born to life.

13. Is it coincidental or intentional on Singer's part to have chosen the name Katzenellenbogen? For there actually was a Rabbi Ezekiel Katzenellenbogen who, like his fictional counterpart, opposed the study of the Cabala by young men and resisted those who sought to hasten the coming of the Messiah.

14. What is striking about Singer's presentation of Asa Heshel's religious background is that it is perceived and presented with the same honesty as are the anarchistic tendencies of the secular world. The past is never hallowed merely because it is the past, just as rabbis are never presented as angels because they are rabbis. Or as the narrator of "The Wife Killer" briskly puts it, " 'Today people talk of love. They think once upon a time men were angels. Nonsense!' " (46) Nevertheless, the accusation that Singer has violated the sacred memory of the past still persists. Recently, Singer replied to that charge: "My judgment is that good does not always triumph, that this is far from the best of all possible worlds. That's why my Jews are not all good Jews. Why should they be different from everybody else?" (Quoted from Richard M. Elman, "The Spinoza of Canal Street," *Holiday*, 38 [August, 1965], 851.)

15. Solomon Maimon (c. 1753–1800) assumed his last name after Maimonides. A cynical philosopher, he was a favorite of Goethe and Schiller, but brought great harm to the Jews through his *Autobiography* by exposing the weak points of Polish Jewry; his sample was restricted to his own contacts and far from representative of Polish Jewry.

16. In Hermann Hesse's *Steppenwolf* (New York, 1927), one finds a nearly perfect expression of Asa Heshel's dilemma. Speaking of his protagonist, Hesse says that his "affliction was not due to any defects of his nature, but rather to a profusion of gifts and powers which had not attained to harmony." Later on, Hesse adds perceptively, "self-hate is really the same thing as sheer egoism, and in the long run breeds the same cruel isolation and despair" (11, 13).

Human life is reduced to real suffering, to hell, only when two ages, two cultures and religions overlap. A man of the Classical Age who had to live in medieval times would suffocate miserably just as a savage does in the midst of civilization. Now there are times when a whole generation is caught in this way between two ages, two modes of life, with the consequence it loses all power to understand itself and has no standard, no security, no simple acquiescence.

———Hermann Hesse, *Steppenwolf*

3.

The Family Moskat:
Secular Metaphysics and Messiahs

The family chronicle form in general combines eulogy and elegy; it records both gain and loss. *The Family Moskat* in particular transcribes an arc that runs from tradition to the individual talent, from Orthodoxy to eclecticism, from the Torah to literature. Breaking free from the tight confines of traditional Judaism and Tereshpol Minor, Asa Heshel joins the open, multiple streams of modern Warsaw. His varied political views, his endless philosophical speculations, his many and temporary love affairs, his messianic and metaphysical substitutions, his literary kinships represent Singer's version of the European *Zeitgeist* in the first three decades of the century. Modern Warsaw provides the geography for Singer's vision of Europe in transition; and Asa Heshel is his *Steppenwolf*.

Wherever Asa Heshel turns he encounters so many variations of his own fragmentation that he feels he is living in a hall of mirrors. He makes friends with Jewish artists and finds that they, too, are caught in the crosscurrents of freedom and religiosity (297). Beset by contradictions, he laments his suicidal talent to perceive further dualities: "he was meditating on Spinoza and Darwin. How could these two philosophies of life be reconciled? How could the pantheistically static be squared with the Heraclitean dynamic?" (374) He envies those who can simply choose between Spinoza and Darwin. But caught between heaven and earth, he himself cannot accept a half that passes itself off as a whole.

The same two pulls he feels toward the past and the present appear in the education of many of his contemporaries. Abram Shapiro, with characteristic gusto and impatience, puts the blame on the older generation for starting the confusion and then exonerating themselves of the consequences:

> "The damn fools. First they send their daughters to decent, modern schools and then they expect them to forget everything they've learned and suddenly become old-fashioned, orthodox, meek Jewish housewives. From the twentieth century back to the Middle Ages." (138)

Even in the midst of the Hasidic Bialodrevna synagogue, the personal dislocation of Asa Heshel finds its multiple echoes in the children of that holy and pious congregation:

> What things had not happened in Warsaw since the Revolution of 1905! Chassidic youth had cast off their gaberdines, shaved their faces, become strikers,

Zionists. Daughters of respectable homes had fallen in love with university students and had run off with them to New York, Buenos Aires, or Palestine. Mothers of children had discarded their matron's wigs and let the whole world see their naked hair. It was these worldly books, printed in Yiddish that everyone could understand, that had poisoned decent people's minds. And these "reformed" schools, where parents were sending their daughters lately, were nothing but nests of paganism and wantonness. . . . Almost every one of the worshippers had a son or daughter at home who was falling victim to the new ways. They brought home novels from the libraries. They went to all sorts of meetings. Speakers were thundering that Jews should not wait for the Messiah to come, but build the Jewish homeland with their own hands. Boys and girls met in secret cellars and attics and conspired against the Czar. The truth was that the Jews were being persecuted more and more. Day by day it was becoming harder to earn a living. What would be the end of it all? (165–66)

In Egypt the Jews had been afflicted with slavery. In twentieth-century Europe, the burden is freedom. Moses pleaded with Pharaoh to let the chosen people go to the promised land. Darwin, Freud, Marx, Herzl, et. al. plead with the czar, the Pope, the Polish counts, the old rabbis to let the people go from the intellectual and cultural ghetto. Awaiting the Ten Commandments at Mount Sinai, the Jews worshipped the Golden Calf. Expecting justice and world brotherhood in Moscow, Warsaw, Vienna, Berlin, and Jerusalem, the Jews study and write secular books, create new metaphysical idols, and worship new political or zionistic messiahs.

Clearly, the pattern is not limited to the Bible or to the twentieth century; for an eternal cycle of slavery and freedom runs throughout history. The breakup of an intact order leads initially to an exciting renaissance but then rounds off to a disintegrating or lamentable close. This tripartite arc, presented in miniature in Singer's family chronicle, appears with cyclic regularity. Thus, describing pretty much the same legacy of disorder that followed in the wake of late eighteenth-century revolutions, Samuel Taylor Coleridge in "Religious Musings" (1796) cries out:

> I will raise up a mourning, O ye Fields!
> And curse your spells, that film the eye of Faith,
> Hiding the present God; whose presence lost,
> The moral world's cohesion, we become
> An Anarchy of Spirits! Toy-bewitched,
> Made blind by lusts, disinherited of soul,
> No common centre Man, no common sire
> Knoweth! A sordid, solitary thing
> Mid countless brethren with a lonely heart
> Through courts and cities the smooth savage roams
> Feeling itself, his own low self the whole. . . .

In "Sailing to Byzantium," William Butler Yeats provides the modern analogue:

> Things fall apart; the centre cannot hold;
> Mere anarchy is loosed upon the world,
> The blood-dimmed tide is loosed, and everywhere
> The ceremony of innocence is drowned;
> The best lack all conviction, while the worst
> Are full of passionate intensity.

But what in particular creates this wasteland of twentieth-century Europe? What spawns the modern "Anarchy of Spirits" and gives birth to the new devil, the smooth savage? In Chapter 2 of this study, the emphasis was on the origins of Asa Heshel's religious despair as he moved from the Jewish cohesion of Tereshpol Minor to the modern confusion of Warsaw. Now Asa Heshel's Jewish dislocation is a passport to other-than-Jewish dislocation. Shorn of his gaberdine and dressed in modern clothes, living in the city, the dominant environment of this century, Asa Heshel is indistinguishable from all other individuals whose pursuit of identity is uninvolved in familial or religious identity and who busily prepare masks to meet other masks. Above all, Singer weaves Asa Heshel tightly into European modernity by detailing his reading of Yiddish and European literature and philosophy.

I

The Family Moskat contains more than fifty allusions to secular works, more than in all of Singer's books combined. To be sure, it is an understandable dimension for Singer's most autobiographical novel and for a family chronicle which documents the transformation of the Jews through the means of secular knowledge and schools. But its ultimate function goes beyond the contemporary to the historical, for through these secular readings Singer essentially has presented the Jewish version of the Battle of the Books.

Initially, the rationalization for writing secular works in Yiddish was not to fragment but to preserve a Jewish culture, both folk and intellectual, through the language of exile—Yiddish. Indeed, it was formalized in a movement known as Yiddishism. I. L. Peretz buttressed the movement by proclaiming that Jewishness need not be solely a matter of religion but also could be represented as a culture. And, in fact, he became the father of so-called

"Worldly Jewishness." Singer's judgment of this movement is ambivalent: "This expression is in itself contradictory. It is akin to saying: worldly religiosity. But the
contradiction springs from the contradiction that exists in
the heart of every modern Jew." [1] Moreover, although the
proponents of nonreligious Jewish movements argued that
no reduction or violation of the ancients was intended by
the moderns, the results are otherwise.

At just about the same time that Peretz was formulat-
ing his philosophy of "Worldly Jewishness," the American
Marxist, Feigenbaum, published an article called "The
Poetic Rebirth of Religion" in *Zukunft* (1912). Feigenbaum called for Judaism to be poetically reclaimed by
lighting Sabbath candles but not saying the benediction,
drinking wine but not reciting the *Kiddush,* and eating
matzo balls without holding a *seder* or Passover service.
Indeed, these suggestions were accepted by many and ritual
observance yielded to the elegance of candles on the table
and wine with meals and the ease of culinary identity. A
witness to the minimum, even reductive ends of such enlightened philosophies that promised so much, Singer
came to understand better his parents' reactions to his
becoming a Yiddish writer:

> It was a great shock to them. They considered all
> secular writers to be heretics, all unbelievers—they
> really were too, most of them. To become a *literat*
> was to them almost as bad as becoming a *meshumed,*
> one who forsakes the faith.[2]

> My parents opposed me terribly because they wanted
> me to be a rabbi and a writer of religious books. To
> them, a secular writer meant unbelieving. . . . They
> were never proud of the fact that I wrote. As a mat-
> ter of fact, my parents tried to hide with all their

power, the fact that they have two sons writers. . . .
So they had in their family, a double shame.[3]

Characteristically, Singer himself is caught between the
views of his parents and those of the Yiddishists; indeed,
in his own person he comprehends the impulses of both
the ancients and the moderns. But such ambiguity is not
extended to those total irreligionists who turn completely
to the pursuit of the secular moderns.

As Asa Heshel discovers, the problem with secular
knowledge is that it has no end. Thus, he reads and studies
only to find that he finishes nothing and achieves nothing.
The promise of the brilliant scholar begins to fade. Actually, Asa Heshel is but one specimen in Singer's fictional
gallery of frustrated secular scholars and philosophers.
Another student of Spinoza, Dr. Fischelson of "The Spinoza of Market Street," had "drawers full of notes and
drafts, but it didn't seem that he would ever be able to
complete his work" (9). The Talmudic scholar who converts to Christianity, Zeidel of "Zeidlus the Pope," worked
on his

> treatise, but still it was not finished. His standards
> were so high that he was continually finding flaws,
> yet the more changes he made, the more he found
> were necessary. . . . His drawers were stuffed with
> manuscript pages, notes, references, but he could not
> bring his work to a conclusion. After years of effort,
> he was so fatigued that he could no longer distin-
> guish between right and wrong, sense and nonsense,
> between what would please and displease the Church.
> (185)

Another character who closely echoes Asa Heshel is Dr.
Solomon Margolin who as a child was considered a prod-

igy. But his pursuit of women combined with his secular knowledge frittered away his potential:

> At seventeen he had attempted a translation of Spinoza's *Ethics* from Latin to Hebrew, unaware it had been done before. Everyone predicted he would be a genius. But he had squandered his talents, continually changing his fields of study; and he had wasted years in learning languages, in wandering from country to country. (193)

Finally, Dr. Margolis of "Caricature" has been at work on an enormous opus which seeks to unify all existing systems of philosophy. But he "was uncertain whether his philosophy, a return to metaphysics, had any value. At sixty-nine he no longer had any need to see his name in print. If he could not bring out a consistent system, it was better to keep silent" (90). A few pages later, in that same story, Singer provides the classic biblical statement on incompletion: the quotation is from Ecclesiastes which, as Milton Hindus has noted, is Singer's favorite biblical book: "And further, by these, my son, be admonished: of making [many] books there is no end" (93). The frustration that Asa Heshel and all the other abortive scholars experience underscores one of Singer's central themes: the pursuit of secular knowledge involves man in his own dissolution and brings him face to face with his limits, the intellectual version of death. To be sure, the same holds true in religious areas, but there failure is followed by the consolation that the limits of man's knowledge establishes the boundary of God's.

The Jewish relationship between God and man is based on a mutual impasse. It is a partnership which respects and reveres the integrity of each. For it to work

God has to acknowledge and be responsive to man's humanness. In part the function of the various covenants is to formalize and legalize that divine obligation on God's part and to demonstrate that man's burdens are not greater than he can humanly bear. In turn man must acknowledge and be responsive to God's divinity, an obligation he honors in negative fashion by not exceeding or degrading his humanness. The important point, however, is the acknowledgement of a permanent and unbridgeable gap between God and man, and an acceptance of the uniqueness of each. Paradoxically, therefore, "Men must act as though all depended on them; and sit and pray as though all depended on God." [4]

Keats urged man to exist in contradiction without irritably seeking after final or facile answers. Singer urges man to exist with the knowledge of the impasse and to refrain from the satanic urge to straddle. Whenever Singer, like John Milton, comes to the edge of that gulf he surrenders the solution of the problem to God. Indeed, that act of surrender marks the renewal of the covenant as well as the eternal re-creation of God. Isaiah says, "You are My witnesses saith the Lord and I am God" (43:12). The commentaries explain it further: "If you are My witnesses, then I am God, and if you are not My witnesses, then it is as if I am not God." [5] God is not created in the image of man; rather God is sustained by the image man creates of himself. As long as man thinks he is God or no longer needs Him, God is denied His body in man's history. The image of God and the image of man are defined by the mutual gulf that separates divinity and humanity. The Faustian search for forbidden knowledge straddles the gap and burdens the song of the self with the psalm of the Godhead. Because secular knowledge or utopias have no God, they have no end, and the pursuit of either involves man in the cycle of self-consumption or the strategy of the perpetually postponed goal.

Clearly, Singer prefers God's silences to man's mani-festoes, especially those that speak for God. Equally as important is the way Singer arrives at this position, for the form it takes provides the key to its content. Characteristi-cally, he does not legislate his preferences or serve as his own commentator. On the contrary, he withdraws in order to give full room and play to all the secular substi-tutes and alternatives for God. Indeed, all of Singer's heroes are embarked on journeys of exhaustion. Every protagonist is granted the freedom to alter and redeem the world. Each one journeys from the center of contradic-tion to the periphery of resolution; there each one bridges the gulf and and returns with his piece of heaven to be realized on earth. In other words, Singer grants his heroes the opportunity to try out all that men can devise so that, in the enlightenment born of desperation, they may con-template what God conceals. Toward the end of the novel, Hertz Yanovar, while in jail awaiting interrogation by the Polish police, begins to contemplate such alterna-tives: "To fall into God's hands was one thing, but to fall into the hands of man was fearful" (510).[6] When Yanovar considers all that men do, God by contrast takes on the stature of the divine and His silence and even in-accessibility establish His wisdom.

All Singer's works thus are informed by the parable of the prodigal son; a recent short story is entitled "The Prodigal Fool." They are structured by the foreknowledge that for the modern Jew the longest way around is for him the shortest way home. To be sure, for those Jews who totally pursue secular knowledge and substitutes for God, the arc of their journey does not conclude with a final return to the fold but takes a deflective turn to limbo. Indeed, a major historical concern of *The Family Moskat* is to show how secular prophets of brave new worlds borrow all the apparatus of religion except its end in God. For that absolute, they substitute Communism, Bundism, Yiddishism, Zionism, occultism, etc. That their fervor and messianic zeal are often accompanied by a rejection of religion is of course not a new insight. But what is perhaps original or at least comprehensive about Singer's exploration of the roots and fruits of secular knowledge, especially its secret kinship with what it rejects, is his notion that the essence of all modern Jewish and European history can be found in this pervasive quest for new secular metaphysics and messiahs. Once again, Asa Heshel is his touchstone.

II

Significantly, Asa Heshel's first exposure to the substitutive metaphysics of Communism begins with books, especially the works of the Polish short story writer and novelist, Stefan Zeromski (1864–1925). By grafting the messianic impulse of religion onto the missionary zeal of Communism, Zeromski typically eases Asa Heshel's transition from earlier beliefs.[7] From that point on, Zeromski works out a complete equivalency: the state becomes God; classless society, heaven on earth; and worldwide brotherhood, messianic fulfillment.[8] Substitutions or not, these are no mean ideals and it can be understood why Asa Heshel and many other Jews were drawn to Communism. In fact, the creation of a distinct Jewish form of socialism known as Bundism gives some credence to the statement, not the twisted interpretation, made in the novel by the Polish chief of police that the percentage of Jewish Com-

munists is so astonishingly large that as a result it provokes
an even more virulent anti-Semitism (517). But it is precisely the contradictory presence of anti-Semitism among
those who espouse world brotherhood that precipitates
Asa Heshel's disillusionment.

Asa Heshel cannot comprehend the point in supporting those who wish to overthrow the czar when they in
turn plan pogroms of their own. Moreover, even though
the Bundists demonstrate that socialism and anti-Semitism
are not inevitable bedfellows, he finds that all socialists
have learned the scapegoating lesson so well that whatever
is wrong with society or encumbers their own efforts is
automatically and irrevocably the fault of the capitalists.
Thus, at one point Asa Heshel complains, " 'Just the same
as the anti-Semites put the blame for everything on the
Jew, that's the way you leftists put all the blame on the
capitalists. There's always got to be a sacrificial goat' "
(533). But what ultimately leads Asa Heshel to reject
Communism is nothing so abstract as ideological differences but his presence at the Russian Revolution of 1917.[9]
Outdoing the barbarousness and greed of the czars, the
Bolsheviks release a bloodbath that so disgusts Asa Heshel
that he concludes, as does Dr. Samoylenko of Chekhov's
prophetic *The Duel,* that if murder and torture are required to save Western civilization or to bring about a
new order, then such a civilization is not worth saving
and such an order does not deserve to be born. Having
played out the journey of exhaustion with Communism,
Asa Heshel shocks Barbara by informing her that he has
gone completely the other way: " 'the capitalist system is
the best. I don't mean that it's good; it's very cruel, but
it's human nature and the economic law' " (495). As Marx
turns out to be a false messiah and Communism modern

idolatry, Asa Heshel chooses a system that is at least hon-
estly corrupt and unfair.

Like a stronger wave cresting out of one that is spent,
Zionism emerges as an alternative messianic possibility.
Revolted by the anti-Semitism of the Bolsheviks and of
his fellow Polish soldiers, Asa Heshel becomes convinced
that the only hope for the Jews is to get out of Europe
altogether and establish their own country. Moreover, the
fact that many of the Zionists are also socialists, as witness
Moses Hess, the "Communist Rabbi," intensifies the at-
traction. All seems right at last, but as Asa Heshel becomes more intimately involved, he discovers that the
Zionist movement is encumbered from within and com-
promised from without. Internally, the Zionists are split
over where to settle and how to go about it. Then, too,
many of the Zionists are not socialistically inclined and
resist and resent those who are. And those who are, are
opposed by their fellow gentile and Jewish socialists who
regard Zionism as a break from and weakening of the
socialist movement. Externally, the opponents of Zionism
are so strong that war, a solution Asa Heshel because of
his own experiences as a soldier can never sanction, seems
inevitable. Finally, some of the most vocal and powerful
anti-Zionists are the Jews themselves. Hertz Yanovar
typically indicates that being a Zionist creates a conflict
of double loyalties, a burden he would rather do without.
A more militant rejection appears in an article, "Jews
with a Mission," which Singer excerpts in the novel:

> We Jews are tired of all these metaphysical missions
> which the German rabbiners and the other Jewish
> leaders have saddled on our weak shoulders. We
> reject the argument that we must turn back the clock

of history and return to Palestine. The Jewish masses
love their homes. They want to live in brotherhood
with their neighbors and to fight shoulder to shoulder
with them for a better world, where there will be
neither nations, classes, no religion, but only one
united, advancing humanity. (242)

Once again Asa Heshel's disenchantment with Zionism, though not as complete as that with Communism,
comes from more concrete sources.[10] He indicates to his
grandfather that he is thinking of going to Palestine to
participate in the building of a Jewish state. But aware
that Asa Heshel no longer believes in the Torah and is
sceptical about the existence of God, Rabbi Katzenellenbogen questions him on the logic of his decision. The
choice of Palestine makes sense only as the *biblical* land
of the Jews. Moreover, it is the land where Jews should
go only if they plan to remain Jews—witnesses of God.
Initially, Asa Heshel shakes off his grandfather's arguments, but as he becomes more intimate with Zionists he
acknowledges the rightness of his grandfather's reasoning.
Specifically, he discovers that most of the Zionists are irreligious and if they worship anything it is work. Indeed,
he begins to wonder whether their real reason for establishing a Jewish state is to denude themselves of all religious
associations which Asa Heshel, his scepticism notwith-
standing, still takes to be the heart of Jewishness.[11]

Asa Heshel is clearly too much of a purist and too
soft for the hard realities the Communists, socialists, and
Zionists had to face. If it were up to him, *Das Kapital*
would be an interesting textbook to study and Israel still
the dream of an exiled people. Nevertheless, his disillusionment proceeds from legitimate insights which tran-
scend his personal bias and weakness. In particular, Asa
Heshel discovers that all modern utopian movements have

borrowed all the essentials of religion except one: in place of a religion of God and man they have created a religion restricted to man only—a religion of humanity. Moreover, the common aim of all the religions of humanity is secular conformity. The anti-Zionist author of "Jews with a Mission" invokes an apocalyptic vision of "one united, advancing humanity," as if the mission of the Jews were to become non-Jews. The Communists yearn for a classless society in which all will be equal, especially members of the party. The Zionists seek a state made up exclusively of Jews, especially Zionists. But such uniformity is inconsistent with Singer's own notion of the uniqueness of each self and people,[12] and unreflective of the diverse, often conflicting factions within each of the movements themselves. Moreover, brotherhood formed in this way would not bind individuals together but blur them into each other; and if it could be created, it could come about only through dictatorship.

Like Dickens in *Bleak House* and Dostoevsky in *The Brothers Karamazov*, Singer portrays philanthropists and humanitarians as able only to love mankind in the abstract but not in the particular. Many of the zealots Asa Heshel meets are failures, sexually, paternally, and domestically. It's as if for the secularists it is easier to love mankind than one's wife or neighbor, just as the temptation for the Orthodox is that it is easier to believe in God than in man. But the most unexpected insight Asa Heshel has is that the supreme threat to all secular messianic causes is the prospect of success. The problem with a dream of perfection is that it sometimes comes true. Unlike religious deliverance, which is genuinely final, the secular versions are realized in the midst of flux. Thus, even in an ideal classless society or in the state of Israel one still has a toothache, a reminder that recalls the classic blindness of John Stuart Mill who, when he projected the fulfillment of all his utilitarian projects and speculated on whether he then would be happy, suffered a nervous collapse. Asa Heshel, for all his confusion, does not make the same mistake of equating a social ill with the existence of evil. Even in an utopia, perhaps even in Heaven itself, the eternal questions still persist. The traditional Orthodox position is not to seek an answer: Rabbi Yanai in *The Ethics of the Fathers* puts it succinctly: "The reason for the prosperity of the wicked, and also for the troubles of the good, is not in our hands."

Asa Heshel starts off with an enormous capacity for belief, first in God, then in humanistic deliverance, and ultimately in very little. Geographically, he travels from Tereshpol Minor to Warsaw, but chronologically he has moved from the Middle Ages to the twentieth century; historically, he has traversed an arc that runs from the ancient Bible to the modern *Das Kapital* and *The Jewish State*. He begins with the cosmos, levels the vertical to the horizontal in an embrace of humanity, and terminates with only the embrace of himself. Symptomatically, Asa Heshel, disillusioned with all communal efforts, turns to private, selfish, and often precious solutions. Pursuing such ends, Asa Heshel moves into the most decadent, perverse, and nihilistic final phase of the novel. To be sure, the novel concludes with the onslaught of the Nazis, but, as Singer especially indicates in this last section, the enemy is not only without but also within.

III

Hertz Yanovar has founded a "metaphysical society" which has recorded and documented stories of "dybbuks, poltergeists . . . a fish who called 'Hear, O Israel!'"

(542). He holds seances during which he reaches out not just for truth but for " 'new truths' " (107). What are these new truths? Yanovar's explanation is as elusive as his rallying cry: "If there was any meaning at all in existence, it would only be comprehended beyond the bourne, in the darkness that knows no knowledge, creates without a plan, and is divine without a god" (510). Singer himself on numerous occasions has expressed his interest in occultism; and dybbuks, poltergeists, and demons abound in his own work. But his identification with Yanovar is not complete, for Yanovar's faith in occultism though not misplaced is misdirected. He employs it as a means of transcending reality whereas Singer uses it as an access to reality. By severing the mysterious bond between illusion and reality, Yanovar ironically impoverishes that reality. To Singer much of the awful power of the supernatural derives from the secret and familiar correspondences it maintains with illusion. Just as man's spirit was breathed into clay, so spirits in general need illusion as their body of incarnation. Or to sum up Singer's own position through the by now classic sanity and fullness of Gimpel, the wise fool: "No doubt the world is entirely an imaginary world, but it is only once removed from the true world" (21).

Yanovar's escapism is of a piece with the excessive otherworldliness of the mystical cabbalists. Indeed, as noted, Singer's ability to perceive excesses and dodges in the secular realm was prepared for by those in the religious. In any case, both groups meet in Singer's fullest portrait of the escape artist, Yasha the magician of Lublin. A less sensational and more rational example of the deflective turn from the duality of reality and illusion is provided by Asa Heshel. His scepticism about God leads him to the Faustian enterprise of replacing the concept of divinity altogether with an autonomous, totally comprehensive philosophic system formulated under the guiding influence of Spinoza (an ironic mentor from the Jewish point of view). Ironic, too, is Singer's timing: the revelation of Asa Heshel's system is first presented to the reader on the day of the "Rejoicing of the Law." That is, on the day that commemorates the Jews' receiving of the Ten Commandments, Asa Heshel's substitutive testament is unveiled.

The title of his unfinished opus is "The Laboratory of Happiness." On a scrap of paper Asa Heshel has written the following outline:

> (1) time is an attribute of God; (2) the Godhead is the sum total of all possible combinations; (3) the truth of falsehood; (4) causality and play; (5) paganism and pleasure; (6) transmigration of the soul in the light of Spinozaism. (316)

These six theses transcribe the deflective and increasingly escapist direction of Asa Heshel's life. The first two are safely traditional and thus acceptable to both religion and philosophy. The third, however, veers off into cleverness and opens the anarchistic door to a verbal reality artificially sustained by semantic gymnastics. Four and five reflect the pseudoscientific title, and their excessive involvement in earthly and mortal matters is unscientifically countered and released by the escape hatch of reincarnation. No wonder Asa Heshel never finishes his work: externally, it has no foreseeable or respectable end; internally, its many contradictions create an endless maze without an exit. Above all, what regularly impedes Asa Heshel's progress are his arguments with his philosophical guide.[13]

Although Spinoza advises against feeling pity for the infirm, Asa Heshel is moved against his reason to give a cripple a copper coin. Asa Heshel trembles at the slaughter of animals for food, and is shocked by Spinoza's notion that man can do anything he wants to the animals, for he need not fear their retaliation.[14] He questions Spinoza's exhortations to joy when he sees so much cause for despair, and resists the philosopher's injunction to achieve relationships when all that Asa Heshel has experienced indicates that relationships do not last. Finally, toward the end of the novel, Asa Heshel, contemplating the impending Nazi holocaust,

> thought about Hitler; according to Spinoza, Hitler was part of the Godhead, a mode of the Eternal Substance. Every act of his had been predetermined by eternal laws. . . . Every murderous act of Hitler's was a functional part of the cosmos. If one was logically consistent, then one had to concede that God was evil, or else that suffering and evil were good. (596) [15]

Horrified by the implications of Spinoza's logic, Asa Heshel finds that his attempt to reconcile religion and philosophy has in the final analysis rendered them irreconcilable. Even more disturbing, it has led him to a metaphysics without morality and to the scientific logic of making an evil a good. Having journeyed so far from the common sense of Gimpel in his cosmic overreaching, Asa Heshel, like many extremists, counters with an excessive commitment to the earthly which aborts all metaphysics. Indeed, there is a direct correlation between Asa Heshel's acceptance of the honest ruthlessness of capitalism and his choice now of the tough-minded pragmatism of

Malthus. Spinoza needs to be tempered and ballasted by Malthus, although in the process the original Laboratory of Happiness is reduced to the Laboratory of Sexuality. Asa Heshel's final philosophical position stresses sex control, by which he means, " 'More sex and fewer children. The bedroom is the key to all social and individual problems' " (497). Earlier, and more cynically, Asa Heshel had indicated that the commandment against murder should be supplemented by an injunction against reproduction.[16]

Lest Asa Heshel's final position appear to be merely an eccentric notion born of personal despair or too trivial to be taken seriously, Singer, through numerous literary and philosophical references, indicates that his hero's metaphysical paganism was very much a trend of his day. An author frequently mentioned in *The Family Moskat* is the Russian novelist Michael Petrovich Artsybashev (1878–1927) whose famous or infamous *Sánin* (1907) caused a sensation when it appeared. Its message is simple: sex, not love or marriage, is reality. When Hadassah tells Abram Shapiro that she considers marriage a mockery, he correctly guesses that she has been reading *Sánin*. Having presented the "metaphysics of sex" in that novel, Artsybashev went on in *At the Brink* (1911–1912) to present through an avalanche of suicides the other reality of his world: the metaphysics of death. In this, he was joined by Leonid Andreyev (1817–1919) whose linkage of sex and death, especially *In the Fog* (1902) and *The Governor* (1906), was matched in his own life by sensational thrill-seeking and scandalous Byronic behavior. The modern metaphysics of Artsybashev and Andreyev hearkens back to the decadent and melancholy Pechorin, the Hamlet-like protagonist of Mikhail Lermontov's *A Hero of Our Times* (1840). But Pechorin is no match for the new hero of nihilism, Eric Falk, the Nietzschean protagonist of *Homo*

Sapiens (1898), written by Stanislaw Przbyszewski (1868–1927). Falk, who regularly compares himself to an eagle, transforms the earlier romantic worship of nature as a means to brotherhood to the amorality of the *übermensch*.

To intertwine sex and death in this way is to describe a sexuality which is ultimately too distortive to be redeemed by the punning power of a John Donne. It is a sex essentially restricted to mutual masturbation. Each one takes what he needs for gratification and, like a relationship with a paid partner, leaves in the dark as intact and unencumbered as when he came. Asa Heshel discourages Hadassah from getting a divorce because he enjoys the temporary and yoke-free relationship of having a mistress. His desire not to have children is not motivated by a concern for overpopulation, but by a desire to terminate population. As a correlation, his temporary arrangement with Hadassah and others is more a way of postponing than having a relationship; more an expression of self-hate than of love; more a way of dying than living. Moreover, just as sexual promiscuity often masks sexual impotence or revulsion, so Asa Heshel's philosophical ability turned to the same cynical ends becomes not a means to power but a rationale for inaction:

> Always the argument wound around the same question: did people know enough about human history to be able to predict its course? Asa Heshel maintained that since not all the factors were known, it was impossible to foretell any outcome. The idea of a kingdom of freedom stood in opposition to the concept of causality. (560)

If it is true that God alone knows all the factors, what then is man to do in the meantime? Wait for a moment that will never come when he will know what his mortality precludes him from knowing—and then act? Asa Heshel rejects Orthodoxy because of its obedience to traditional injunctions only to embrace ironically an emancipated philosophy which results in the morality of inertia. Moreover, it is doubly ironic for Asa Heshel and Eric Falk to signal their achievement of power and independence with the cry that God is dead when, by rejecting interdependence for transcendence and the community for the superman, they have discovered the impotence of not being God. Asa Heshel has journeyed from the center of active obedience to the periphery of enlightened paralysis. The bridge of self-sufficiency gives way and he falls into "the abyss of the free will."

In the final anaylsis, what happens to Asa Heshel and to all those who are involved in the cult of self-sufficiency[17] can be summarized as a confusion of the crucial differences between individuality and independence. That the two are not synonymous and that an equation of the two impoverishes both, appears in the following distinctions of a late-nineteenth-century religious poet:

> A man *should* be individual, but not independent. . . . Independent, he puts forth no influence; he is as sterile as the sands of the desert. . . . There is but one thing you can do for yourself; you can kill yourself. Though you may try to live for yourself, you cannot, in any permanence, live by yourself. You may rot by yourself, if you will; but that is not doing, it is ceasing.[18]

A further indication that the way to independence is the way to death appears in the following passage from Hesse's *Steppenwolf:* the Steppenwolf was ever more independent. He took orders from no man and ordered his ways to suit no man. Independently and alone, he decided what to do and to leave undone. . . . But in the midst of the freedom he had attained Harry suddenly became aware that his freedom was a death and that he stood alone. (61)

Asa Heshel does indeed rot and decay in his self-sufficiency. Pursuing secular knowledge, he finds his work without end. Embracing secular messiahs and metaphysics, he regularly encounters the imperfections of mortal heavens without the consolation of divine continuity and finality. Constantly intellectualizing and philosophizing his experience, he enfeebles his heart and his power to act; and he falls subject to John Stuart Mill's diagnosis of spiritual dryness: "the habit of analysis has a tendency to wear away the feelings: as indeed it has when no other mental habit is cultivated, and the analysing spirit remains without its natural complements and correctives." Above all, by rejecting God, he is sentenced, as Hesse puts it, to the "pangs of being born ever anew." [19] Near the end of the novel, when his wife comes to him for help, Asa Heshel, who has embarked on many journeys of exhaustion, rightly confesses that he is physically and spiritually weary and sick. When she then urges him to see a psychiatrist, he replies, " 'Then every Jew in the world would have to go to one. I mean every modern Jew' " (544). In the Bible, Asa was a King of Judah and his name means physician.

In Asa Heshel, Singer has sought to normalize certain insanities of the twentieth century. Caught between the two worlds of heaven and earth and situated between the two ages of the ancients and the moderns, Asa Heshel experiences moral schizophrenia—a perfectly normal affliction for a dislocated product of a displaced generation. According to Singer, "Enlightenment created a host of split personalities among its adherents." [20] Later, with the onslaught of the Nazis, the Jew will again typify another form of modern madness: for him a persecution complex will unfortunately be a normal state of mind. In his first role, Asa Heshel is a prophet of things to come; in the second, a victim of things to come. As a homeless wanderer between heaven and earth and the past and the present, he sums up the terrible freedom of being broken off from God. As an object of inhuman persecution without parallel in history, he begets an unforgettable and perhaps unforgivable source of guilt for all men who in forgetting God have forgotten to be men. [21]

Notes

1. I. B. Singer's review of Peretz's *My Memoirs* in *American Judaism* (April, 1966), p. 21.

2. Joel Blocker and Richard M. Elman, "An Interview with Isaac Bashevis Singer" *Commentary*, 36 (November, 1963), 368–69. With sardonic humor, Singer explores the same problem in "The Last Demon." The last demon complains that man has taken away most of the work of the Devil; he is so adept at damning himself that Satan may become obsolescent. In particular,

> The Jews have now developed writers. Yiddish ones, Hebrew ones, and they have taken over our trade. . . . They know all our tricks—mockery, piety. They have a hundred reasons why a rat must be kosher. All they want to do is to redeem the world. (122)

3. "A Conversation with Isaac Bashevis Singer," *The Eternal Light*, 2.

4. Emil Fackenheim, "Judaism," in *The Meaning of Life in Five Great Religions*, edited by R. C. Chalmers and John A. Irving (Philadelphia, 1965), p. 77. I am deeply indebted to Professor

Fackenheim's presentation of the Jewish partnership between God and man.

5. For a fuller treatment of this notion, see Ernst Simon, "The Jews as God's Witness to the World" *Judaism*, 15 (Summer, 1966), 306–18.

6. As its title suggests, the entire story "I Place My Reliance on No Man" revolves around this theme. In "The Unseen," Singer not only returns to this notion, but also provides its ultimate biblical source: "Do you remember the words of King David: 'Let me rather fall into God's hands, than into the hands of the people?' " (203)

7. That harmony could exist between religious and social messianic ideals is demonstrated in the person of Moses Hess, the founding father of German socialism, who was dubbed by his comrades of the 1840's the "Communist Rabbi." Indeed, to complicate the matter even further and to disturb the false neatness of categories, Hess was also a Zionist. In fact, his *Rome and Jerusalem* is considered, along with Pinsher's *Auto-Emancipation* and Herzl's *Jewish State,* one of the three classic texts of Zionism. For a more detailed account of Hess's career as well as how Bundist and Zionist elements could be sustained, no matter how precariously, within traditional Judaism, see Jonathan Frankel's " 'The Communist Rabbi': Moses Hess," *Commentary,* 41 (July, 1966), 77–81.

8. The specific novel of Zeromski's mentioned in *The Family Moskat* is *The Labors of Sisyphus* (1898) which has been characterized as the Polish *Nicholas Nickleby*.

9. Similarly, Singer's disillusionment with Communism comes from personal sources:

> This reviewer bore witness, while he was living in Poland in the 30's, to the way in which young Yiddish writers became drunk with Communism. They left Warsaw, forsook us, the "capitalist lackeys," the servants of imperialism, the preachers of fascism. From Soviet Russia, the land of the bright future, they sent letters, at first enthusiastic, urging their friends and family to follow them. As time passed, their letters came less frequently, and carried cryptic passages and ominous expressions.

Singer goes on to describe how those writers were terrorized into becoming informers against their fellow Jews (*Commentary*, 33 [March, 1962], 268). He subsequently enlarged upon this view:

I always felt about the Soviet Union that it would never come to any good. From its very beginning it was a butcher shop [the worst curse of a vegetarian], and it has remained so even today . . . even if there has been some "improvement." When people have extreme power over other people, it's a terrible thing. I always pray to God (and I do pray because I am in my own way a religious man), don't give me power over any other human beings.

Quoted from Blocker and Elman, 369.

10. Approached by one seeking to go to Palestine, Singer's father replied, " 'A man must be a Jew before he can go to the Holy Land' " (*In My Father's Court*, p. 85). Although Singer believes that Zionism is far superior to Communism, and the state of Israel a much better place than Russia, his scepticism is the prevailing note:

> For some strange reason, just as I was sceptical about religious dogmas, so I was sceptical about political dogmas. Certainly, I was very close to these people, and maybe that was the trouble: you know, sometimes when you see the cook, the food doesn't seem very appetizing. While the ideologies sounded very attractive, I was close enough to see who was preaching them and how these people fought for power among themselves. The truth is, if you ask me, that the aches and troubles of this world cannot be cured by any system.

Quoted from Blocker and Elman, 369.

11. Just as Rabbi Katzenellenbogen maintains that Palestine has meaning only for Jews who desire to remain Jews, and just as recently David Ben-Gurion indicated that a Jew can call himself a Jew only by coming to Israel, so Singer applies the same principle to the use of Yiddish:

> Thus, since the Yiddish of East European Jews has been, above all, an instrument of their Jewishness, it becomes flat and barren when used for the denial of Jewishness. One might say that the language cannot organically tolerate atheism. Purged of the religious sentiment which gave it cohesion, Yiddish is reduced to a conglomerate of disparate elements, and only then justifies the accusations of its adversaries that it is gibberish, jargon.

Singer concludes by asking, "If Jewishness is neither religion, nor Zionism, nor a sense of being a part of world Jewry, what is it?" (Quoted from *Commentary*, 33 [March, 1962], 266, 269.)

12. In the "Author's Note" to *In My Father's Court*, Singer maintains, "Only that which is individual can be just and true."

13. It is at this point that Dr. Fischelson, the other major devotee of Spinoza, and Asa Heshel part company. Both cling to Spinoza but Asa Heshel does so in the face of despair whereas, with unaware pathos, Dr. Fischelson does so in the face of happiness.

14. According to Singer himself, it is this notion of Spinoza that finally made him a vegetarian.

15. Dr. Gombiner of "The Séance" shares Asa Heshel's sexual and fascistic philosophy:

> There was a time when he had tried to understand all things through his reason, but that period of rationalism had long passed. Since then, he had constructed an anti-rationalistic philosophy, a kind of extreme hedonism which saw in eroticism the *"Ding an Sich,"* and in reason the very lowest stage of being, the entropy which led to absolute death. His position had been a curious compound of von Hartmann's idea of the Unconscious with the Kabbalah of Rabbi Isaac Lurie, according to which all things, from the smallest grain of sand to the very Godhead itself, are Copulation and Union. . . . According to his own philosophy, he had believed that all suffering was nothing more than negative expressions of universal eroticism— Hitler, Stalin, the Nazis who sang the Horst Wessel song and made the Jews wear yellow armbands, were actually searching for new forms and variations of sexual salvation.

Encounter, XXV (July, 1965), p. 15.

16. Dr. Yaretzky of "The Shadow of a Crib," in following the philosophy of Schopenhauer, comes to the same conclusion about having children as Asa Heshel does. Yaretzky says, " 'How does it go: The luckiest child is the one not born?' " (77)

17. Martin Buber presents the Orthodox point of view on this matter: Jewish "teachings contest the self-sufficiency of the soul: inward truth must become real life, otherwise it does not remain truth. A drop of messianic consummation must be mingled with every hour; otherwise, the hour is godless, despite all piety and devoutness" ("The Silent Question," *Judaism*, I [April, 1952], 103). Recently, Eric Partridge found evidence for the

reappearance of the cult of self-sufficiency and in the process pointed out that for all its lofty overreaching, the cult ironically produces contraction and reduction: "The danger lies in the fact that it is not a leveling upwards, a raising of standards, but a leveling downward, a lowering of standards" ("Speaking of Books: Degraded Language," *New York Times Book Review* [September 18, 1966], p. 2). Although the context is different, Saul Bellow comes to the same conclusion in almost the same terms: "Yet what our literary intelligentsia does is to redescribe everything downward, blackening the present age and denying creative scope to the contemporaries" ("Speaking of Books: Cloister Culture," *New York Times Book Review* [July 10, 1966], p. 2).

In other words, the deification of the self, which was part a general expansive and liberating movement, ultimately turns out to be self-consuming and even brutal. Indeed, Singer's exposure of Asa Heshel's metaphysical sexuality, perhaps, can now be applied to the so-called sexual revolution, and in particular to its two English and American prophets, D. H. Lawrence and Henry Miller. Although, to be sure, the metaphysics, especially of Lawrence, may be more spiritually conceived and broadly based than that of Asa Heshel and his literary counterparts, that did not avert the same downward reductiveness. What has happened to Lawrence's mystique is presented sensitively in a recent poem by the Swedish poet, Henry Martinson:

> The hour you waited for, when things would assume
>   soul anew
> And their interiors visited by soul and sensation
> on the day of inward turned sensuality.
>
> But the world was turned outward.
> Only misunderstanding ripened fully.
>
> The new, deep communion you sang never happened.
> The table was spread inside,
> but only a few came
> and only a few could eat.
> The others came out of a curiosity that meant nothing.
>
> Your church within the flesh must close.
> Now it stands abandoned in steel storm
> on the devil's heath of the outward turned.

(*Times Literary Supplement* [September 3, 1964], p. 820. Translated by Morton Seif.) Recently, Henry Miller in an interview indicated that he has washed his hands of the entire sexual revolution because it has become "a new tyranny, a tryanny of the flesh." In place of the old Victorian hush-hush attitude toward sex, there is now, according to Miller, an equally reprehensible mechanistic preoccupation with sex. But it is all dead —all technique and commodity—and not what he intended at all (David Drury, "Sex Goes Public: A Talk with Henry Miller," *Esquire*, LXV [May, 1966], 118 ff.).

18. Francis Thompson, *The Life and Labours of Saint John Baptist de la Salle* (London, 1911), p. 77.

19. Hesse's influence on Singer is reinforced by the wild chaotic balls in *The Family Moskat*, "The Gentleman from Cracow," and "A Wedding in Brownsville," all of which resemble the famous surrealistic ball and theater at the end of *Steppenwolf*.

20. Singer's review of Peretz's *My Memoirs* in *American Judaism* (April, 1966), p. 21.

21. Singer concludes the novel and the search for secular messiahs and metaphysics with the words of Hertz Yanovar. Running around war-torn Warsaw like a crazed man, Yanovar meets Asa Heshel who ironically is shocked by the final nihilism of the occultist: " 'Death is the Messiah. That's the real truth' " (611). In the original Yiddish version, which appeared in two volumes in 1950, Yanovar's words are not the final ones. Singer went on for eleven more pages to relate how a group of Zionists manages to escape from Warsaw as the shattered house of Meshulam Moskat collapses. Then, too, alongside Yanovar's final nihilism, there is the soul-searching discussion of intellectuals who speculate whether their flirtation with modern learning has not contributed to the plight they are facing.

On the occasion of the reissue of the 1950 English version, Milton Hindus lamented the continued abridgment of the original ending (*New York Times Book Review* [March 14, 1965], pp. 4, 44–45). I agree. Singer, in general, has problems with endings. The particular problem here is that Yanovar's pessimistic summation while accurate is partial; it does not mirror the mixture of pessimism and optimism both in the original ending and throughout the novel. Or to put it another way, because Asa Heshel for all his failures does choose to be chosen by remaining in Warsaw with his fellow Jews, Yanovar's words should not obscure that last exhausted gesture. Perhaps a summary, which more comprehensively reflects all that has taken place and is more faithful to Singer's ambiguity, is provided by Wallace Stevens in a poem appropriately entitled, "Connoisseur of Chaos," and appropriately dated 1942:

> A. A violent order is disorder; and
> B. A great disorder is order. These
>   Two things are one.

4.

Satan in Goray
and the Progression of Possession

The most striking aspect of *Satan in Goray* is that
although it is Singer's most thoroughly satanic novel—
the title alone heralds that—the Devil does not manifest
himself until near the end of the book. It is almost as if
the archfiend requires a maturation period before he can
be fully incarnated. To avoid the common extremism of
removed symbology on the one hand and of the mechanical
escapism of a *deus ex machina* on the other, Singer needs
time and events to create a cosmic expectation from which
the Devil can emerge pristine and terrible. Preparation is
required for the coming of the Messiah; the same holds
true for the Devil. Indeed, Singer handles both through
the novel's special mode and movement.

Satan in Goray begins as saga or chronicle—objective,
factual, detailed, and restrained. The setting is the isolated
village of Goray in mid-seventeenth-century Poland. The
stress is communal; the characterization multiple and
panoramic. Events occur in homes, the marketplace, and

the synagogue. But gradually, almost imperceptively, the novel shifts realms and modes and concludes as a surrealistic gothic tale—grotesque, fevered, baroque, and insane. The emphasis then is cosmic and historical; the characterization archetypal and cabalistic. Events occur in souls and spiritual realms; lives are concentrated to their cosmic essences. In the first half, the internal is rendered psychologically: Rabbi Benish succumbs to melancholia. In the second half, the internal is rendered apocalyptically: Rechele is impregnated by Satan.

This movement from fact to vision, from chronicle to psychic fable, supports the novel's emotional progession from hope to hysteria, from rumors and portents of messianic deliverance to shocks and realizations of satanic entrapment. The cumulative effect is the gradual adjustment of the reader to the experience of evil and subsequently to the recognition of Satan's existence and power. As if that were not formidable enough, Singer also urges a receptivity to messianic promise. In other words, Singer is aware that the believability of Satan is contingent on the more comprehensive acceptance of a spiritual realm which presupposes and gives substantiality to both good and evil, the Messiah and the Devil. But Singer is too respectful of his reader to assume or to demand such beliefs of him and too wise to make a direct assault on his credulity. Instead, he obliquely brings the reader to the threshold of the otherworldly by presenting the mediating experiences of terror and indecision.

Near the end of the novel, when Rechele has prophetic visions and is visited, tortured, and raped by a satanic dybbuk, the reader balks and exclaims: "How can this be?" But almost as if Singer had anticipated that resistance and wished to undermine it, he creates a series of incidents throughout the novel which are no less horrible

or unbelievable but which are factually unchallengable.
First, we learn of the atrocities committed by Chmielnicki,
the Cossack *hetman,* and his barbaric army of *haidamak*
troops in 1648–1649. Children were impaled on lances,
women were violated and then their bellies slit open and
sewn up with cats inside. Are Rechele's experiences less
believable or horrible than these? Second, one of Singer's
recurrent situations or obsessions is the ritual slaughtering
of animals (like Kafka, Singer, significantly, is a vegetarian). With his merciless eye for realistic detail, Singer
presents scenes in which blood-drenched butchers, with
razor-sharp knives between their teeth, do their bloody
work while the eyes of cows glaze and chickens, with their
heads off, run wildly and blindly about like puppets. And
throughout all this slaughter there is the Jewish scrupulos-
ity for purity or *Kashruth!* Is there any more vivid example of religious paradox than this? Third, Rechele's
upbringing recreates the special terror of childhood that
is so much at the heart of Dickens's power. Raised by an
uncle who is a ritual slaughterer and exposed to sights
like the above, she is also told harrowing tales of witches,
hobgoblins, and demons by a grandmother who herself
is a grotesque. Clearly, by the end of the novel Singer
suggests that such otherworldly horrors not only are
echoed in this world, but also are available to others, in
addition to the very young and old. Finally, the rumors
and portents of the self-proclaimed Messiah, Sabbatai Zevi
(1625–1676),[1] are rendered in the ornate and fantastic
language of the Cabala and conjured up with such an
authentic atmosphere of apocalyptic deliverance that all
revelations seem possible and plausible. Indeed, by the
end of the novel, the reader trembles along with the Jews
of Goray sitting on rooftops and waiting for the dark
cloud to come and release a pillar of fire. In short, Singer

employs events of this world and those akin to it as a base for a step-by-step initiation into cosmic mysteries. At the beginning of the novel, a historical gap is not only acknowledged, but also welcomed because of the protective distance it affords. But by the end of the novel, there is no longer any such gap, and there is little safety. Initially, a suspension of disbelief is required; ultimately, there is little disbelief to suspend. In the process, the reader is converted from a sceptic to a believer or, at least, a sceptical believer.

At the same time that Singer provides, through a series of ascending analogical planes, an exposure to terror, he uses the concept of the Messiah to present the companion experience of indecision. Throughout the novel the nagging problem is whether Sabbatai Zevi is a true or false Messiah. Actually, Singer has selected this messianic focus in order to dramatize a favorite concern that involves and yet goes beyond the messianic dilemma: the difficulty of discerning the holy from the unclean, the sacred from the profane. The experience of indecision which is essential to his focus appears in the main characters who, like one dissolving wave after another, so disappoint all initial hopes and judgments that one is as unsure as the people of Goray as to who is godly and who is satanic, and as to what is right and what is wrong.

The first character in this cycle of confusion is Rabbi Benish. In spite of his age and the attractive offers he has received elsewhere, he has returned to Goray after the pogroms to rebuild the Jewish community. Indeed, he now feels that after such suffering the people are ripe for a return to God. Orthodox, learned, somewhat severe, Rabbi Benish, like Rabbi Katzenellenbogen of *The Family Moskat,* insists on the strict observance of the law and prohibits the study of the mystical commentaries as a substitute for basic Hebrew studies. And yet, although he has all the appeal of a patriarch and seems to command Singer's support, he is unequal to the task of holding the Jewish community intact and harmonious from the discordant intrusions of the Messiah. He lapses into melancholy which, according to the commentaries, is the prelude to lust or despair, depending upon one's age and temperament.[2] In Benish's case it is the impotence of despair.

But as Benish's star descends, that of Itche Mates ascends. An intensely holy and pious ascetic, who fasts endlessly and who seldom sleeps, Mates is a cabalist who believes in the authenticity of Sabbatai Zevi. Although his devotion appears excessive and even punitive, there again seems to be no question of his righteousness. But then he marries Rechele and the marriage is unconsummated. Mates' disciples are shocked; and so are we. As he loses favor, his impotency coincides with that of Benish and thus underscores the cycle of reversal. Finally, one other character follows the trajectory that moves from certainty to disillusionment. Reb Gedaliya is Mates' opposite. A Hasid, devoted to joyous and generous service of God, Gedaliya comes to Goray like a wave of the Enlightenment. Mirroring the liberality of the Devil in "The Gentleman from Cracow," Gedaliya loosens restrictions, encourages the enjoyment of the body and the world, and ecstatically heralds the coming of Sabbatai Zevi. But what initially appears as liberal morality rapidly becomes anarchistic permissiveness.[3] Unclean animals are passed off as pure; wholesale sinfulness is encouraged. Gedaliya seduces many women, including Rechele, and turns out to be as promiscuous as Mates was abstinent. Finally, his position is unmasked when Rechele is impregnated by Satan and Sabbatai Zevi is converted to Islam, the two developments being correlations of each other.

Clearly, Singer has plotted with great care if not with sorcery. Aware that no discussion of the Messiah is meaningful apart from the turbulence of uncertainty, Singer presents a series of characters all of whom on the surface appear to be holy or righteous but under pressure betray extremism which is the sign of sinfulness. In other words, without compelling a direct belief in a Messiah, Singer tilts his work in that direction by involving the reader in a dialectic between appearance and reality, surface and substance. The debate yields enough doubt to sustain not only the reality of a Messiah, but also the criteria for determining his truth or falsity. Thus, in many ways, the central subject of the novel is not restricted to Sabbatai Zevi, but extends to the entire Jewish concept of the Messiah which, in turn, represents Singer's ultimate answer to the secular messiahs of *The Family Moskat.*

I

The Jewish messianic notion is an epitome of Judaism. According to tradition, God, not man, decides when the Messiah will come and His decision is motivated either by His sense of Justice or of Compassion. Man, in turn, is free to create the conditions for God's action. The Messiah will come either when the world is so righteous that it deserves redemption and God grants it out of His Justice; or when the world becomes so evil and suffering so intense that it needs redemption and God grants it out of His Compassion.[4] Although the concept appears clear and comprehensive, the alternatives actually are so inextricably tangled that one understands why the rabbis prohibited all attempts to calculate the end of days.

Each condition for the coming of the Messiah presupposes knowledge of the other as a realistic corrective.

Thus, although the rabbis also claim that a single day of wholehearted obedience would be sufficient for the Messiah's immediate arrival, the coexistence of both conditions constantly keeps before us the question of man's capacity for such sustained or shared fidelity. In other words, what community could ever be capable of a single day's devotion either to good or to evil? How, for example, could the righteous or the sinful ever persuade their opposites to be either *totally* repentent or self-indulgent?[5] In short, on the one hand, Judaism presents an ideal of righteousness which compels the Jew to seek justice and which thus makes his individual life a meaningful part of an eternal continuum preparing the way for final deliverance. On the other hand, Judaism offers a fundamental orientation to the human which recognizes that absolutes, either of good or evil, are essentially incompatible with life and human nature as we know, and history records, them to be.[6]

Traditional Judaism exists in the center of this contradiction and so does Singer's vision. Indeed, much of the purpose of the novel is to defend the traditional view and to justify the ways of unresolvable duality to man. Characteristically, however, Singer's way of supporting Orthodoxy is to give full play to all those who oppose or demand clarity of it. And when their arguments are spent, then the contradiction, though still difficult and maybe even impossible to comprehend, appears as a preferable and affirmative alternative. Indeed, the return to the traditional contradiction is like a return to the fold.

The character who comes closest to embodying that traditional view is Rabbi Benish. It is, of course, significant that Benish and Orthodoxy do not prevail in Goray. Nevertheless, the particular nature of his failure underscores the central sin of hastening the Messiah: the breakdown of community. "Worst of all, at this time when

unity was most necessary, every man went his own way,
no longer willing to share the common responsibility"
(34). Significantly, Benish is not master of his house and
his sons fail to provide leadership for theirs. The result
is discord in the household of Israel. Indeed, to get some
peace Benish orders his bed removed to his study and
becomes more and more a solitary. His descent into melancholy is thus accompanied by the historical sin of isolation from the family and the community. Individuality
and Judaism are far from being mutually exclusive, but
self-development pursued in isolation is suspect from the
Jewish point of view.

To Singer the family represents the Jewish community in miniature. The Jewish community in turn is the
stepping-stone and basic unit of history. When the family
is fragmented, the communal ties are broken and the historical analogue between the two is shattered. Benish's
particular failure thus deprives Judaism of its providen-
tial extension and power. Indeed, when Benish withdraws
both from his family and the Jews of Goray, he becomes
increasingly weak, "his face yellowed and grew wrinkled,
and old age overtook him at once" (97). Benish severs a
tie which is a source not only of historical continuity,
but also of life.

Benish's descent is hastened externally by Mates' rise
to leadership in the Jewish community. Earlier, Mates
and Gedaliya have been discussed in terms of their roles
in the cycle of confusion. Now those comments must be
amplified and brought to bear on the matter of the Messiah. The basic reason both Mates and Gedaliya initially
command respect or fail to invite suspicion is that each
dramatizes one of the two conditions for messianic deliverance. Through self-mortification, Mates attempts to move
the world toward righteousness. Through self-indulgence,

Gedaliya seeks to hurry the world toward sinfulness. Their common errors, however, are twofold: first, each makes his half the whole; second, in order to attain such totality, each pushes his half so far from the center that excess results. Thus, for all his piety, Mates is a sadistic ascetic; for all his joy, Gedaliya is a decadent sensualist. The details of each one's journey to distortion not only are revealing in themselves, but also point up the unexpected fate both characters share.

II

Throughout the novel Mates is associated with death and corpses. Rechele, in fact, shortly before their marriage, explains her reluctance by saying, " 'He has dead eyes' " (83). On their wedding night, Mates claims that he sees Lilith lurking in the dark corners of the bedroom. He then turns to Rechele and says that Lilith looks like her: " 'Long hair like yours. Naked. Concupiscent' " (133). And he cannot be a man to her.

Singer makes Mates impotent in order to expose asceticism as a secret hatred of life, the disgust with sex being its most powerful manifestation. Like Kafka's Hunger Artist, Mates is obsessed with cleanliness. Like the ascetic in "The Fast," he fasts so often and for such long periods that he appears to be trying to keep his insides free and clean of decay or dirt. Because the ascetic sees little value in his body and therefore in the body of this world, he is to Singer essentially a secret blasphemer. Such repudiation is appropriately released by the Messiah, for what the ascetic really yearns for is not life but its cessation.

In terms of the traditional notion of the Jewish Messiah, Mates has contracted its duality to singularity—

its troublesome entanglement to simplified perfection.
Such a view also violates or terminates human history
because, in its commitment to purity, including sexual
abstinence, it precludes the procreation of the race. In
exposing Mates' impotence, Singer is thus making a judgment not only on the sterility of Mates's asceticism in
the special context of the seventeenth century, but also
on the general nature of asceticism from the Jewish point
of view. Self-denial is a virtue and its sacrifices are enormous, but pushed to excess asceticism not only impoverishes the rich ambiguity at the heart of Judaism, but also
turns out to be an easier way of life than existing in contradiction.

Gedaliya is as robust and generous as Mates is joyless
and stingy. Everything about Gedaliya is rich and full—
his gorgeously embroidered clothes, his love of food, his
enjoyment of dancing, his devotion to the body. Wherever
Mates sees pain, Gedaliya sees pleasure. Mates' sexual
fears and frigidity are countered by Gedaliya's sexual freedom and even promiscuity. If Mates represents the attempt to hasten the Messiah by making the world perfect
and pure, Gedaliya takes the opposite tack and seeks to
hurry deliverance by committing every sin. It is significant that in the process Gedaliya draws more disciples
than Mates; he, after all, represents a more liberal and
generous spirit that ministers to the modern.

To Singer, however, Gedaliya is proof of the Orthodox Jewish position that the law of crash is slip. Initially,
all of Gedaliya's liberalizing adjustments are small and
harmless. Little boys pinching women are first excused
by Gedaliya as being merely mischievous. Later they become Peeping Toms and go upstairs to the women's bal-
cony of the synagogue to commit acts of homosexuality
and sodomy. Sessions that Gedaliya conducts with young

women on how to inflame their husbands rapidly degenerate into illicit gatherings. Lights are turned out and husbands exchange wives, a seventeenth century version of the modern key game. Finally, two beggars wander into Goray and are married on a dunghill by some mischiefmakers.

If Mates represents the perversions of being a slave to the soul, Gedaliya symbolizes the perversions of being a slave to the body. Mates lives as if life were nothing; Gedaliya as if it were everything. If Mates produces a distorted image of man when he tries to be more than human, Gedaliya produces a distorted image of man when he tries to be less than human. During Gedaliya's reign, moral anarchy triumphs. The Jews of Goray commit every sin imaginable and emerge as a collection of monstrosities and gargoyles.

Singer's central insight seems to be that the artificial or pathological hastening of the Messiah breaks open the dualistic center of Judaism into irreconcilable and antagonistic poles. The Messiah becomes not a harmonious but a discordant force. It makes enemies out of faculties that should be allies, sets members of the community at odds with others, and transforms good into evil. Asceticism turns out to be secret impotency; sensualism idolatrous lust. The former precludes the family; the latter diminishes or blurs it.

The unfortunate fulfillment of Rabbi Benish's prophecy of disunity serves Singer's end of compelling a more receptive and urgent reappraisal of the Orthodox position. Indeed, the contradiction at the heart of the Jewish concept of the Messiah seems, from the vantage point of the distortive ending, less terrible and obtuse. Basically, that dualistic knot represents to Singer the point at which man's understanding terminates and God's originates.

Such a limit is difficult for man to accept, but without such gulfs there can be no genuine strain to faith and no divine object of his surrender. Indeed, as long as man thinks he is supreme, God does not stand a chance. Singer's way of underscoring the necessity of God is to allow man to play out all his desires to achieve final resolution. And then, because his solutions generate only discord to the Jewish soul and community, the traditional position, for all its severity and even impossibility, emerges as a statement of sanity and a refuge for faith. What then are Singer's final notions of the Messiah? Will he come? Of course. When? In God's own good time. How? Only God knows. Indeed, perhaps only when man attributes such final knowledge to God and evidences a belief in Him that is stronger than his belief in himself, will the Messiah make himself known or already be present. Meanwhile, Lucifer strides forth at every sunrise, refreshed and formidable, with his temptations of certainty and peace.

III

Although this summary of the messianic theme deals with the center of the novel, it leaves relatively untouched a crucial aspect of the work—the role of Rechele. At this point the omission appears slight. After all, her story covers the same ground as that of Mates and Gedaliya. However, there is one dimension to the novel which has not been fully examined and which may justify Rechele's apparent redundancy.

Throughout the novel and, indeed, throughout Singer's works there are recurrent references to the people of Israel as a woman who is divorced, widowed, abandoned, or raped. Imparting immediacy to the abstract historical notion of the Household of Israel, Hadassah bears the same symbolic burden in *The Family Moskat;* and so do Hindele in "The Black Wedding" and Wanda-Sarah in *The Slave.* In addition, the coming of the Messiah is likened to the birth pains of a woman in labor. Rechele in many ways collects and embodies these allusions and becomes a collective symbol of the people of Israel, just as more gloriously the beloved symbolizes Israel in the "Song of Songs." [7] Significantly, she was born in 1648, the year of the massacres. Her origin, in other words, is associated with rape. The child of a rich, grubby man who, nevertheless, is pious in his devotions, she bears all the confusion of that mixed heritage. Her mother died when she was five and her father disappeared during the years of flight from the Cossacks. In her youth she thus appears as the orphaned, violated image of Israel after the pogroms.

Raised to adulthood by a ritual slaughterer who, like Gedalyia, is bestial and by a granny who terrifies her with supernatural tales, she emerges slightly deranged. Even her loveliness is marred by the fact that she is crippled. As a maiden, Rechele is a portrait of the abandoned and unwed Israel, waiting for love and a bridegroom. Wed first by Mates, she tastes the impotence of asceticism. Seduced later by Gedaliya, she experiences the fruitlessness of lust. Living in an atmosphere of messianic conjurings, she believes she sees visions. Gedaliya quickly and opportunistically proclaims her a prophetess and treats her like an idolatrous object or Golden Calf. Attired like an Eastern princess and carried around in a golden chair, she "looked like one of those icons that gentiles bear in church processions during their festivals" (183). Finally, just as the Jews of Goray are possessed by evil, Rechele is impregnated by Satan and carries within her womb a blaspheming dybbuk. Behind all false Messiahs stands the true Satan; such messianic labor pains gave birth to discord in the community and to blasphemy in the soul. Embodying the trial of the Messiah, Rechele, whose life began in violation, ends that way.

Rechele serves both as the microcosm of the community of Goray and a macrocosm of the Jewish community in history. Her life and fate become the record not only of the Jews of Goray in the seventeenth century, but also of the entire Jewish people before and after that nexus. Times may change and Messiahs may alter; they may be Napoleon or Hitler. The Messianic impulse may assume different and even more respectable utopian forms—Marxism, Zionism, scientific perfectibility. But to Singer these are merely variations on an eternal formula and the insights that sustain the story of Rechele remain firm and penetrating.

The basic insight is that the messianic urge is a request for a clarity or perfection that is not only beyond man's means, but also in the process tarnishes what is within his power. It is an attempt to unburden the world of its permanent mystery and to escape the dread of living in unresolved and perhaps unresolvable duality. But to Singer, as long as man is alive he is hemmed in by death and by its finite agent, doubt. Man's place is on a tightrope which runs from the human to the divine, from individuality to community, from self-criticism to self-fulfillment. The desire to perfect the world is the desire to conclude it. To get off the precarious tightrope [8] for the more solid footing of certainty delivers man into the hands of Satan and to his temptation of peace. Once the dualistic partnership, which fully mirrors existence, is broken, each camp parades off crying it has the answer. And between false prophets, the result is not deliverance but discord, not heaven but hell.

What Mates and Gedaliya separately embody must be reintegrated in meaningful tension. If Mates and Gedaliya could be coalesced into one soul, then each half would rid the other of its excess. The self-punishment of asceticism would be constrained to proper self-criticism; the self-indulgence of sensualism would be restrained to legitimate self-satisfaction. Ironically, their common extremism blinds them from recognizing that each has what the other needs. But, blindness or not, extremes unexpectedly bend and meet; in the novel they join at the common point of impotency, which makes frigidity and promiscuity in the final analysis familiar bedfellows.[9]

Rechele is crucial in all this because she serves as the haunting image of lovelessness in the novel. At the hands of Mates and Gedaliya, she either is a maiden or a harlot, untouched or raped. Such are the fruitless and false alternatives of extremists, for when Satan triumphs he triumphs through divorce. In the face of such evil, Singer holds to the wider promise that the love between a man and a woman, hopefully between a Jacob and a Rachel, knits the community together and serves as the Jewish threshold for a harmonious proximity to history and to God. And in this promise of self-fulfillment coupled with a faith in messianic deliverance that requires self-restraint, Singer strikes a final Jewish balance between the human and the divine through the medium of history.

Notes

1. If it were not for Nathan of Gaza (1644–1680), a disciple of Sabbatai Zevi, who spread his reputation and doctrines widely, this false Messiah would have been relatively unknown. His notoriety, however, accounts for his being also treated in fic-

tion by Israel Zangwill in *Dreamers of the Ghetto* and in dramatic form by Sholem Asch in *Sabbatai Z'vi.*

2. Melancholy is a perennial disease of the religious, just as Rabbi Benish's family situation and the setting in Bilgoray serve as Singer's archetypal family and landscape. Gina's melancholy in *The Family Moskat* leads to insanity (64); amongst the younger generations it serves as the threshold of idolatry and conversion (408). It also renders Rabbi Naptali of "The Black Wedding" impotent; that story, incidentally, is a miniature version of *Satan in Goray.*

3. The progression of satanic possession is always as subtle as it is disguised. Thus, at the beginning, Gedaliya does not so much lie as twist or curtail the whole truth. In "A Tale of Two Liars" the Devil begins his narration of the story by saying, "A lie only can thrive on truth; lies, heaped one upon another, lack substance" (36).

4. The Jewish concept of the Messiah is such a complicated and dangerous subject that I have leaned heavily on what seems, at least to me, to be one of the clearest and most articulate presentations—that of Emil L. Fackenheim, which appeared under the title "Judaism and the Meaning of Life," *Commentary,* XXXIX (April, 1965), 49–55.

5. In *In My Father's Court,* Singer, speaking of the contrast between Wolf, a loudmouthed, profane coal dealer, and his patient mother, puts the problem succinctly and with appropriate scepticism: "The Messiah will not come until Mother became like Wolf the coal dealer or Wolf the coal dealer like Mother" (194).

6. That this dualistic notion of the Messiah is at the heart of Judaism and extends beyond messianic application may be suggested by the first book of Numbers, which deals with priestly assignments. The three tribes of Levi were led by his three sons: Gershon, Kohath, and Merari. The Kohathites were entrusted with the task of transporting the holy furniture: the Ark, the Tablets, the Menorah, the Altars. Each son of Kohath was assigned a specific item. The rabbis of the *Midrash* raise the question why the Torah is so specific—why each son is given a precise assignment? Two answers are given which initially appear antagonistic but under closer scrutiny are as complementary as the two conditions required for messianic deliverance.

One explanation argues that if the assignments were not specific, there would be dissension. All or many would want to carry the Torah and consider themselves as, or more, worthy than the one given the task. Hence, to eliminate such discord, specific responsibilities were fixed. The other explanation stresses that many hold the holy items in such awe that if they were not ordered to carry them they would refuse to do so.

The Torah is a tree of life. It is meant to be respected but not to the point of paralysis. On the other hand, one must never forget its sacred origin or nature and thus be totally comfortable in its presence or use. Hence, the rabbis move from opposite ends to converge toward a point of tension through which an ideal is suggested, although never stated.

7. In Jeremiah (31:2:20) Rachel is spoken of as the mother of Israel. Another famous biblical allegory of this kind is to be found in Hosea (II:1–22). There, Hosea bemoans the infidelity of his wife Gomer and, in the process, finds that his personal tragedy symbolizes that of the entire people of Israel who have been unfaithful to God. And just as Hosea's love for, and forgiveness of, Gomer persist, so does God's. Employing the prophetic voice, Hosea concludes: "And I will betroth thee unto Me in faithfulness; and thou shalt know the Lord."

Building upon this concept of God as a lover, later Church Fathers figured Christ as a bridegroom pursuing man's soul, His beloved; special emphasis also was put upon the nun as Christ's bride. A medieval version of this love relationship between Christ and man appears in the allegorical poem, "Quia Amore Lanqueo"; a better-known late-nineteenth-century version, perhaps, is Francis Thompson's "The Hound of Heaven."

8. The image of the tightrope is Singer's definition of man's precarious state in this world and is treated with great detail in *The Magician of Lublin.* Ultimately, that image generates the notion that man is a slave to God, a concept that is glowingly and appropriately embodied in a love story, *The Slave.*

9. The Talmud nicely sums up the progression of satanic possession by describing sin first as a stranger, then a friend, and finally a master.

*In the last analysis, to attempt ultimate
integration through self-realization is
an attempt to escape human nature.*

———Emil L. Fackenheim,
"Self-Realization and the
Search for God"

5.

The Magician of Lublin:
The Religion of the Picaresque Artist

In *The Magician of Lublin* Singer presents his characteristic journey of the prodigal son. The novel opens with the buoyant, frequently immoral Yasha the Magician moving freely and deftly from one circus engagement and love affair to another. It concludes with the ascetic figure of Yasha, now called Jacob the Penitent, literally entombed in a brick prison and undergoing mortification. The transformation takes place during a twenty-four hour period when Yasha attempts to rob the safe of the wealthy Zuraski. With the money he hopes to be able to divorce his wife, marry the elegant widow of a Warsaw professor, convert to Christianity, and pay for the cost of preparing a new act to be performed before the crowned heads of Europe. But all his plans are laid to rest in the tomb Yasha has chosen as his punishment or his life; perhaps, for him and for Singer they are one and the same.

The Magician of Lublin falls into three parts, like a three-act drama, except that the structural divisions sup-

port three different aspects of reality. The first deals with
Yasha in a situation that is characteristically modern in
its mixture of freedom and restraint, adultery and fidelity,
secularity and religiosity. The second part is wild and
surrealistic. All bars are down and the full play of the
picaresque hero is released. The conclusion arrests all
motion and presents the penitential portrait of imprisonment and slavery to God. The problem of accepting the
ending is thus contingent once again on comprehending
the total arc of Singer's vision.

When we first meet Yasha the Magician, he is lively
and engaging, always the master of complicated locks and
situations, and looks and acts ten years younger than his
forty years. Moreover, what rapidly becomes clear is that
Singer has selected Yasha's profession with symbolic care,
for it characterizes not only his way of earning a living,
but also his way of life. Thus, Yasha "had tangled and
disentangled himself on numerous occasions" (13). He
juggles various love affairs and walks an emotional tightrope as deftly as the one he performs on in the circus. In
the house of Zeptel, one of his mistresses, Yasha partici-
pates in the local ritual of entertaining the villagers by
opening a lock which they feel will stump his skill. But
Yasha says, " 'A lock is like a woman. Sooner or later it
must surrender. . . . It'll give, it'll give. You only need
to squeeze the belly button' " (57).

Although Yasha manipulates people as he does locks
and carries on with other women, Singer does not present
his hero as without virtue or conscience. He has affairs
with many women, but his love for his wife remains intact, and he holds his marriage sacred. Although he mixes
with thieves and low life, he refuses to employ his lock-
picking talents for dishonest ends. Finally, Yasha is not
without respect for God, although it is colored by his

profession. Driving along the road in spring, he surveys the budding fields, inhales the scent of growing newness, and spontaneously exclaims: " 'Oh, God Almighty, You are the magician, not I! . . . To bring out plants, flowers and colors from a bit of black soil' " (60). Although he treasures his belief in God, he often plays the role of the Devil's advocate in taverns, scoffing at the pious certainty of believers. In short, in the first part we have the portrait of an appealing scoundrel who is no fool. Sensitive to conscience and responsive to the godly, he is nevertheless too confident of his magical powers, too flushed by the strength of his still youthful body, and too skeptical of glib religious answers to accept any restrictions of life, love, and marriage. Singer sums him up:

> He was a maze of personalities—religious and heretical, good and evil, false and sincere. He could love many women at once. He was ready to renounce his religion, yet—when he found a page torn from a holy book he always picked it up and put it to his lips. (58)

Yasha is fully and humanly greedy. He is involved in everything, in the body and the spirit, in this world and the next. His ruling mode is "play" and his success at "play" is the picaresque answer to the Horatio Alger myth of success through work.[1] Devoted to the pleasure-principle as his reality-principle, Yasha in many ways is a perpetual adolescent or a character who constantly recovers his adolescence. As a result, he is promiscuous in the profound sense of the term, for he generates an image of endless life and infinite possibilities. In his animal health and confidence, Yasha is akin to Abram Shapiro of *The Family Moskat,* who significantly is dubbed the "Flying Dutchman" (54). Abram, endlessly inventing schemes of seduction, knows his powers: "In his years of women-chasing Abram had learned that a man's will always prevails. If a man makes up his mind, a woman will happen along. It was a kind of magnetism" (483). Similarly, Yasha could "never understand how other people managed to live in one place and spend their entire lives with one woman without becoming melancholy. He, Yasha, was forever at the point of depression." Relieving his depression by pursuing women, Yasha succeeds, like Abram, because it "was one of his attributes to adjust to any character. It was a useful factor when applied to the act of magnetism" (44). The only difference between Yasha and Abram is that Yasha employs magnetism in both his play and work. Indeed, Singer's way of coming to the religious as well as sexual heart of his *picaro* is through his series of love affairs.

In all, there are five women with whom Yasha maintains an actual or desired sexual relationship. There is his wife, Esther; his assistant, Magda; his mistress, Zeptel; the woman he has fallen in love with, Emilia; and Emilia's daughter, Halina. Obviously, Yasha's way of remaining young and unfinished is to insist there are many Yashas, each woman reflecting merely one facet of his multiple character or multiple ego as Hermann Hesse describes it:

> In reality, however, every ego, so far from being a unity is in the highest degree a manifold world, a constellated heaven, a choas of forms, of states and stages, of inheritances and potentialities. (79)

But though Yasha manages his love affairs to reflect flatteringly on his manifold exterior, Singer arranges them in a significant pattern to reflect on his psychological and religious interior. First, the women fill out a religious spectrum. Esther is a pious Jewess, Magda is Christian, Zeptel is a wayward Jewess, Emilia is a converted Jewess who now wants to recant, and Halina, symbolic of the new generation, has no firm religious commitment. Second, that religious varietism is accompanied by a psychological spectrum which relates the physical differences of the women with the different roles Yasha assumes with each. His wife is barren; as a result, when Yasha put "his arms around her she was aroused like an adolescent— since a woman who has not been pregnant, remains virginal forever" (23). Yasha then exchanges the role of a young bridegroom for that of a lover-father with Magda who is so young and painfully thin that she appears to be his daughter. Zeptel, on the other hand, whose hips are too broad and whose bosom is too protuberant, is like a mother. Finally and significantly, his relationship with the mature Zeptel and the girlish Magda is carried over to that with the middle-aged Emilia and her adolescent daughter, Halina.

Singer has made Yasha a magician to dramatize his role as a promiscuous chameleon who seeks to escape time's net by being an artist of many devices, disguises, and lives.[2] Thus, Yasha's multiple flirtations with Judaism, Christianity, conversion, and agnosticism are correlated to his variegated roles as son, adolescent, lover, and father. The religious danger of conversion finds its sexual counterpart in the threat of incest. What Yasha resists above all is being fixed with a permanent identity, as if that act of definition also would mark his demise. As long as he can manipulate his various love affairs, like pins in his juggling act, and be different persons or wear different masks—boy, lover, father; and Jew, Christian, convert, sceptic—to different women, he is unfinished, still to be defined, still in a state of becoming. This is the domain of comedy, for tragedy represents the sharp pressure of finality. Comedy measures the span and possibilities of life; tragedy the span and inevitability of death. Variety to Yasha is not just the spice of life; it is his answer to and substitute for termination. But whereas in the first part of the novel Yasha magically seems to be able to play both sides of the moral and religious fence, his relationship with Emilia in the second part threatens his dualistic straddling. Specifically, Emilia, who moves among cultivated circles of Warsaw, makes not only marriage but also conversion a condition of sexual surrender. Thus, for all his deft sidestepping, Yasha finds the pressure of identity intruded into his life in the form of Emilia's demands.

I

Although in the second part the comedy shifts to tragedy, Yasha is unaware that Emilia's wishes represent a damnation in disguise. All Yasha knows is that Emilia reflects his own aspirations to rise above the petty life he has been leading and to reach for the artistic recognition he believes he deserves. If anything, Emilia appeals to Yasha's desire for more freedom, more variety, more secularity. Ironically, however, in rejecting the duality of liberality and restraint that characterizes the first part for the harmonious singularity of complete freedom, Yasha far from gaining more life nearly encounters his death. Here is a brief catalog of what happens to Yasha by the end of the second part: he ages rapidly, becomes a thief, nearly cripples himself, drives Magda, his gentile mistress, to suicide, and hastens his Jewish paramour, Zeptel, into a house of prostitution. Add to all of this the night-

marish night he spends after the robbery—the fear of
detection, the encounters with the twitching cripple, the
humiliation and disgrace, the experience for the first time
of impotency—and one has the sense of an enormous collapse. It is necessary, then, to see the expansive and worldly
reality that Emilia offers to Yasha as essentially a temptation.

At the heart of that temptation is Emilia's request
for conversion. Significantly, that request involves another
which Yasha previously had resisted—the temptation to
steal.[3] Indeed, one wonders whether this is not a symbolic
connection. Thievery seems to be Singer's way of stigma-
tizing conversion as the act of taking something that does
not belong to you. Evidently, to Singer a Jew is free to
be a Jew or to be a nonbelieving Jew but he is not free
to be a Christian. This is not mere chauvinism, for it
applies to any conversion in which one takes what is not
his to take. The issue of conversion serves as Singer's
special way of approaching the modern and eternal problem of identity. Central to Singer's notion of identity is
the image of the tightrope which reverberates throughout
the novel.

Just as earlier aspects of Yasha's craft were extended
to characterize his attitude toward others and God, so his
walking the tightrope is not limited to his performing as
a magician. "He constantly felt that only the thinnest of
barriers separated him from those dark ones who swarmed
around him, aiding and thwarting him, playing all sorts
of tricks on him. He, Yasha, had to fight them constantly
or else fall from the tightrope, lose the power of speech,
grow infirm and impotent" (112). Yasha is aware that the
aim of the devil is to throw him off his moral balance.
In fact, just before the robbery, Yasha "felt its presence—

a dybbuk, a satan, an implacable adversary who would disconcert him, while he was juggling, push him from the tightrope, make him impotent" (142).

Walking the tightrope is Singer's image of what it is to be alive, not only as a Jew but as a man. It represents the precariousness of identity which has no authentic meaning without dangerous duration. Moreover, identity is not a product but a process. It is not achieved once and for all time but is the endless task of making and remaking the self. Weary of the perilous equilibrium between faith and doubt and of the endless struggles within him, Yasha seeks instead the peace, permanence, and new prospects that he believes conversion will grant him. He also hopes to escape from the tantalizing void of the Jewish God who has no face or form and has never accommodated Himself to man by assuming mortality. In addition, because, as Singer notes, God revealed himself to no one, gave no indication of what is permitted and forbidden, Jewish identity historically has been characterized by an endless and indecisive dialogue between *men* about *God*. Indeed, at one point in the novel when Yasha, out of his desperation, pleads with God to give him a sign, he is essentially requesting God to make himself tangible and unambiguous. The absence of peace in this life and the constant doubts that assail men's minds and hearts are the reflections of an absence of metaphysical clarity in Judaism. Indeed, Singer's notion of the tightrope is a traditional Jewish one and undoubtedly goes back to the sage, Eleazer of Worms, who claimed that man is a rope whose two ends are pulled by God and Satan; and in the end God proves stronger.[4]

Reflecting on that ceaseless warfare, Rabbi Katzenellenbogen of *The Family Moskat* confesses

All his life he had hoped that in his old age all
worldly temptations would depart from him so that
he might be able to serve the Eternal in full faith.
But even now, at the very threshold of the grave, he
still found himself carrying on interminable wrangles
with Satan. . . . (229)

In contrast to Rabbi Katzenellenbogen's desire to hold on,
Yasha's desire to convert represents his wish to throw off
the special Jewish burden of seeking fullness in the face
of lifelong limitation and unconfirmation. To Singer the
final strain that is put upon Jewish identity comes from
God's terrifying Oneness—a relentless singularity that refuses to yield or adjust to human and social pluralism.
Indeed, after the robbery, Yasha, who now feels the terrible burden of freedom from God, cries out, "This is
no life! . . . I don't have a moment's peace of mind anymore. I must give up magic and women. One God, one
wife, like everyone else . . ." (159).

In Singer's world the Devil's way of seducing Yasha
from the tightrope is to offer him metaphysical amnesia
which Singer, in *The Family Moskat,* defines as the state
of "plunging into the abyss . . . of the free will" (212).
The Devil himself symbolizes a cosmic loophole in that
he represents the opportunity to escape the endless battle
between good and evil, between God and Satan, waging
within and constituting the identity of the Jew. To Singer,
evil thus appears not only in the obvious forms of immorality and disobedience, but also in man's striving to
be more than he can be or settling for less than he is. In
either case, the satanic aim is to free man from his dependence on God. Such freedom makes man the total
magician—the adept performer who pushes self-reliance
to the point of picaresque self-sufficiency. However,

Yasha's desire to be fully emancipated and to express his animalistic nature actually incarnates the Devil, for as Emil L. Fackenheim notes:

> when health becomes the ultimate law, the "blond beast" is set free for breaking the fetters of morality; when the spirit is its own unqualified measure, Satan, the perverted spirit, is free also, transforming a mere urge for security into a metaphysical lust for power. . . .[5]

Moreover, as Singer warns, the result of stepping off the tightrope is not power but impotency. At the end of the second part, Yasha, in fact, discovers that in trying to become more than a man—a god—he has become less than a man—a twitching, impotent cripple, like the ones he and Asa Heshel encounter. Instead of freedom, he lives a life of imprisonment; at the end of the novel Yasha, far from expanding his existence, ends up contained in a "living grave."

Before going on to a consideration of the final third of the novel, one might speculate on an unexpected yield from the image of the tightrope and the issue of conversion. Perhaps, Singer has allegorically built into the situation of Yasha the Magician his own situation as a Jewish writer. Perhaps, to Singer the basic temptation offered to the Jewish writer is also conversion—the temptation to turn away from his special Jewish materials for the wider world of American or world experience—to give up the stubborn, nagging yearnings of the Jewish soul for an historical and cosmic identity and choose instead the social and political variety of New World culture.[6] To Singer, at least, the Jewish artist who does so is a thief and runs the risk of producing work that is crippled or impotent. Whether this allegory has application to other Jewish writers, it certainly has meaning for Singer. By remaining within the sharp and troubling confines of his own special Jewish area, Singer is proof of the paradox that intense narrowness may be the surest avenue to comprehensive statement. Moreover, he appears to be recommending to Yasha his own solution; namely, that in slavery Yasha will find his true freedom.

It is at this point that we come full circle and back to the problem of the ending. Not only is the ascetic figure of Yasha the Penitent a painful contrast to that of the vital Yasha the Megician. Even more objectionable, Yasha's retirement from the world seems not only in excess of his crime, but also fails to reflect it. In Singer's behalf, however, it should be noted that the ending not only is consistent with his vision, but also can be defended against charges of escapism or punitive orthodoxy.

First, Singer makes it quite clear that Yasha's attempt to escape the temptations of the world by self-imprisonment fails. The tightrope is portable—the temptations go wherever Yasha does. Like Rabbi Katzenellenbogen, Yasha, in fact, admits, "No, the temptations never cease" (232). Second, Yasha's prison is Singer's metaphor of man's slavery—to one wife, one life, one God. At the beginning of the novel Yasha was content to stay on the tightrope as long as he was in control and as long as no choice of a fixed identity was forced on him. In the process, he is interested only in having rather than denying. The temptation of Emilia and of Satan is to get off the tightrope altogether and to pursue a life of freedom without any inhibitions. The end of the novel redresses the imbalance. Having yielded to all satisfactions, Yasha turns to burdens not so that he may choose one or the other, but so that both may be once again brought together in a reconstituted and more informed human and Jewish identity. In these terms, the prison is merely the most intense form of the tightrope.

At the beginning of the novel, Yasha jokingly predicts the end of the novel and in the process indirectly reveals Singer's source. Yasha teasingly asks his wife, " 'What would happen if I became an ascetic and, to repent, had myself bricked into a cell without a door like that saint in Lithuania? Would you remain true to me?' " When his wife indicates that it is not necessary to entomb oneself in order to repent, Yasha replies, " 'It all depends on what sort of passion one is trying to control' " (25). To this might be added, it all depends on what hero one wants to humanize. Singer has sentenced his picaresque hero to a life sentence, or rather a sentence of life, in order to generate the most severe metaphor for the Jewish journey from the circumference of freedom and self-expression to the center of slavery and inhibition. That these harsh ends, nevertheless, may serve as the threshold for genuine freedom and expression is affirmed by Yasha. Asked by a friend why he has entombed himself, Yasha-Jacob replies, " 'I could no longer breathe' " (236).[7]

Notes

1. Robert Heilman, "Variations on Picaresque (*Felix Krull*)," *Sewanee Review* (Autumn, 1958), pp. 547–77. I am indebted to this comprehensive and often brilliant survey of the *picaro* and his long literary life.
2. John le Carré, author of *The Spy Who Came in from the Cold*, recently described the artist as a combination of magician and spy: "He is an illusionist. He will show you an egg, and ask you to believe in the parts you cannot see." Applying the analogy to the artist, Le Carré continues: "he is a chameleon in search of a color. . . . In the process he may wear many

disguises, according to his mood. He will change his identity as he changes his stories, as other people change their clothes" ("The Underground Man," *New York Times Book Review* [June 27, 1965], p. 2).

3. Similarly, Koppel Berman of *The Family Moskat,* who is presented with the same religious multiplicity and picaresque sexuality, robs the safe of the wealthy Meshulam Moskat, divorces his wife, and flees to America.

4. Described in Gershom Scholem, *Major Trends of Jewish Mysticism* (New York, 1959), p. 92.

5. "Self-Realization and the Search for God," p. 293.

6. In this connection, Singer remarked in an interview to Brian Glanville, "It's true that being a Jewish writer you limit yourself. . . . In a way, I feel that to be a Yiddish writer is to be isolated in a very terrible way from the world of literature." Similarly, Kafka, whom Singer admires, was described by Thomas Mann as expressing "the solitude, the aloneness of the artist—and of the Jew, on top of that. . . ." (From "Homage" to *The Castle* [New York, 1951], p. xi.)

7. In Singer's recent story, "The Slaughterer," Yoineh Meir, who has been persuaded to become a ritual slaughterer, comes to detest his job. He yearns for release: "Yoineh Meir understood now why the sages of old had likened the body to a cage—a prison where the soul sits captive. . . ." The parallel to Yasha's situation is extended when Yoineh Meir cries out, " 'Father in Heaven, I cannot breathe!' "

When the Baal Shem had a difficult task before him, he would go to a certain place in the woods, light a fire and meditate in prayer—and what he had set out to perform was done. When a generation later the "Maggid" of Meseritz was faced with the same task he would go to the same place in the woods and say: We can no longer light the fire, but we can still speak the prayers—and what he wanted done became reality. Again a generation later Rabbi Moshe Leib of Sassov had to perform this task. And he too went into the woods and said: We can no longer light a fire, nor do we know the secret meditations belonging to the prayer, but we do know the place in the woods to which it all belongs—and that must be sufficient; and sufficient it was. But when another generation had passed and Rabbi Israel of Rishin was called upon to perform the task, he sat down on his golden chair in his castle and said: We cannot light the fire, we cannot speak the prayers, we do not know the place, but we can tell the story of how it was done. And, the story-teller adds, the story which he told had the same effect as the actions of the other three.

——Gershom Scholem, *Major Trends of Jewish Mysticism*

9.

Singer in Miniature:
The World of the Short Stories

Singer is a master of the short story form because he regards caricature not as an aberration but as a norm. In his hands, the short story is not so much a slice as a twist of life. Not accidentally, his shorter novels—*Satan in Goray, The Magician of Lublin, The Slave*—are, in my judgment, his best. Indeed, *Satan in Goray* is essentially a long short story and, like Singer's best tales, is a gnarled sampling that displays the conventional gothic preference for both terror and brevity. Obviously, this does not mean that all Singer's short works are flawless. Jonathan Baumbach, for example, in his review of *Short Friday* (1964), found only three stories memorable and one, "Jachid and Jechidah," an "extraordinary clinker." [1] (Not really; it is an overworked metaphor for an essay not a story, just as "The Warehouse" (1966) [2] is more a sermon than a tale.) Then, Michael Fixler, complaining of Singer's lamentable tendency to force a "quizzical" effect, rightly questions why

> demonic narrators are used gratuitously to bracket stories compelling in themselves. The demons simply offer a coy point of view where Singer could have done as well or better with some old peasant or beggar. "The Unseen" and "The Destruction of Kreshev" are good examples of first-rate works with trivial narrators. [3]

But Singer's most serious flaw is his marred endings. We already have quoted and supported the objections of Milton Hindus to the revision of *The Family Moskat. Satan in Goray* also is badly terminated: it concludes with an epilogue which seeks to "explain and document" the possession of Rechele by a dybbuk. Forgetting the advice of Henry James, who rightly maintained that for evil to have any force its origins and motives must be indefinite, Singer follows the bad example of Faulkner who ruined the splendid gothic quality of *Sanctuary* by adding a case history to account for Popeye's malevolence. *The Magician of Lublin*, too, concludes with a totally irrelevant and dramatically abortive letter from Emilia. Finally, *The Slave* comes to a labored end as a result of Singer's almost sentimental insistence on documenting the "miracle" of

Jacob's burial next to Sarah. The same charges can be directed at a number of the short stories, especially "Yachid and Yechidah," "Short Friday," and "A Wedding in Brownsville." The only explanation for the pervasive presence of this structural failure is Singer's resistance to the harsh dictates of his own vision. The same desire to soften tragedy results in the sentimental gesture of concluding works with miraculous happenings. But whereas this flaw characterizes all his novels, many of his short stories are rounded out to a perfect fullness, consistent both with their narrative impulses and those of Singer's vision. On this matter, Singer himself said:

> Actually, I prefer the short story because only in a short story can a writer reach perfection—more than in a novel. When you write a novel, especially a larger novel, you are never the ruler of your writing, because you cannot really make a plan for a novel of say, 500 pages, and keep to the rules, or keep to the plan. While in a short story, there is always the possibility of really being perfect.[4]

Moreover, the short stories are different not just in degree but also in kind from the novels. Singer's longer fiction is dominated by a traditional and masculine point of view (often, the two are synonymous). But a great many of the short stories are dominated by an untraditional and feminine point of view; Singer's first story to be published was "Women." Indeed, as a correlation, although there are hardly any evil women in Singer's novels, they abound in the tales. Thus, Singer's tales of the *shtetl,* like Chaucer's *Canterbury Tales,* fall into groups and, initially, the most sensational is that of the evil Amazons.

I

Part of the traditional cast of Singer's vision appears in his acceptance of the subservience of women. He frequently reminds readers that woman was created second, out of Adam's side, and dependent. In the life of the *shtetl* it was not unusual for a wife to work so that she could boast that her husband is free to study the Torah. In the households of Rabbis Katzenellenbogen and Benish, the wives inhabit the background to their husbands' foreground and serve as the peripheral and occasional objects of their interests. But when she breaks free of that masculine tyranny, woman, Singer reminds us, often recovers her original role as temptress. Indeed, as an evil force she is such a scourge that the Devil appears benevolent by comparison. Thus, in "The Gentleman from Cracow" (1957), Hodle, the daughter of a ragpicker and drunken father, is the town witch, wanton, and thief; and her curses are so biting and imaginative that the townspeople proverbially dread to fall into her mouth.[5] Significantly, when evil is unmasked in Frampol, Hodle marries Satan and emerges as her ancient prototype, Lilith. An older, more gnarled version of Hodle is Cunegunde, who appears in a number of stories as well as one in her own right, and who is visited by another shrew, appropriately named Zlateh the Bitch, to cast spells on her husband and enemies in "The Wife-Killer" (1955). But the supreme feminine devil, who also stakes out Singer's total spectrum of distorted women, is Risha of "Blood" (1964).

"Blood" powerfully weds the familiar theme of the progression of perversion with the notion of bloodlust. Singer begins the story by documenting the fusion:

The cabalists know that the passion for blood and
the passion for flesh have the same origin, and this is
the reason "Thou shalt not kill" is followed by
"Thou shalt not commit adultery." (26)[6]

Twice widowed and now married to an old pious Jew,
Risha, like the Wife of Bath, is still frisky and eager. One
day while observing Reuben, the ritual slaughterer, effi-
ciently going about his bloody business, lust rises in her.
Singer does not permit the reader to forget the cabalistic
connection, for he describes Reuben's seduction of Risha
in terms of the former's craft; Risha says, " 'You certainly
murdered me that time' " (33). Before long, the identification becomes total, and Risha and Reuben copulate
in the midst of the slaughtered animals:

While the beasts were bleeding, Risha threw off all
her clothes and stretched out naked on a pile of straw.
Reuben came to her and they were so fat their bodies
could barely join. They puffed and panted. Their
wheezing mixed with the death-rattles of the animals
made an unearthly noise; contorted shadows fell on
the walls; the shed was saturated with the heat of
blood. (39)

Having reduced her human nature to that of an animal,
Risha then demands that Reuben allow her to assume the
man's role of slaughtering the animals. Finally, she caps
her adulterous betrayal of her husband by being unfaithful to the Jewish community: she sells non-kosher meat
as pure.
    Whatever personal reasons motivate Singer's vegetar-
ianism, the slaughtering of animals and fish serves as his
theological metaphor of a fallen world. Prior to the fall,

Adam and Eve were vegetarians, and Isaiah's prophecy of the lion lying down with the lamb was accompanied by his vision of the lion once again eating grass. But though fallen, man's further descent to the level of the beasts was arrested by means of moral controls, not the least of which are the laws of *Shehitah* or ritual slaughtering. Specifically, in Judaism detailed ritualistic rules are prescribed, perhaps as an expression of guilt for the slaughtering act itself, which are governed by the principles of mercy and purity. The animals must be killed rapidly and, within a restricted group, those selected must be without blemish.

To be sure, even these redemptive strictures fail to satisfy the pitying soul of Yoineh Meir who, in "The Slaughterer" (1967), envisions the entire world as a slaughterhouse. Indeed, in his final madness and blasphemy— to Singer the two are one—Yoineh Meir accuses God of being the supreme slaughterer of all. In "Cockadoodledoo" (1964), the narrator, a rooster, claims, as does the hero of "The Parrot" (1966), that all animals have souls and "If your human ears could hear our weeping, you would throw away all your slaughtering knives." [7] In other words, Singer, whose preoccupation with the slaughtering of animals begins with *Satan in Goray* and continues in even his most recent stories, regards the killing of animals as the expression of fallen man's potential murderousness. To be sure, there is a world of difference between Yoineh Meir and Risha; for whereas Yoineh's tortured *weltschmerz* is informed by heavenly or paradisical standards, Risha's sexual slaughter is perverted to hellish and bestial ends. Indeed, Singer caps Risha's descent to the level of the beasts she kills by having her sell non-kosher meat to indicate that historically and cosmically there is no such thing as a terminal or minor sin.

Every personal indiscretion rapidly gains momentum and swells to a communal and biblical betrayal. But to Singer the most serious betrayal of all and the one that prepares the way for all the others is the blurring of masculine and feminine clarity. From Singer's point of view, the temptation of Eve is an invitation to violate both the boundaries of obedience and of masculine dominance. Significantly, Risha grows stronger as Reuben grows weaker; increasingly, she becomes the more aggressive of the two. That external exchange mirrors a more basic internal substitution that employs lust as a transitional agent.

Physical sensations by their nature are immediate and short-lived. When accompanied by love in Singer's world, those sensations travel through the fullness of the partners and thus are given a longer, reverberating life. But Risha and Reuben are like animals and they rapidly reach points of satisfaction which require perversions to be extended. In the process, they hurry their lives away and become "prematurely old"; glutting themselves, they become so fat they can hardly come together. Ironically, their bloodlust has involved them in a self-consuming cycle; their sexuality, in truth, has become slaughter. By surrendering his masculinity to Risha, Reuben has essentially turned his soul over to his body. Allowing women, in D. H. Lawrence's terms, to stray outside the bounds of man's beliefs and gods, Reuben has created a sexual Frankenstein—a mannish woman.

Risha serves to establish a crucial nexus for a special group of women in Singer's stories. On the one hand, she provides a more naturalistic base for comprehending Singer's cabalistic and already fully-formed devils like Hodle and Cunegunde. On the other hand, Risha serves as an extreme in her own right to a host of mannish women. They include Hindele of "The Black Wedding" (1961); Lise of "The Destruction of Kreshev" (1961); Yentl of "Yentl the Yeshiva Boy" (1962), who actually dresses and passes herself off as a boy; Mrs. Margolis of "Caricature" (1961), who increasingly resembles her husband; and Zeitl and Rickel of "Zeitl and Rickel" (1968).

The full arc of the group mirrors the span of Singer's chronology and visionary theology. One extreme is embedded in the past and in demonology—in the Garden of Eden and in Lilith. The other is anchored in the modern world and in emancipated types—in an increasingly nonhierarchial and mobile society and in Madame Bovary, Nora, Sister Carrie, Lady Chatterley, and Temple Drake. Risha is the go-between, just as Satan is Singer's eternal panderer. Like Janus, Risha faces in two directions. On one side, she adjusts the absolute incarnations of evil to recognizable human distortions; on the other, she collects and projects the feminine incursions into traditionally masculine realms to their ultimate cosmic ends. To be sure, the latter group of mannish women is not evil per se. Nor are they grotesque like Risha. Nevertheless, she serves as a warning and terminus for one of Singer's recurrent themes: the dilemma of the intelligent woman in the man-dominated world of traditional Judaism.

Undoubtedly, Singer was attracted to this familiar literary theme by personal reasons. In *In My Father's Court* he relates how his mother was preferred by her father even above her brothers because of her learning (50). Singer's sister evidently was also well read. Indeed, what all of Singer's mannish women have in common is their love of books which, in turn, leads to the loss or obscuration of their femininity. Thus, Adele, Asa Heshel's wife in *The Family Moskat*, is a serious student and as a

result there "was something mannish and rationalistic
about her forehead, her lifted eyebrows; it was as though
behind the familiar facade, the spirit of her father, the
scholar, had broken through" (319). Similarly, when Lot-
tie in the same novel is told by her father that a Jewish
daughter's duty is to marry, she retorts: " 'What is there
in marrying? I want to learn, to get knowledge' " (454).
In a lighter vein, Mr. Margolis of "Caricature," coming
home late one night, finds his wife wearing his robe,
smoking his cigar, and working on his unfinished scholarly
opus. Struck by her resemblance to himself, Mr. Margolis
recalls the "saying of Schopenhauer: Woman has the appearance and mentality of a child. If she becomes intellec-
tually mature, she develops the face of a man" (91). In
"The Black Wedding" Rabbi Naphtali has only a daughter. But Hindele "at fifteen, was already reading esoteric
books and periodically went into seclusion like a holy
man. It was rumored that Hindele wore a fringed gar-
ment under her dress . . ." (26). Reb Bunin's daughter,
Lise, in "The Destruction of Kreshev" (1943; 1961) also
evidences at an early age an intense interest in books.
Although her father warns her that studying is not the
way to the marriage altar, he nevertheless confesses, " 'It's
a shame that she's not a boy. What a man she would have
made' " (149). Finally, Yentl of "Yentl the Yeshiva Boy"

> preferred men's activities to women's. Her father Reb
> Todros, may he rest in peace, during many bedridden
> years had studied Torah with his daughter as if she
> were a son. He told Yentl to lock the doors and drape
> the windows, then together they pored over the
> Pentateuch, the Mishnah, the Germara, and the Com-
> mentaries. She had proved so apt a pupil that her
> father used to say:

"Yentl—you have the soul of a man."
"So why was I born a woman?"
"Even Heaven makes mistakes." (132)

In *The Family Moskat* the People of the Book were weaned away from the Torah by books. A reminder of this broader context is important because it reveals that the dilemma is not solely a feminine but essentially a Jewish dilemma. To be sure, Singer adjusts the feminine version: Hindele, Lise, Yentl, and Zeitel read not secular but religious works. Standing behind men so long, they are forced initially to channel their desires for independence and individuality into less dramatic areas of contrast. Nevertheless, by extension the full arc is open to them, and as mannish women they are on the way to making synonomous the acquisition of knowledge and of masculinity. In the process, Singer in the novels often indicates that behind every amazon or mannish woman there often is a barbaric or weak man driving her to it. In the short stories, that notion is given a curious psychological twist: all these young girls have scholarly or rabbinical fathers who do not just pass on their knowledge but like dybbuks appear to deposit their natures in the souls of their daughters. In other words, the weak or barbaric man who invites or compels his wife to become mannish finds his counterpart in a strong father who, through excessive involvement, leads his daughter not only towards masculinity but also by guilt to sexual abstinence or by transference to homosexuality. What finally emerges is Singer's characteristic correlation of the pursuit of forbidden knowledge with the release of forbidden desires. Clearly, therefore, Singer's apparently unreasonable and archaic condemnation of women acquiring learning is merely his Jewish means of examining all ways in which women, in trying to become what they are not, blur their sexual clarity. Thus, Hindele marries an evil man and, like Rechele, is beset by a dybbuk in her womb; Lise engages in a steady series of sexual perversions and even becomes a sanctioned whore; and Yentl, who dresses as a young boy, enters a Yeshivah and marries a girl.[8] Indeed, Yentl admits that in wearing man's clothes she has perplexed her soul and invited the possession of a dybbuk:

> Only now did Yentl grasp the meaning of the Torah's prohibition against wearing the clothes of the other sex. By doing so one deceived not only others but also oneself. Even the soul was perplexed, finding itself incarnate in a strange body. (140)

Like Swift and Carlyle, Singer employs clothes as man's second creation. The first was God's, and just as He meant flesh to contain the organs of the body, so appropriate clothes serve to restrain man in the world. To Singer, "a rabbi in a long cloak, a beard and side-locks, is not likely to dally with a girl on the street corner. . . . Clothes guard a person just as words do." [9] In donning man's clothes, Yentl dislocates her sexuality. Like a dybbuk, the alien clothes perplex and possess her until she becomes what she wears. It is almost as if the real Yentl has been taken over by her shadow. Indeed, clothes and shadows are made metaphorical equivalents of each other in Singer's tale of "Getzel the Monkey" (1964).

Getzel, a mild, observant Jew, suddenly decides one day to ape the gay life of Todros, the local man-about-town. But the narrator warns:

> A man should stay what he is. The trouble of our world comes from mimicking. Today they call it

fashion. A charlatan in Paris invents a train in front
and everybody wears it. They are all apes, the whole
lot of them. . . . I am afraid of a shadow. A shadow
is an enemy. When it has a chance, it takes revenge.[10]

In the process of mimicking Todros, Getzel, who previously had kept to his Jewishness, becomes an irreligious
fop. In other words, the confusion of Yentl's sexuality
finds its ultimate equivalent in the surrender of Getzel's
Jewishness.

In "Getzel the Monkey" Singer presents the notion
that all men exist in two forms: in an actual form which
its fixed and more or less known; and in a secret form
which is unformed and more or less unknown. The former
is always specific and an original; the latter mysterious
and a shadow. To Singer, a shadow is each personality's
intimate dybbuk or secret sharer. Dreams, fantasies, sinful desires—all are the expressions of a shadow and represent what an individual might be if he and his shadow
exchanged roles and clothes. Indeed, the narrator of
"Getzel the Monkey" supplements the main tale with two
others. One is about twin sisters who, strangely, die on
the same day but in different towns. The reason? Not
coincidence, but rather "They were two bodies with one
soul. . . . Perhaps, one sister was real and other one was
the shadow." The other tale is equally harrowing:

> Yes, mimicking is forbidden. If you imitate a person,
> his fate is passed on to you. Even with a shadow one is
> not allowed to play tricks. In Zamosc there was a
> young man who used to play with his shadow. He
> would put his hands together so that the shadow on
> the wall would look like a buck with horns. . . .
> One night the shadow jumped from the wall and
> gored the young man as if with real horns.

Singer's progression is shrewd. He begins with clothes,
extends them to shadows, and finally moves to ghosts.
One may be possessed by a transmigrated soul in gothic
terms or be taken over by the secret soul of one's shadow
in psychological terms. But whatever the form, Singer
maintains versimilitude, for the possessed individual does
not become what he never could be but potentially what
he secretly is. The known and the unknown are held together by a secret continuity which it is the story's aim
to reveal. Thus, Yentl disguises himself as a man not so
that she can become a Casanova or a rabbi but so that
she can remain a scholar. But what Yentl and all trans-
gressors cannot foresee is what happens when a familiar
personality resides in an alien body. To guard against
such exchanges and confusions of substance and shadow,
biblical tradition severely judges homosexuality and other
sexual blurrings to be abominations, and biblically inspired custom requires the wearing of appropriate cloth-
ing. Characteristically, Singer interprets these prohibitions
as another indication of man's slavery. Specifically, man
is shackled to one religious identity, one sex, one personality, one God—in short, to singularity. To be sure, Singer
is aware that such chains are difficult to bear, especially
when one is regularly tempted by the unlived possibilities
of one's shadow. And again Singer does not legislate traditional views but instead gives free rein to the playing
out of all the secret alternatives. In fact, his presentation
of Yentl's plight is initially sympathetic. After all, what
is so terrible about a woman pursuing knowledge? But
to achieve this good end, Yentl must trangress; she must
surrender herself to her shadow or rather to her father
who serves as her shadow. As a result, by the end of the
story, what first appeared to be reasonable turns out to
be insane: Yentl gets married. As Yentl switches sexes,

sympathy correspondingly shifts from Yentl to Hadass. Whatever Yentl's needs initially, what about Hadass's now? A single step has been taken but released a "multitude of transgressions." Through the shock of recoil at the end of the story, Singer points to the wisdom of keeping one's shadow in its place.

Yentl also is Risha's counterpart in a curious partnership of extremism. Risha's distortion of her femininity rises to the hysterical, cabalistic pitch of bestiality. In Yentl's case it sinks to the quiet undertones of homosexuality. Together, both stake out the cosmic heights and psychological depths of Singer's vision and, in the process, make religious and psychological distortions, not alternatives but versions of each other. The one through lust, the other by biology, preclude the family and thereby terminate the community. Clearly, the implications of distorted femininity, whatever the cause, are ultimately too serious to be bandied about in terms of masculine dominance and feminine subservience or as the battle of the sexes in which neither party is the victor. Behind the bloodlust of Risha and the homosexually inclined scholarship of Yentl, there lurks the ultimate perversion: the refusal to be dependent and vulnerable. To Singer a man truly achieves his manhood and a woman her womanhood only when both realize such goals are unachievable alone. Singer values the traditional subservience of women not because he is a male chauvinist or wishes to perpetuate the evil image of Eve but because that capacity for dependence and surrender created a model for men. But when men forget to be men and good fathers, the women understandably throw off their yokes and ape the dislocated freedom of their mates. In the process, Risha and Yentl reveal that sexual promiscuity and sexual abstinence meet on the common ground of spiritual virginity, and further, as women increasingly become men, so cosmically Satan becomes God. Indeed, love is such a rarity in Singer's world (and perhaps in the world in general) that when it does appear, it takes such radical forms that another group of his stories accurately might be called gothic love tales.

II

To Singer man's two most private and powerful worlds are those of love and belief. Man's secret longings, his sexual fantasies, his forbidden desires are of a piece with his private conversations, arguments, and prayers to God. Often, what a man will say to a woman in the intimacy of love is what he would say, if he could enjoy the same intimacy, to God. In such transcendent eulogies to unity as "Joy" (1951), "A Wedding in Brownsville" (1964), and "Short Friday" (1964), it is impossible to tell where love leaves off and belief begins. But when the mutuality of both private worlds is not acknowledged, or harmonized, the result is a discordant yoking of curious opposites. Such fragmentations of man's basic duality find frequent external embodiment in Satan's area of mismatching couples in marriage. In a recent story, "The Warehouse," [11] Singer even heretically suggests that heaven eases the Devil's task of mismatching.

The warehouse is a heavenly clearing station where souls await new bodies. Bad souls are punished in two ways: first, traditionally, in Gehenna or hell; second—and here is Singer's twist—by being given new bodies that are the inverse reminders or matches of their prior sinfulness. Thus, a whore is given the ugly body of a spinster; a miser that of a eunuch, etc. But over and above these individual ironies, there is the general problem that whereas long ago bodies and souls used to fit nicely together, now they do not. All kinds of mistakes are made; genitals are mixed up or not attached properly. In other words, what becomes clear in "The Warehouse" is that Singer's theme of mismatching couples builds on and compounds the basic mismatching of body and soul. But, unpredictably, he also counterpoints the theme in a number of love stories that present the surprising power of deflected love and belief.

In all these gothic love tales, love is the dream of one who is awake, or of one's shadow. But like all star-crossed lovers, those in Singer's tales are unaware of the extent to which their deepest conscious desires are in contact with their deepest unconscious desires. It is as if the dreams of love reach down to such a basic core that in Helegian fashion they release their antitheses. The desire for another unexpectedly releases the unknown otherness of the desirer. Often, he anchors this odd coupling in the occult. Thus, the hero of "Powers" (1967) states that "in each great love there is an element of telepathy." [12] Indeed, in an excellent long story, "The Letter Writer" (1968), the hero, in fact, does achieve the great love of his life through the benevolent intervention of a departed grandmother.[13] In other words, Singer's occultism functions as his gothically inspired psychology and, as such, represents the secular version of his demonically centered theology. Above all, love offers a double mirror: one clear, the other shadowy. It reflects what the dreamer knows about himself and what he does not. Singer's way of imparting terror to love dreams is not to deny but to grant their fulfillment. Thus, "Alone" (1962) opens as follows: "Many times I have wished the impossible to happen—and then it happened. But though my wish came true, it was in such a topsy-turvy way that it appeared the Hidden Powers were trying to show me I didn't understand my needs" (48). The hero of the story wishes that he could be alone, understandably, in Miami Beach. And it happens. Suddenly, the hotels are closed, the tourists leave. Significantly, now without the restraint of "society," the solitary survivor feels free to release what really was behind his first wish—the desire for sexual surrender. And that, too, nearly happens when a grotesque Cuban cripple tries to seduce him. She argues that he can afford to be unfaithful to his wife this one time because no one is around to see. But he replies, " 'God sees.' " (God is the ultimate Jewish version of the one who sees but is not seen.) Whereupon she spits on him and adds that if she were not a cripple he would not speak of God. Indeed, her parting fillip edges the hero's moral triumph with irony and reveals that he has escaped infidelity only by the narrowest and luckiest of margins.

In "Alone" the revelation of love strikes a compromise between the unknown and known. First, the hero recognizes that his initial capricious wish to be alone actually masked his real desire to be unfaithful: that revelation surprises him. The second, however, confirms his nature. To Singer, the sign of a devout or moral man is not the absence of desire but rather that the antithetical side of his nature is not beyond his powers of restraint. In consequence, the story concludes neither on a sensational note of absolute discontinuity nor on a moralizing note of total continuity but on an adjustment of what the hero knows and does not know of his nature and dreams.

The same release of fantasy into reality characterizes "Taibele and Her Demon" (1953). The wife of an ascetic and melancholy man who deserts her, Taibele, at thirty-three, faces the lonely life of a grass widow without children to comfort her. One summer evening while sitting with some young matrons, Taibele recounts a tale she has read of a demon who ravished a young Jewish woman and lived with her as her husband. While Taibele describes all the details with relish, Alchonon, a Hebrew teacher's helper, overhears it all. Miserably poor and a widower, Alchonon has the reputation of being a prankster and somewhat deranged. And because he is also dreadfully lonely, he decides to pretend he is a demon and seduce Taibele. Taking on the name of Hurmizah and using his knowledge of cabalistic demonology to convince and frighten her, he has his will of her. Initially, Taibele responds only because he is a devil, but soon her fear of his return is transformed into the fear he may not. In short, they become lovers. The story concludes with the death of Alchonon and thereby of Hurmizah. Ironically, Taibele, bemoaning the loss of her demon lover, takes pity at the absence of mourners at Alchonon's funeral and serves as the only follower to his burial.

"Taibele and Her Demon" turns on the power of love not only to fulfill the dreams of the loveless, but also to release their unknown capacity for love. Taibele yearns for a ravisher as an extreme answer to her impoverished sexual life with an ascetic; instead, she gets more than she bargained for. Her demon-lover turns out to be tender as well as potent and brings her full domestic happiness far beyond her sexual expectations. Alchonon begins as a prankster and an opportunist, only to find the unexpected responsiveness of Taibele transforms him into more than he ever dreamed of. Singer is not suggesting that love is so paramount and rare that any means, including evil ones, may be employed to bring about its fruition. His closing reference to eternal judgments and his repeated moral strictures preclude such justifications.

Nor does he cater to his characters. He could have presented the entire story as an actual dream but that would
have put Taibele in complete control; the outcome would
have been as obvious as Taibele's identification with the
young Jewish woman of the tale she relates. Instead,
Singer acts in collusion with and stands apart from his
characters; he sympathizes with their plight and yet is
aware of divine judgment. In this story, what softens that
judgment is that the emotional and sexual deprivation
of Alchonon and Taibele is so acute that it dictates the
narrow scope of their dreams. In "Alone" the revelation
was limited; the tale moved toward a readjustment of the
known and the unknown. In "Taibele and Her Demon"
it is total and goes far beyond the expected. In donning
the mask of Hurmizah, Alchonon transforms the role of
the seducer into that of husband. In surrendering to a
demon, Taibele goes beyond the role of an adulteress to
become a wife. Indeed, Alchonon and Taibele, in their
gothic way, tilt an extramarital love affair toward the
sanctity of marriage and thus graphically move from the
circumference of demonic extremism to Singer's human
center. That the demonic overreaching leads to such ends
is as far as Singer will go in countenancing the immoral
means employed to achieve it. Ideally, it should have been
that way without such subterfuges but when it is not, love,
like truth, will out, and often in grotesque shapes.

The most severe test of the power of love, however,
appears in stories whose heroes are strong intellectuals
or devout believers. Indeed, "The Spinoza of Market
Street" (1961), "The Shadow of a Crib" (1961), and "The
Fast" (1964) hinge on the perversion of too much strength
and self-knowledge. Thus, in the first tale, the sage Spinoza is the sole buttress of the scholarly Dr. Fischelson;
in "The Shadow of a Crib" the physician Dr. Yaretsky

leans heavily on the cynical attitude of Schopenhauer toward sex and propagation; and in "The Fast" Reb Nokham, imitating the ascetic sages, tries to deny the power of love through fasting and self-flagellation. But in each case love overwhelms reason and forces a corrective extreme upon the hero's excess as a means of restoring dualistic balance.

Dr. Fischelson of "The Spinoza of Market Street" is another of Singer's deflective scholarly Jews who in turning from religious to secular materials, like his idol Spinoza, encounters in his incompleted work the face of his own mortality. But his infatuation with Spinoza finds competition from a most unexpected source. He becomes ill and his next door neighbor, Black Dobbe, an ignorant, swarthy, unattractive spinster, comes to nurse him. They talk and one thing leads to another; they become engaged, to the gossiping delight of the tradespeople of Market Street. But on the wedding night, the copy of Spinoza's *Ethics* falls from Dr. Fischelson's hands as Dobbe embraces him:

> What happened that night could be called a miracle. If Dr. Fischelson hadn't been convinced that every occurrence is in accordance with the laws of nature, he would have thought that Black Dobbe had bewitched him. Powers long dormant awakened in him. Although he had only a sip of the benediction wine, he was if intoxicated. He kissed Dobbe and spoke to her of love. Long forgotten quotations from Klopstock, Lessing, Goethe, rose to his lips. The pressures and aches stopped. He embraced Dobbe, pressed her to himself, was again a man as in his youth. Dobbe was faint with delight; crying, she murmured things to him in a Warsaw slang he did not understand. Later, Dr. Fischelson slipped off into the deep sleep

young men know. He dreamed he was in Switzerland
and that he was climbing mountains—running, falling, flying. At dawn he opened his eyes. . . . Dobbe
was snoring. (24)

Dr. Fischelson goes to the window, gazes at the awakening
cosmos, and falls into his philosophizing habit. The story
concludes with his pathetic apology: " 'Divine Spinoza,
forgive me. I have become a fool' " (25).

The perversity of man's strength—that he cannot accept happiness at the hands of another. The perversity of
the Faustian intellectual and Ivan Karamazov—that they
can love only what they first understand. The perversity
of Pangloss' slavery to consistency—that he is shackled to
a philosophical identity. Dr. Fischelson undoubtedly will
live out his life convinced that he has betrayed Spinoza
(whereas the reverse is true) and that his life has been
turned off from its proper direction (whereas here, too,
the opposite is the case). The corrective power of love is
applied gently in this story, for it respects Dr. Fischelson's
delusions. That is not the case in either "The Shadow of
a Crib" or "The Fast."

Dr. Yaretsky is a cynic who shares Schopenhauer's
dictum that a woman is merely a "wide-hipped vessel of
sex, which blind lust has formed . . . to perpetuate the
eternal suffering and tedium." Moreover, like Asa Heshel
of *The Family Moskat,* Dr. Yaretsky is determined not to
add to the cycle of birth and death, and supports the proverb that the "luckiest child is the one not born" (77). A
Christian, he cannot understand why the Jews, who have
suffered so much, continue to propagate more victims. But
Dr. Yaretsky's philosophical security and insularity are
shattered one night at a ball, when Helena, a stylish young
maiden of the town, startles everyone including the doctor,

by kissing his hand. That aggressive act disturbs Yaretsky and gives him bad dreams, including a prophetic one of her being ill. In any case, they become engaged, but before the wedding can take place, Dr. Yaretsky slips out of town and is never seen again. The story concludes many years later with the apparition of Dr. Yaretsky returning to haunt the rabbi of the town and Helena's house. Many swear that in Helena's bedroom there was visible the eerie shadow of a crib on the wall.

The ghost of Dr. Yaretsky represents that half of his nature which, though awakened by Helena's love, was suppressed by Schopenhauer's castrating cynicism. But that capacity comes to life after Dr. Yaretsky is dead to play out its unfulfilled dreams. Every unlived love begets a ghost which waits patiently to be incarnated in a natural or unnatural form. With Dr. Fischelson, Spinoza was pushed to the side so that the stored-up love of Black Dobbe could unite with the unlived youth of the scholar while both were alive. But Dr. Yaretsky's Schopenhauer is too strong to be dislodged and as a result the physician's strength turns out to be a source of inadequacy. The distinction of love is that of reality: it assaults. Dr. Yaretsky would not kiss Helena's hand so she kisses his. But though he resisted being violated while alive, so stirring was that kiss that it imparted life after death; and the ghost of Dr. Yaretsky returns to visit his unborn child.

One additional story which is closely related to those above and also provides a transition to two final gothic tales is "The Fast." Itche Nokhum proudly discovers after his wife has divorced him that "a man can curb every desire" (69). Itche's way of triumphing over the lust of the flesh is to overcome the needs of the flesh for food. Like Kafka's Hunger Artist, Itche finds exquisite pleasure in pure bowels. Assailed by dreams of his ex-wife, Roise

Genendel, appearing as Eve, he puts pebbles in his shoes, flagellates his chest and arms with nettles, and slaps his face and calls himself wanton. Envying the ascetics of old who fasted from Sabbath to Sabbath, Itche embarks on a week-long fast only to find that as his control gets stronger, so do his evil inclinations. Finally, toward the end of the fast, Itche is visited by Roise, who hysterically accuses him of being a devil and visiting her so that she does not have any peace. The story then concludes:

> "Roise Genendel, I cannot . . . I cannot forget you!"
> "Miserable leech! I'm in your power . . ."
> Roise Genendel's mouth twisted. She covered her face with both hands and broke into a hoarse wail. (118)

William Blake proverbially remarked, "If a fool persists in his folly he will become wise." Singer seems to believe that if one aspect of man's nature is pushed far enough, although its initial intent was to eliminate the other, it, in fact, recovers duality but in such extreme form that it results in the schizophrenia of becoming a transmigrated soul. Thus, as Itche's capacity to control his desire increases, his lust, which originally was never strong, suddenly acquires a strength it never had. Like a man split in two, Itche embarks on a journey of cross-purposes. All the while he is moving toward ascetic sainthood and away from Roise, his unlived sexual life, like a demon, has been visiting, courting, and tempting her. The shock of the story is not that asceticism to Singer is an evil—that is obvious and already familiar in Itche Mates of *Satan in Goray,* with whom Itche Nokhum has a great deal in common.[14] The surprise is that Itche's asceticism is actually a

warped form of love which ironically finds its potency only
in transmigrated sexuality. The final portrait of the wasted
Itche straining his parched throat to tell Roise that he
still loves her, coupled with the wailing wife now tortured
by his frigid potency, symbolizes the waste through extremism of love's wholeness. Unity, external or internal,
is no longer possible, for there is now not enough between
them to put together one soul, let alone two.

The punitive love of Itche Nokhum is Singer's version
of the eternal fusion of hate and love, a fusion which characterizes the two remaining stories in the group of gothic
love tales: "Under the Knife" (1964) and "The Unseen"
(1943). Hate and love exist in inevitable proximity and
collusion because they reflect man's basic desire both to
be needed and to resent being in need. Indeed, the more
dependent the greater the hate, just as Itche's rejection of
the body does not consume but feeds its antithetical acceptance. On love's power to release opposites, Singer, in
acknowledging the influence of Knut Hamsun, speaks in
particular of Hamsun's *Pan* (1894) which he translated:
"Knut Hamsun is a master of describing great love and
the contrariness that often accompanies it. Glahn and
Edvarda wage sexual war. The ambition of each is to drive
the other insane." [15] Similarly, in "Under the Knife,"
Leib's hatred of Rooshke is so intertwined with his love
of her that it colors the way he plans to murder her: "In
the dark, Leib returned to his cherished vision: Rooshke,
deathly pale, lay there, dress up, legs stretched out, the
yellow-blonde hair in disorder, the knife in her stomach
with only the metal handle sticking out" (93). Indeed, in
another recurrent dream of sexual murder he slits her
throat and makes love to her at the same time; and wakes
up claiming "there were two Rooshkes" (93). Similarly,

Nathan of "The Unseen" who leaves his wife, Roise, to run away with his whore-servant, Shifra, dreams that they

> were one woman with two faces. . . . He kissed the two-faced female, and she returned his kisses with her doubled lips, pressing against him her two pairs of breasts. . . . In her four arms and two bosoms, all his questions were answered. There was no longer life and death, here nor there, beginning nor end. "The truth is twofold," Nathan exclaimed. "This is the mystery of all mysteries!" (205)

The apocalyptic or Blakeian image of the twofold woman serves in the context of the gothic love tales to establish duality as a permanent condition and norm of human nature. Paradoxically, love alone has the power both to release and to harmonize hate and love, desire and violence, asceticism and sensualism in a partnership of cooperating contraries. Love provides an additional revelation only hinted at in the other stories but fully articulated in "The Unseen." The acceptance of the tightrope of duality leads to a vision beyond all duality. For the first time, Nathan is aware that the principle of opposition dictates that there are no ends or beginnings. Every thrust of life partly derives its force and meaning from the counterthrust of death so that nothing in creation is singular or even terminated so long as it remains dualistic. Love, which compels the ultimate relationship of human opposites, man and woman, violates man as a solitary unit so that he may experience unity and cosmic coincidence. As such, Love is an agent of God, for her efforts to have man recognize his double nature culminate in his acceptance of this world as a mirror of that nature. When love fails, man is deflected from the cycle of unity and either falls to

the level of an animal that regards this world as everything or ascends to the level of an angel who regards this
world as nothing. Singer's gothic love tales define love's
wholeness through a refraction of fragments.

III

The publication of Singer's newest collection of short
stories, *The Séance and Other Stories* (1968), serves not
only to confirm his mastery of the short story, but also to
designate what now appears to be his essential stylistic
range. A survey of Singer's nearly seventy-five collected
and uncollected stories reveals a prose style woven of four
main strands: the realistic, the philosophic, the demonic,
and the apocalyptic.

The realistic strand is never absent from Singer's
works. Even his holiest rabbis suffer from stomach
cramps, and his most grandiose devils endure the ignominy
of warts. The saintly Rabbi of Marshinov, near death,
contemplates heavenly realms and has difficulty passing
water. Dr. Fischelson, on his honeymoon, gazes up at the
expanse of the universe with the rush of a young man's
love while his bride snores in bed. As a result, what is
rapidly established is that for all Singer's sensational
demonism, religious transcendence, miraculous happenings, and gothic psychology, this world is lodged firmly
and permanently in the center of his vision. To be sure,
although the realistic style, especially in the historical novels, often stands by itself, more characteristically it is in-
terwoven in tension with the remaining modes. Indeed, in
large part, the purpose of the other styles is to tease and
tug at the substantiality of this world and to beset with
shadows and qualifications its ally, realism. Thus, the
philosophical mode, which sustains *The Family Moskat,*

The Manor, and many short stories, seeks to turn substance into sand. It supports Singer's characteristic sceptical ambivalence and his favorite theme of the collusion between life and death. It generates and buttresses heroes who, as fools or saints (perhaps one has to be one to be the other), wear the mantle of melancholia and serve as the Jewish versions of Hamlet and Yorick spawned in the grave of the ghetto. The philosophical mode bends the realistic to its *weltschmerz* and heralds Ecclesiastes as Singer's supreme authority on the subject of appearance and reality.

If the philosophical point of view tends to put the world under wraps, the demonic heightens and electrifies even the ordinary. A capricious, buoyant mode, it accounts for much of the freshness and vividness of *The Magician of Lublin* and many of the demonic tales. Indeed, the style is the image of Satan himself. Cocky and brash, Satan wastes no time trying to persuade the reader that he exists. Instead, he disarmingly introduces himself as the Evil One and then promptly sets about proving it. He takes credit for mismatching couples in marriage, for instilling faith in the poor so that their lives may be wretched, for inspiring the pursuit of justice in a world in which the "wicked make history." Above all, Satan's claim that he has access to man's most secret desires appears unchallengable. In one story, the Devil confesses, "Evenings, I watch the women at the ritual bath, or make my way into the bedrooms of pious folk and listen to the forbidden talk between man and wife. . . . So sharp are my ears that I can hear thoughts behind the skull." Combining the voyeurism of the peeping tom with the privileged knowledge of the psychiatrist, Satan is the perfect omniscient narrator, for he is free to go everywhere, and no secrets are safe from his prying curiosity. Indeed, to

Singer the world is set up to betray secrets; in "The Mirror" (1955) he states:

> everything hidden must be revealed, each secret longs to be disclosed, each love yearns to be betrayed, everything sacred must be desecrated. Heaven and earth conspire that all good beginnings should come to a bad end. (78–79)

The demonic mode not only embodies that conspiracy, but also presents the temptation of self-betrayal.

Finally, the apocalyptic mode, which glowingly informs *The Slave* and a number of affirmative short stories, provides the maximum opposition to all the other styles. In the process, this ecstatic style also presents a crucial corrective to the notion that Singer's supernaturalism is exclusively demonic. His supernaturalism is a bridge not only to a permanent past—seventeenth century Poland and biblical times—but also to a permanent future—the afterlife. The Devil is Singer's means of recovering the terror of the past; postmortal visitations are his means of anticipating the future. Indeed, such visitations in *The Slave,* "Joy," "A Wedding in Brownsville," and "Short Friday" dramatically reveal that the present does not really exist in Singer's time scheme. His visionary preoccupations with the past or the future preempt the present and leave it as the exclusive province of Satan: "I speak in the present as for me time stands still" (120). To Singer, if the present has any reality it has so only outside this world as the time of eternity.

The contraries of his style support the contraries of his vision. Each mode opposes, questions, and collides with its alternates: devils are answered by angels, sceptical philosophers by visionaries, rationalists by occultists, the

Golden Calf by the Ten Commandments. Stubbornly and defiantly, each mode refuses to yield its ground and its claim to the whole truth. The result is an artistic vision locked in battle with itself. Singer's stylistic world is precariously poised for disintegration, just as many of his protagonists teeter on insanity. But because each mode will not surrender its claim to totality, Singer sets them permanently at odds with each other and ultimately employs unrelieved tension as his only guarantee against excessive or distortive partiality. Or as Gimpel the Fool neatly puts it, "No doubt this world is entirely an imaginary world but it is only once removed from the true world" (21).

Curiously, Gimpel's foolishness ultimately leads to balance. Gimpel believes "everything is possible, as it is written in The Wisdom of the Fathers" (4). As a result, the pivot of this deservedly famous story seems to be that Gimpel's gullibility is actually the overflow of faith. Scepticism, which supports the toughness of Singer's morality, need not harden into cynicism or nihilism. That scepticism may be poised as qualified belief is, in fact, one of Gimpel's conclusions and perhaps Singer's as well:

> the longer I lived the more I understood that there are really no lies. Whatever doesn't really happen is dreamed at night. It happens to one if it doesn't happen to another, tomorrow if not today, or a century hence if not next year. (20)

In more philosophical terms, Singer presents the same argument in *The Family Moskat*:

> [all] inadequate and confused ideas arise from as real a necessity as adequate and clear ones, and nowhere in the world of ideas is there anything positive that

can be called false. . . . In God every idea is true.
(558)

The aim of "Gimpel the Fool" and many of the other
stories is to invest the strange with the familiar and to
normalize dislocation. *In My Father's Court* begins:
"There are in this world some very strange individuals
whose thoughts are even stranger than they are" (3). And
in "The Boudoir" (1966), the narrator opens by saying,
"No, one needn't be insane to get a crazy idea into one's
head." [16] Later, a key distinction is made: "When a mad-
man is mad, that's one thing, but when a sane person acts
crazy, one gets completely confused." To Singer one need
not be insane to harbor madness nor unusual to have a
shadow. The day is solid and reassuring; the night murky
and threatening. One works and one dreams; one wears
clothes and makes love without them. Singer's stylistic
interchanges make the apparently separate worlds of
realism and demonism continuous. The secret dreams of
Taibele are rendered with all the solidity of daytime fac-
tuality; the philosophical abstractions of Dr. Fischelson are
braced by the vital gift of Dobbe's realism. Characteristically, Singer, like Gimpel, seeks the totality of a world continuous with the past and future, originals and shadows.
Moreover, that sylistic totality supports a thematic totality.
Nothing less than that both the experience of love and
belief will fulfill man and woman and impart any justification for the world being created in the first place. That
many of the stories dramatize not the fulfillment but the
fragmentation of such harmonious ends is perhaps his way
of representing the rarity of both love and belief and
justifying his use of the short story and demonic narrators
as appropriate modes of refraction. If there is one controlling notion that binds all the separate tales and groups of

stories together, it is undoubtedly the notion that impotence is the bitter fruit of independence. To Singer impotence is the result of willing what cannot be willed and of seeking wholeness that cannot be achieved alone. The wisdom of Gimpel the Fool dictates that surrender often requires greater strength than self-reliance, and that certain illusions are more real and difficult to sustain than the facts of life. Stylistically, too, Singer resists the independence of any one mode by binding them all together in a textual knot whose tension renders his vision in miniature.

Notes

1. *Saturday Review* (November 21, 1964), p. 49.
2. *Cavalier* (January, 1966), pp. 40, 88–89.
3. "The Redeemers: Themes in the Fiction of Isaac Bashevis Singer," *Kenyon Review*, XXVI (Spring, 1964), 373.
4. "A Conversation with Isaac Bashevis Singer," *The Eternal Light*, p. 11.
5. The supreme feminine curser in Singer's tales is Henne of "Henne Fire" (1968). The traditional image of anger is fire. But Singer, like Poe, Kafka, and other gothic writers, makes the symbolic the literal. Thus, Henne earns her nickname of Henne Fire not only because her tongue is vile and inflammatory, but also because she causes fires to break out wherever she is. Indeed, ultimately she herself is consumed by fire, and all that is left for the burial society to handle are her charred bones.
6. In "The Plagiarist," which appeared in *Israel Magazine* (November, 1967), Rabbi Karriel Dan Kinsker curses his plagiarizing disciple for stealing from him. Soon after, his disciple dies. To do penance for the sin of judging and condemning a sinner, Rabbi Karriel resigns his post and concludes: " 'The Commandment "Thou shalt not kill" includes all sins.' "
7. "The Parrot" appeared in *Harpers* (June, 1966), pp. 59–66; "Cockadoodledo" in *Hadassah News* (November, 1964), pp. 9, 27–28; and "The Slaughterer" in the *New Yorker* (November 25, 1967), pp. 60–65.
8. Singer's only story of explicit homosexuality is "Zeitel and

Rickel" (1968). Initially, it follows the pattern of the transgressions of Singer's mannish women. Zeitel's father was a follower of the false Messiah, Jacob Frank, and instructed Zeitel, behind draped windows, in the mysteries of forbidden books. After his death, Zeitel rejects all marriage offers, invites Rickel to live with her, and finally they both sin together. Their version of the slaughtering of animals is that of self-slaughter; both girls finally commit suicide in their desire to ascend to heaven and possess sexless souls. (Curiously, there are no examples of male homesexuality in Singer's works. The worst thing that happens to his males is deviation from belief and sexual impotence.)

9. "The Extreme Jews," *Harper's* (April, 1967), p. 57.
10. *American Judaism*, XIV (Fall, 1964), 12–13, 53–56. In "The Plagiarist" Singer weaves an interesting variation on Getzel's aping and even his name. There, Shabasi Getsel, the disciple of the Rabbi of Machlev, plagiarizes the unpublished *responsa* or commentaries of his master and hopes thereby to take over his position as rabbi. Indeed, in this story and in a few others, Singer's favorite theme of Jacob supplanting Esau seems to be secretly propelled by the Kafka-like obsession with the son supplanting the father. A different though still related version of the theme that what one plays at one becomes, appears in "The Wager" in the *Saturday Evening Post* (November 18, 1967). There, Avrom Wolf, who perhaps echoes Wolf the Coal Dealer in *In My Father's Court*, along with his brother and a group of boisterous freethinkers and practical jokers decides to trick a newcomer to their society. They wager that he will be unable to remain in the same room with a corpse for an entire night. Avrom Wolf is elected to play the part of the corpse, but his stirrings and sneezings so terrify the newcomer that he is literally frightened to death. The situation now reversed, Wolf is forced to spend the night with a real corpse. The next morning, fearful of what may happen to them, Wolf and his brother leave town never to return. Many years later, having been separated from his mother and father, from his brother and his friends, and having led a miserable and lonely life, Avrom Wolf finally realizes that he has been separated from life itself. In short, he is a living ghost; he really died that night.
11. *Cavalier* (January, 1966), pp. 40, 88–89.
12. *Harper's* (October, 1967), pp. 76–87.
13. The hero of "The Letter Writer" is Herman Gombiner who shares with Dr. Zorach Gombiner the same last name and the same interest in the occult. Dr. Zorach Gombiner of "The

Séance," which appeared in *Encounter* (July, 1965), pp. 14–19, is told by Mrs. Kopitzsky: " 'There is no death, there isn't any. We live forever, and we love forever. This is the pure truth.' "

14. Itche Nokhum, like Itche Mates, also is a secret worshipper of the false Messiah, Sabbatai Zevi.
15. "Introduction" to *Hunger,* trans. Robert Bly (New York, 1967).
16. *Vogue* (April, 1966), pp. 148–49, 214.

7.

The Freedom of *The Slave*

The central political experience of the nineteenth century was the pursuit of freedom. But before the century was over, the earlier demand for freedom from the long-standing abuses of authority became converted into an invocation of authority against the new abuses of freedom. Ibsen turned back on the middle class its own previous historical weapon. The bourgeois, who earlier were champions of the cause of individuality, had become in Ibsen's day the suppressors of individuality; the victims were now the victimizers. In *The Brothers Karamazov* Dostoevsky provided existentialism with its fundamental premise when he proclaimed that freedom was the greatest burden man ever was given. Surveying modern trends, Karl Jaspers agrees: "Everybody covets freedom so much that even despotic systems are obliged to traffic under the banner of liberation; and yet so many people cannot endure it. They feel an inner constraint to go where, in the name of freedom, they will be delivered from freedom." [1]

Forsaking the authority of God or that of a God who is dead (actually, it was not a cry of triumph but of despair for Nietzche), men made gods of men or ideologies and slipped into the bondage of totalitarianism. That, in turn, was followed by the great world wars which, borrowing the trappings of religious crusades, revealed the chaos of uncontained and unresponsive authoritarianism. Indulging in the passion of violence, men sought martyrdom both by suffering it themselves and inflicting it on others. Each war was then followed by the construction of antidotes of universal authority. But the creation of each worldwide institution was more symptomatic of the need for authority than it was an effective or genuine medium of that authority. Indeed, the ironic cycle of the nineteenth century reappears in the excesses of emerging nations in the twentieth. In short, the dilemma of freedom without bounds and of authority without respect remains the political and moral crisis characteristic of the modern world.

To be sure, the Jews also were involved in the same liberating movements. As noted, in large part the task of *The Family Moskat* is to chronicle the historical "abyss of the free will." Nevertheless, there are certain aspects of Jewish tradition which stress the necessity of slavery in the very midst of freedom and which, theoretically at least, checked the Jew's commitment to any liberating cause that was unresponsive to authority. In Judaism, Passover, which commemorates the release from Egypt, is linked to Shavuot, the Festival of Weeks or the First Fruits. Indeed, to maintain the connection, the days between the two festivals are counted. The rabbis, however, never refer to Shavuot, which heralds the giving of the Ten Commandments, as the Festival of the First Fruits but by a term which literally means "holding." The reason is instructive. The Jews were released at Passover from the wrong kind of slavery so that they could be "held" or hemmed in by the right kind of slavery—the Ten Commandments.

The slavery to an oppressor establishes a condition of historical exile which can be ameliorated or terminated; or if neither, hopefully endured. But the slavery to God is permanent and beyond all mortal relief. To be sure, exile was often comprehended as a punishment of God. But its termination only meant that the Jew was freer to choose religious bondage. Democracy, Communism, Zionism are not equated with the millenium. Freedom from the czar did not break the shackles of slavery to God anymore than freedom from the Pharaoh was a substitute for the Ten Commandments. In other words, long before freedom historically emerged as a real and comprehensive prospect, Jewish tradition never conceived freedom as an end in itself, or regarded it as meaningful apart from authority. On the contrary, authority is genuine only when it calls forth freedom. Freedom is meaningful only when it yields to a liberating authority. Passover finds its fulfillment in Shavuot.

I

More than any other notion, the concept of slavery gathers and binds together the central strands of Singer's vision. To him, slavery dramatizes the experience of otherness. Because man is neither perfect nor perfectible, the image of man in fetters reflects his permanent condition of incompletion. Seeking the wholeness of love, he pursues his complement—his soulmate. Seeking the totality of personality, he tries to come to grips with his unconscious —his secret sharer. Seeking to last, he turns to the continuity of community—his historical alterego. In addition to these bonds, and also as a way of imaging them all, Singer presents the special Jewish versions of bondage. The Jew is a slave to a God who sees but is not seen. The Jew is chained to a Messiah whose coming is unknown and unknowable. The Jew is a slave to the repetition of history and thus to the constant incarnation of the past in the present. The typical Jewish protagonist is presented as a melange of child, boy, and man—son, lover, and father. He accepts the notion that the child is the father of the man because the child is still alive in the man. All previous states exist contemporaneously with any present state in the evolution of the human personality. Such is also the case in the historical personality, for the coexistence of the child in the man finds its extension in the aliveness of the Jewish past in the life of the contemporary Jew. In *The Slave,* Singer invests the pull of the past with absolute power—Jacob is pulled back to and relives biblical bondage.

One of the most striking aspects of *The Slave* is the extent to which its evolution follows the calendar of Jewish holy days. Thus, the novel opens with Jacob a slave to Polish peasants who in turn are presented as seventeenth century Egyptians. Although he tries to remain pious, Jacob lusts after Wanda, the daughter of his overseer, and finally seduces her at the holiest time of the year—Rosh Hoshanah (New Year) and Yom Kippur (Day of Atonement). Significantly, Jacob is ransomed from slavery just before Passover (which commemorates the release from Egyptian slavery). Later, he returns to Wanda or, as he puts it, to the Egyptian bondage of lust during the month of Av which includes the fast day of Tishav Be'Av to lament the destruction of the temple. His son is born just before Yom Kippur and he steals him away before Succoth, which marks the birthday of the Torah, in order to flee to Palestine which marks the birthplace of the Torah. Finally, the novel concludes with Jacob returning and dying in the month of Av. In other words, in the same month that he went in search of Wanda, he is reunited with Wanda-Sarah. In the midst of a time set aside to lament the destruction of the temple, the "miracle" of his being buried next to his wife brings the Jewish calendar which has governed the entire novel to its most affirmative climax and coincidence.

Ostensibly, *The Slave* is set in seventeenth century Poland; ultimately, however, it rests in biblical times and places. Singer's intermediary is an eternal Jewish calendar. By linking the life of Jacob and that of the Jews of Pilitz to major Jewish festivals, Singer is able not only to recover the biblical events they commemorate, but also to impart permanence to the seventeenth century. As a result, the chronology is actually allegory. The novel begins with Jacob a slave to pagans in Egypt. It concludes with Jacob a slave to God in Palestine. This movement is matched by that from the yoke of lust to that of love, a transformation reflected in the change of names and roles; the pagan Wanda becomes the Jewish Sarah (the name given to all female converts). Indeed, in the progress of the novel the arc of biblical recovery coincides with that of conversion; that alignment is set bit by bit in place through a series of intervening and reinforcing events. Thus, Jacob's seduction of Wanda during Rosh Hoshanah and Yom Kippur is perhaps answered and redeemed by the birth of his son at the same time of the year. The intertwining here of guilt and forgiveness, of violation and continuity, establishes the ambiguous character of the entire novel and surrounds Jacob and Wanda with the protective paradox of holy sinners. Then, in returning to Wanda, especially during the month that includes Tishav Be'Av, Jacob seems to be repeating the sin that led to the original destruction of the temple. Yet, his desire is to rescue his son from the pagans and to insure the continuity of the temple. The same desire later leads him to return to the exile of the Polish town of Pilitz to retrieve his son and take him to Palestine where continuity had its origin. In other words, throughout the entire novel Jacob's bondage to Wanda is linked to his obligation to his son so that every desire to return to the past is inextricably involved in the promise of the future. In the process, Wanda throughout the novel is associated with the lost, the impure, the desecrated temple—in short, with the remnant in search of a bridegroom. Benjamin, born of sorrow, is tied to the future, the guiltless, the promise of continuity—in short, to the orphan in need of a father. In ministering to both, Jacob lives up to his name and prototype by being the supplanter—the one who seeks, no matter how deceitfully or unheroically, to rescue the pagan Wanda so that she can become Sarah, the mother of the Jews; and to outwit Esau so that he and his son can enjoy the primal birthright.

The Slave is thus distinguished from most reworkings of biblical or mythical materials in that the focus is not so much on a hero as a people. Indeed, it is this traditional framework that makes intelligible Singer's otherwise confusing evocations of biblical events that occurred before or after the story of Jacob in the Bible. Moreover, *The Slave* is distinguished from all of his works in that it is the only novel in which nature is described in other than predominantly demonic terms.[2] Actually, the two differences are related, for Jacob's slavery to Polish peasants simultaneously evokes both the oppression of the Jews in

Egypt and the freedom of Adam in a newly created Eden.

The novel opens with Jacob gazing at a sacramental world:

> He threw open the barn door and saw the mountains stretching into the distance. Some of the peaks, their slopes overgrown with forests, seemed close at hand, giants with green beards. Mist rising from the woods like tenuous curls made Jacob think of Samson. The ascending sun, a heavenly lamp, cast a fiery sheen over everything. Here and there, smoke drifted upward from the summit as if the mountains were burning within. A hawk, wings outstretched, glided tranquilly with a strange slowness beyond all earthly anxieties. It appeared to Jacob that the bird had been flying without interruption since creation. (4–5)

Caring for his master's cows at the top of a mountain, Jacob experiences a proximity to original creation and to "that primeval substance which . . . gave birth to all things" (13). Again and again Singer paradoxically describes the world as eternally new because it is eternally old: "The mountains remained as deserted as in the days of creation" (13). Through the pristine, Eden-like setting, Singer ties Jacob's evolution as a Jew to the genesis of his race: "He was as solitary here as the original Adam" (135). Like his ancestor, Jacob calculates the months according to lunar movements and is a vegetarian (17).

Singer has stripped Jacob of all the complexities of society and history so that he may experience directly the divinity of original creation. Above all, to anchor Jacob's newly-discovered love of nature to that of the human, Singer describes Wanda in the same terms as he does of nature: "Her body exuded the warmth of the sun, the breezes of summer, the fragrance of wood, field, flower,

leaf, just as milk gave off the odor of the grass the cattle
fed on" (71). Allegorically, Jacob's love of Wanda is the
expression of his love for the natural, prelapsarian world
of original creation. A learned, pious Jew, Jacob, against
his scholarly will and hardened heart, is taken back to a
premoral state in order to recover his natural desires for
love and belief. But lest he overshoot the mark or become
totally content with natural religion, Singer provides a
warning in the paganism of the Polish peasants. Although
outwardly Christian, the Polish peasants are grotesque
denials of any religion. They eat the meat of animals not
yet dead. The women are perennially pregnant; the men
cannot remember how many bastards they have sired.
They simultaneously pray to the Virgin and to the "lime
spirits" for rain. On the way to church, they fear attacks
by Kobalt, the devil who speaks with his belly. In short,
they are a throwback to ancient times and practices; and
yet, because they also exist in the seventeenth century,
Singer suggests that they appear throughout history as the
mistakes of creation:

> Shame was unknown to them, as if they had been con-
> ceived before the eating of the forbidden fruit. Jacob
> often reflected that as yet the rabble had not developed
> the capacity to choose freely. They seemed to him
> survivors of those worlds, which, according to the
> Midrash, God had created and destroyed before fash-
> ioning this one. (55)

Singer has set Jacob against the double backdrop of
God's original creation and man's degradation of that
creation in order to demonstrate that nature and freedom
as ends in themselves pervert nature and freedom. The
special Jewish and mythical version of the problem is released by the pagan Wanda. As a knowledgeable Jew,
Jacob is aware that he is flirting with damnation. As a

man experiencing the lust of the flesh really for the first time, Jacob finds it difficult to reject a desire which is called forth and identified with original creation. The God of traditional Judaism requires restraint; the gods of nature urge fecundity. At this point in the novel, Singer's cooperating contraries of asceticism and sensuality, inhibition and expression, appear as irreconcilable extremes. To be sure, by the end of the novel the slavery of Jacob to Wanda and to God meet, like the halves of a sphere, and turn out to be not alternatives but versions of each other. But much of the power and mythical veracity of the novel appears in the meaningful obstacles Singer puts in the way of that analogy.

Another way of describing Jacob's deflective or eclectic journey is to note Singer's rejection of either a completely traditional or modern approach. He does not rapidly or irrevocably condemn Jacob's lust. Indeed, referring to the Cabala, Singer even argues the near-heretical position that lust is of divine origin (133). Nor does he take a modern stand and unreservedly applaud Jacob's sexual liberation. Significantly, after they have been lovers for a while, Jacob forgets to say his prayers and becomes lazy. Typically, he has his novel exist in the tension between both attitudes. On the one hand, he demands that tradition neither be blind to the beauty of the body or of the world, nor forgetful of the extramarital and even illicit love relationships of the biblical patriarchs. On the other hand, Singer rejects any modern paganism which is unaware of the extent to which the love of Jacob and Wanda may degenerate to the level of the human animals in the novel or their biblical prototypes in Sodom and Gomorrah. As a result, Jacob is right to surrender to Wanda and to seek through her to humanize his love for the natural world of God's creation. And yet Jacob is wrong to choose a pagan to love and therefore potentially to surrender his soul to his body, his Jewishness to Egypt.

Just as Singer has had to work out his own religious tradition and to find his own artistic style, so Jacob, his surrogate, has to find his own way with love and with God. His method of acknowledging the difficulty of that task is to surround it with unrelieved ambiguity. Thus, before making love to the gentile Wanda, Jacob asks her to follow the Jewish ritual of cleansing herself. Then, Jacob experiences a delight in his body he never thought possible at a time of the year when Jews are being judged for their sins. Finally, at the same time that Jacob is concerned with the loss of heaven for his lust, a quotation from the *Song of Songs* counterpoints his thoughts. By the end of the first part of the novel, the ambiguities are so thick that no final judgment on Jacob's love is possible. What is therefore poised is the dilemma of Jacob's reconciling his love of both the world and of Wanda with that of God and Judaism. In the second section, the problem Jacob confronts is reconciling his love of God with the suffering of mankind. In the first part, Singer sets Jacob in the timeless realm of myth; in the second part, he moves Jacob into history. There are therefore two stories of slavery in the novel. The first involves man's relationship with God informed by a biblical backdrop; the second involves man's relationship with his fellowman set in the midst of community. Final resolution requires the intersection of both, for the central issue of the novel is whether man can love both God and man.

II

Wanda's name is changed to that of Sarah, and Jacob informs the inhabitants of Pilitz, where they have come to live as man and wife, that Sarah is a mute, lest her good

Polish and poor Yiddish betray her gentile origins. Involved in the communal life of Pilitz in which Jews,
peasants, and aristocrats conspire and intrigue, Jacob, like
Dimmesdale of *The Scarlet Letter,* finds that his secret sin
grants him access to the sinfulness of the men in the community; just as Sarah's dumbness is an open invitation for
the women to reveal their hypocrisy. In the process, Jacob
discovers that paganism is not limited to prehistory but
appears in the social barbarisms of a community bereft of
any morality and fellow feeling. As a correlation, the second section of the novel abounds in doctrines of antislavery against which Jacob has to struggle as strongly as
he had to resist the degradations of his Polish captors.

In essence, the doctrines of antislavery are three in
number and collectively take on the shape of a comprehensive pattern. The first is embodied in the leading
Jewish elder of the community, Gershon, whose name,
significantly, means "the exile" because he was cast out
of his tribe. The second version is presented by Waclaw,
a Polish ferryman and atheist. The last appears with gothic
decadence in Lord and Lady Pilitzsky, the Polish aristocrats who rule the town of Pilitz and who are curiously
devout Christians.

In his corruption and ignorance, Gershon is no better
than the pagan overseers in the first part of the novel.
Gershon collects the taxes but taxation

> in Pilitz worked on the principle that the friends and
> flatterers of Gershon paid little or nothing; all others
> tottered under the weight of his levies. Gershon was
> ignorant but had granted himself the title "Our
> Teacher" and did not allow the cantor to intone the
> eighteen benedictions until he, Gershon, had said
> them over to himself. (165)

Although everyone knows how Gershon has acquired his wealth, the Jews defend his piety by pointing to his regular attendance at prayers and to his observance of the laws of *Kashruth*. But to Jacob that is not sufficient:

> Jacob was continually astonished at how many Jews obeyed only half of the Torah. The very same people, who strictly observed the minor rituals and customs which were not even rooted in the Talmud, broke without thinking twice the most sacred laws, even the Ten Commandments. They wanted to be kind to God and not to man; but what did God need of man and his favors? (219)

Divine bondage, historically defined, appears in dealing with one's fellow man as the way of dealing with God. Indeed, that it is the only means by which God remains alive:

> But now he at least understood his religion: its essence was the relation between man and his fellows. Man's obligations towards God were easy to perform. Didn't Gershon have two kitchens, one for milk, and one for meat? Men like Gershon cheated, but they ate matzoth prepared according to the strictest requirements. They slandered their fellow man, but demanded meat doubly kosher. They envied, fought, hated their fellow Jews, yet still put on a second pair of phylacteries. Rather than troubling himself to induce a Jew to eat pork or kindle a fire on the Sabbath, Satan did easier and more important work, advocating those sins deeply rooted in human nature. (247)

An equally formidable challenge to Jacob's beliefs is provided by Waclaw who, though born of noble blood, has chosen a way of life that is the antithesis of slavery: " 'Here

at the ferry I'm as free as a bird' " (259). Like Ivan Karamazov, who dredges up all sorts of dreadful, blasphemous
stories to unsettle his pious brother, Waclaw plays the role
of Devil's advocate with Jacob. When Jacob maintains the
existence of God, Waclaw asks if he has seen Him. When
Jacob speaks of the one true God, Waclaw counters with
the worship of snakes by Indians. When Jacob talks about
the punishment of evildoers, Waclaw tells him the story
of a Polish count who flogged hundreds of peasants to
death and then lived until he was ninety-eight. To Waclaw, the only thing that is certain is death, and only the
worms are impartial and democratic in consuming both
the good and the bad, the rich and the poor. Waclaw sums
up his philosophy:

> "One thing I've learned in my life: don't get attached
> to anything. You own a cow or a house and you're its
> slave. Marry and you're the slave of your wife. . . .
> What does the priest want? To put another rope
> around your neck." (260)

Waclaw's philosophy is by now a familiar one. It is
embraced by Asa Heshel out of desperation; by Dr.
Yaretsky out of cynicism; and by Yasha the Magician out
of strength. Later, Jacob calls it the philosophy of the
vigorous because picaresque self-sufficiency is contingent
on the total recovery of one's powers as a substitute for a
helpmate. Set in the context of pogroms, however, Waclaw's attractive irresponsibility takes on a more sinister
aspect. It becomes the sin of silence and moral inertia.
Wisely, Singer does not provide Jacob with any answers
to the dilemmas Waclaw poses. What Jacob does discover,
however, is that Waclaw's freedom from dependence not
only deprives him of any extension beyond this life, but

also denies him access to strength when his vigor fails. By serving as a slave to what will outlast him, Jacob not only secures perpetuity through his son, but also inexplicably experiences a strength beyond his own to face the inexplicable dilemmas of this existence.

Gershon's doctrine of antislavery results in a mechanical God who is appeased by ritualistic observances; Waclaw's results in a superman who in being a law unto himself needs no God. Gershon's distortion of God's fullness is matched by Waclaw's distortion of man's wholeness. The distortions of both, however, appear in Lord and Lady Pilitzsky.[3]

Singer's portrait of these two decadent mistakes of creation is presented with unqualified condemnation. To be sure, their perversions echo those of the short stories, especially "Blood" and "The Destruction of Kreshev," and thus reveal that the Jews are not conveniently excluded from such practices. But undoubtedly what accounts for Singer's unqualified indictment is that although the Pilitzsky's act out what the positions of Gershon and Waclaw can lead to, these human gargoyles cap their personal sins with senseless and unforgiveable persecutions. Consequently, the portrayal of Adam Pilitzsky, like that of the tyrant in Plato's *Republic,* is meant to be a psychological and political composite of the perversions of power:

> The revolt of his serfs and the cruelties with which he had suppressed the rebellion had further mortified Pilitsky's spirit. He knew that widows and orphans sorrowed because of him. At night he had visions of bodies hanging from gibbets, their feet blue, their eyes glassy, their tongues extended. He suffered from cramps and headaches; his skin itched. There were days when he prayed for death or planned suicide.

Not even wine and vodka could calm him now. Nor were the pleasures of the body as intense as they had been. He was always on the lookout for new sensations to stave off impotency. Because of the perversities of that witch Theresa, now only her infidelities aroused his lust. He made her describe her affairs in detail. When she had exhausted the catolog of her debauchery, he forced her to invent adventures. Husband and wife had driven each other into an insane labyrinth of vice. He procured for her and she procured for him. She watched him corrupt peasant girls and he eavesdropped on her and her lovers. He had warned her many times that he would stab her, she teased about poisoning his food. But both were pious, lit candles, went to confession, and contributed money for the building of churches and religious monuments. Often Adam Pilitzsky opened the door of their private chapel and found Theresa, her cheeks wet with tears, a crucifix pressed to her bosom, kneeling before the altar deep in contemplation. Theresa spoke of entering a nunnery; Pilitsky toyed with the idea of becoming a monk. (175–76)

Despots are notorious purists. Indeed, much of their appeal stems from the ability to keep apart the image of virtue from the pursuit of power, the ideals of the state from the dreadful acts required to realize them, the soul from the body. Inevitably, such alternatives result not in Singer's resigned acceptance of duality but in a passionate martyrdom to conflict. The image of man on a tightrope is transformed into the stigmata of crucifixion. Thus, the religious devotion of the Pilitzskys is an essential spur to their sexual perversions for, unlike Risha of "Blood," they seek to arrest their descent to the level of animals by refreshing periods of mortification. Insulating their barbarisms with the warming agony of religious devotion, Adam and Theresa Pilitzsky are able to perpetuate their compulsions in a closed cycle of guilt and forgiveness. Their monkish and nunnish ambitions are a sign of their spiritual virginity and infantilism. To them God is all good and the Devil is all bad; man similarly is either all pure or all bestial. The Pilitzskys live as if they have never fallen or have always been depraved. And throughout it all there is the sadistic logic of regarding themselves as victims of persecution at the very moment they watch children being disembowelled. Historically, the Jews have released the fury and insularity of the Pilitzskys by treating the bedroom as a chapel, the body as an agent of the soul, the relationships between men as the expression of God. In short, the traditional slavery of the Jews to the total duality appears to invite the violent freedom and purity of extremists.

Just as Jacob's movement toward biblical proximity is linked to the festivals of the Jewish calendar, so his progress through seventeenth century history is defined by the examples of communal paganism and doctrines of antislavery through which he must pass if he is to come to the end of exile. As Singer's most passive hero, Jacob's standard responses are a series of rejections which collectively serve as Singer's political versions of his religious "Thou shalt nots." Above all, Singer has encumbered the relationship of Jacob and Sarah so that their dislocation can serve as a judgment on both communities. Cut off from the Jewish world by marrying a Christian, and cut off from the Christian world by marrying a Jew, Jacob and Sarah are thus peripheral to both and equitably expose the lovelessness they share. The specific indictments of the Jews of Pilitz is that they have cut Judaism off from biblical ambiguity, alienated themselves from the divinity of original creation, and ignored the godly in man in order to worship the less taxing prospect of the godly in God.

To Singer the infallible sign of God's genuine authority is His rejection of any devotion which serves as a substitute for the love of man. Nor can one love only man
and not God. As he notes in *The Family Moskat,* when
men forget God they soon forget to be men. In other
words, his way of underscoring the need for authority is
to reveal the chaos of the unbound. His way of defining
the virtues of slavery is to have Jacob pass through the
vices of freedom. In the process, lest the reader come to
the mistaken conclusion that Jacob's passivity is synonymous with cowardice or fatalism, Singer reveals that Jacob
is not always long-suffering.

III

Sarah's labor pains are so severe and protracted that
the "mute" cries out, and in Polish. Having betrayed her
gentile origins, Sarah dies, unaware that her son has been
seized by the officials and that Jacob is arrested. Chained
to the horse of a Polish soldier escorting him to jail, Jacob
at first obediently allows himself to be dragged along. But
then he thinks to himself:

> God . . . had formed both the rider and the horse.
> He had made the chain strong. Suddenly it occurred
> to Jacob that sometimes chains could be broken. No-
> where was it written that a man must consent to his
> own destruction. Instantly his mood changed. He was
> angry. Powers slumbering within awoke. He now
> knew what to do. (251)

Jacob breaks the chain and flees into the forest: "He had
outwitted the powerful, broken the chain of slavery, but
despite his escape he felt no elation. . . . The chain
dragged; he felt its weight on his hand" (252). Significantly, the fields he finds himself in recall his slavery to

the Polish peasants. Once again, the sacramental universe glowingly opens before him, but this time the evocation of the past is tied to that of the future: the emergence of the sun is compared to the head of a newborn child. Suddenly, his wife appears to him in a vision as both Wanda and Sarah, addresses him as "Jacob my slave," and urges him to rescue their son and raise him as a Jew.

All that has been endured in the novel is concentrated and affirmed in this incident. The chain still dangling from Jacob's wrist and the lack of elation represent the emptiness of freedom without authority. Following the linkage of Passover and Shavout, Jacob has succeeded in throwing off the wrong kind of slavery as a preparation for assuming the right kind. The right slavery is the one to his son and to future continuity. That a return to the past is the key to the future not only affirms a traditional Jewish approach, but also prepares the way for the fusion of Wanda and Sarah. In the short stories, the dualistic image of woman served to reflect the basic makeup of man. In *The Slave* it more comprehensively reflects the nature of total existence. By marrying Wanda-Sarah, Jacob has married both worlds—the natural and the religious. God gave man two books: The Book of Nature and the Book of the Bible. Wanda-Sarah aligns both, and in the process Jacob the man comes closer to becoming Jacob the Patriarch.

To be sure, Jacob is still in doubt and fearful. Indeed, perhaps as an articulation of his conflict, Singer subsequently has Jacob encounter Waclaw, the ferryman, and an emissary from the Holy Land who is travelling through Poland soliciting funds. Waclaw, as noted, presents the doctrine of picaresque freedom. The old man from the Holy Land listens to Jacob's story and shakes his head in sorrow at what Jacob has done. But then the emissary presents what is perhaps Singer's own judgment of the relationship of Jacob and Sarah:

> "The community is right. Your wife was a gentile and so is your son. The child follows its mother. This is the law. But behind the law, there is mercy. Without mercy, there would be no law." (265)

The emissary further advises, " 'You must save yourself and you must save the child. . . . Let him be brought up as a Jew. It is written somewhere that before the Messiah will come, all pious gentiles will have been converted" (266).

Because obviously the best way for Jacob to save himself is not to rescue his son, what the emissary seems really to be suggesting is that Jacob must rescue his son as his ultimate means of saving himself. Sneaking into Pilitz at night, Jacob steals his son away just before Succoth. By naming his son Ben-oni or Benjamin, a child born of sorrow, Jacob not only further ties himself to his biblical namesake, but also aligns the birth of his son with that of the Torah. Leaving Pilitz with Benjamin, Jacob comes to the Vistula River and surveys again the beauty of God's world. Waiting for the ferry, he begins to meditate not solely on his own past but also "on his past before birth" (278). To Singer everyone has a past before birth; for Jacob it takes the form of his biblical original:

> Jacob remembered the words his namesake had spoken on his deathbed: "And as for me, when I came from Padan, Rachel died by me in the land of Canaan in the way, when yet there was a little way to come to Ephrath; and I buried her there. . . ."
>
> His name was Jacob also; he too had lost a beloved wife, the daughter of an idolater, among strangers;

Sarah too was buried by the way and had left him a
son. Like the biblical Jacob, he was crossing the river,
bearing only a staff, pursued by another Esau. Everything remained the same: the ancient love, the ancient
grief. Perhaps four thousand years would again pass;
somewhere, at another river, another Jacob would
walk mourning another Rachel. Or who knew, perhaps it was always the same Jacob and the same
Rachel. (278–79)

IV

The above passage concludes the second section of
the novel. It should have marked the end of the novel, for
the final section, entitled "The Return," in adding little
takes away much. But if one cannot find artistic justification for Singer's going on, one perhaps can perceive a
religious justification. The last part enables Singer to describe Jacob's having reached the Holy Land and having
raised his son as a Jew; Benjamin, in fact, is a teacher in
a religious school in Jerusalem.[4] Singer thus is able to
contrast the life of Jacob with that of the community of
Pilitz and to reinforce the paradox of bondage: as a slave
Jacob has been able to reach Palestine, whereas those who
have chosen freedom remain in exile. That Jacob's fidelity
both to God and Judaism have more than compensated
for his initial sins is suggested further by his decision to
return to Poland and to disinter Sarah's bones so that they
may be buried in hallowed ground. Because Sarah as a
convert originally was not permitted to be buried within
the borders of the Jewish cemetery, the prospect of her
being buried in the Holy Land contains an implied judgment on those who judged her unfit. However, so many
years have elapsed since Sarah's death that her grave cannot be found. Saddened by the frustration of his desire,

Jacob suddenly becomes weary and dies. When his grave is dug, miraculously, it turns out to be next to Sarah's whose body, although it has lain in the earth for twenty years, is miraculously, too, still recognizable.

Throughout the novel, Jacob has been the means by which the past and the future—Wanda and Benjamin—have been linked. Now the miracle dramatizes the fusion of the past with an eternal future—the afterlife. The deflective journey of love and belief finds its chronological and geographical analogues in Jacob's bridging the Bible and history, Poland and Palestine. The base of the arc is pagan Egypt and the ghetto of Pilitz; there the temple is destroyed. The end of the journey is Palestine and the ghetto of Pilitz; there the temple is recreated. The conversion of the bond of lust to that of love finds its ultimate extension in the conversion of the pagan Wanda to the Jewish Sarah. The real miracle is the transformation of Wanda from the image of the desecrated temple and bride into that of the beloved Sarah, the mother of the Jews. That the destruction of the temple is Singer's pivot for indicating how despair can give way to hope, slavery to freedom, appears in the communal miracle in which the Jews of Pilitz are able to discover communal bonds and affirm God at a time set aside for lamenting the loss of the temple.

Although the last section brings to an affirmative conclusion many of the themes of the first two parts, it is different not just in degree but in kind from the rest of the novel. Unlike the first two parts, the last is exclusively factual and historical. There is almost no conversation or, for that matter, drama or conflict. It essentially records facts and deeds, the miracle being the most dramatic act of all. What all this points to is one of Singer's most persistent themes: just as God sees but is unseen, so He does not speak but acts. Not once in all of Singer's works does God ever manifest Himself in form or speech directly to man. Aside from reflecting the traditional Jewish point of view, Singer has explained God's reticence in his own way:

> God is silent because if He were to speak He would have to in all fairness speak in all the languages and dialects of the world. Besides, God does not use ordinary language or language as we know it to be. God speaks in deeds—that is His language. Now of course the question arises: how do we know what are God's deeds and what are man's? After all, man has free will—he does things, too. The difference is this. God's deeds last. And they always are worthy of being attributed to God.

Having journeyed back to the Bible to invest the story of Jacob with the permanence of the past, Singer took the liberty of gracing the end of that journey with a deed that, like biblical deeds, would be "worthy of being attributed to God."

The epitaph chiseled across the common gravestones of Jacob and Sarah reads: "Lovely and pleasant in their lives, and in their death they were not divided." The passage is from II Samuel 1:23 and is taken from David's lamentation over the death of Saul and Jonathan. It is one of Singer's favorites, for it is employed to conclude the equally affirmative "Short Friday" and to inform "A Wedding in Brownsville." But it seems curious to celebrate the relationship between husband and wife with a passage associated with father and son. And yet has not that been the precisely unexpected yield of that love? It was the prospect of being a father that led Jacob to return to Wanda and the bondage of lust and paganism. Later, it is Wanda-Sarah who again urges him to rescue his son from idolaters. Indeed, by serving as a bridge between father and son, Wanda becomes Sarah and thus further underscores Jacob's role as an intermediary between the past and the future. By assuming the biblical yoke of lover and believer and the historical burden of father, Jacob honors his love of Wanda-Sarah by making it one with the love of God. In giving new life to the past, Jacob of Pilitz becomes Jacob of the Torah, a coincidence that recovers the past and serves as Singer's supreme metaphor of the Jewish journey.

It is appropriate that the final image of *The Slave* is both traditional and individualistic, ancient and eclectic. Indeed, in putting his own stamp on Orthodox beliefs, Jacob reinforces the traditionalism of Singer's vision. Jewish prayers invoke the Deity as "Our God and the God of our Fathers" and even more curiously as the "God of Abraham, Isaac, and Jacob." The rabbis rightly ask: why the repetition? Clearly, there is only one God. The answer given is that each Jew receives the tradition of his fathers as a legacy. But then that tradition must be personally claimed, invested with individual experience, if it is to be alive and if the living God is to survive. This is what all the biblical originals had to do, including the biblical Jacob; this is what Singer has compelled his seventeenth century Jacob to do. Indeed, the religious journey of Jacob toward personal and traditional affirmation mirrors the religio-aesthetic journey of Singer toward the same ends. In surrendering to a silent God, to an inscrutable Messiah, to a love of the Divine which must be embodied in the love of man and communal continuity, to a past which eternally refuses to remain past, both Jacob and Singer are slaves of reclaimed belief.

Notes

1. "Freedom and Authority," *Diogenes,* I (1950), 34. For a fuller and earlier presentation of these notions of Jaspers' see his *Psychologie der Weltanshauungen* (1919) and *Vernunft und Existenz* (1935).
2. Singer's wife, before the composition of *The Slave,* urged him to be more lesiurely in his novels and especially to have more nature scenes. After he wrote *The Slave,* Singer said to his wife, "So this time I listened to you. There are plenty of nature scenes" (Lisa Hammel, "The Novelist's Working Wife," *New York Times* [November 23, 1967], p. 56).
3. The Pilitskys of Pilitz are akin to the Jampolskis of Jampol in *The Manor.* Count Wladislaw Jampolski and his family in *The Manor* embody the same distortions, and their manor similarly is a gothic House of Usher.
4. The biographical connection here is strong: Singer's own son by his first marriage was raised in Palestine and is at present also a teacher in Israel.

> *History is the temporality of the eternal.*
>
> ———J. V. Langmead Casserley,
> *Towards a Theology of History*

> *Eternity is in love with the productions of time.*
>
> ———William Blake,
> *The Marriage of Heaven and Hell*

8.

The Manor Revisited

The Manor, Singer's most recent novel,[1] is his only long work to be set in the nineteenth century. It thus fills a gap in what can be designated as Singer's characteristic chronology. *Satan in Goray* and *The Slave* are set in the seventeenth century and together represent the furthest point back in history to which Singer has travelled. The other end of the arc is relatively close to modern times and is now nicely staked out by three novels: *The Manor,* which begins after the abortive Polish uprising of 1863; *The Magician of Lublin,* which takes place at the turn of the century and just before World War I; and *The Family Moskat,* which concludes with the Nazi occupation of Warsaw.

Whatever general European patterns are operative within this time span of about three hundred years, to Singer the essential pattern is that known as the Jewish Enlightenment. The period of the Jewish Enlightenment, marked the beginning of opposition to Orthodoxy, the dissolution of the ghetto, the first appearance of favorable portraits of Jews in fiction,[2] the emergence of secular Jewish writers, the first admission of Jewish students to previously restricted schools, universities, and professions, the birth of Bundism, Zionism, Yiddishism, etc. In other words, Singer's favorite chronological arc features the tensions of transition. The old is not yet atrophied nor is the new totally triumphant. The initial base of the arc is tied anteriorly to the Torah; the final one to the works of Darwin, Freud, Marx, and Herzl. In addition, Singer's characteristic historical span is bounded at either end by massacres, for parallel with the liberating experience of the Jewish Enlightenment went the unenlightened experience of persecution. The seventeenth century was the time of the Chmielnicki pogroms; the twentieth the Nazi holocaust. In between, and regularly featured in Singer's intervening novels, are echoes of the former or anticipations of the latter. Thus, the pogroms both in Russia and Poland that followed the attempted assasination of Alexander II shock the Jewish intellectuals in *The Manor;* the Dreyfus case informs the atmosphere of *The Magician of Lublin;* the purges of the Bolsheviks dominate the latter half of *The Family Moskat.* Indeed, to Singer the experiences of liberation and persecution are historically tied to each other by an ironic bond. As each wave of emigration from the ghetto reaches a crest, a counterwave of persecution comes to thrust it back and to embarass all prophets of progress. Moreover, the timing is always ironic: precisely at the moment when young Jewish intellectuals in *The Manor* and *The Family Moskat* become "enlightened" to the point of supporting Communism and nationalism, they are assaulted by the Communists and the nationalists. Having shorn themselves of their caftans and earlocks and rejected the antiquated practices of their forefathers, they are forced to wear yellow arm bands.

Although this pattern of ironic freedom embraces with striking chronological fullness the body of Singer's work, each individual work presents the pattern in miniature. Indeed, its reappearance in each generation supports the possibility that it represents for Singer the essential pattern of Jewish history. Thus, *Satan in Goray* moves toward messianic release only to withdraw at the end to the inexplicable traditional notion of final redemption. *The Slave* presents Jacob and his son reaching the Holy Land only to conclude with Jacob's returning to Poland and to death. *The Magician of Lublin* expansively moves out toward the wider circles of cultural and artistic Europe only to terminate with the magician entombed in a brick prison. *The Family Moskat* features the gradual emancipation of Asa Heshel from Tereshpol Minor only to picture him withdrawing to the Warsaw ghetto. *The Manor* records Calman Jacoby's progress through the wider world of European finance only to conclude with his retiring to his private chapel. In other words, Singer's novels are simultaneously progressive and regressive. The forward thrust of the Jewish Enlightenment meets its counterthrust in the historical irony of persecution and in the vitality of past tradition. Above all, Singer's judgment of this entire period is built into the basic structure of all his works. Like a funnel, each one moves from openness to constriction. The unlimited and expansive possibilities at the beginning of a life or an epoch ultimately give way to actual or symbolic graves; to tightropes not rocking chairs; to inexplicable mysteries not rational clarities; to acts of faith not experiences of understanding. Although *The Manor* confirms this overall pattern and thus is essentially similar to all Singer's novels, it does contain a number of elements which make it different, especially from its companion chronicle, *The Family Moskat.*

I

As noted earlier, the two dominant strains in Singer's works are the historical and the demonic. And although his novels can be sorted out between the two, Singer does not so much move from one mode to another as subdue one to the other. Thus, in the historical works, demonism appears as scepticism, especially philosophical scepticism. In the demonic works, history appears in the form of biblical analogues and traditional Jewish notions, especially messianic ones. *The Manor* is no exception; demonically inspired scepticism is a regular feature of this family chronicle. But, in addition, the demonic appears here in another and essentially new form—the form of dreams.

Throughout the novel and often in the midst of a discussion of changing political and economic patterns, Singer suddenly freezes his historical chronicle and moves toward gothic surrealism. Fantastic, marvelously inventive and harrowing dreams and nightmares dramatically violate the impersonal texture of history. Moreover, Singer adjusts the dreams to reflect the psychology of the dreamer. Thus, Count Lucian Jampolski, who is overtly bestial and decadent, dreams quantitatively not qualitatively. He never dreams about illicit relations, which he already has performed anyway, but only about size or numbers: he dreams of wrestling with an enormous, virile ape, of having relations with more than one woman at the same time, with mutilating and killing hundreds of people

(231). Clara, Calman Jacoby's second wife, on the other hand, is only adulterous and therefore can dream of more qualitative possibilities. Specifically, she contemplates drinking blood and sleeping with her son (296). For Calman Jacoby, who is the most Orthodox dreamer of this group, Singer reserves almost explicit satanic visitations. Satan, in fact, speaks to Calman and urges him to murder his wife; and later Lilith, Satan's wife, appears to Calman in a dream.

Clearly, the dreams function not only as a psychological means of exploring character, but also as an historical means of supporting Singer's chronology. Explicitly satanic dreams occur only to Calman Jacoby who, because of his patriarchial traditionalism, is tied to the past. Those who are more emancipated and closer to modern times are disturbed by less explicitly satanic dreams, mostly because what they have done already during their waking hours has in a sense emptied the dark recesses of the mind of its traditional tabooed prospects. In other words, as the novel moves in time from the old to the new, Singer pegs the progress with dreams that range from the satanic to the unconscious. Calman Jacoby, plagued by bad dreams and fears, visits the saintly wonderworking Rabbi of Marshinov. The more modern characters visit a psychiatrist or, as he was called in the late nineteenth century, a specialist in nervous disorders. It is surely significant in this connection that Ezriel Badad does in fact become such a physician; indeed, as the son of a rabbi, Ezriel embodies the transition from demonology to what Dostoevsky called the unconscious, "the satanic depths."

Ezriel Badad is a link to other distinctions of *The Manor*. This chronicle deals more with children than with parents. In *The Family Moskat* the parental stress is multiple. But in *The Manor* Calman Jacoby is the only substantial father figure, and the bulk of the chronicle is preoccupied with his daughters and, through marriage, with his sons-in-law. Then, too, because the drama of the children involves maximum contact with the modern world, it deals more with relations between Jews and non-Jews than did *The Family Moskat*. Finally, the new chronicle is concerned more with institutions—the title itself is reflective of that—and with governmental and economic matters. In other words, the differences of *The Manor* are all variations of a central difference—Singer has moved this family chronicle more toward history than toward fiction. Indeed, in the process, he perhaps has overburdened his narrative, for the heavy institutional and historical stresses tend to put characterization under wraps, impede narrative, and sputter impact. In *The Family Moskat,* although there were nearly a hundred characters, Asa Heshel was central and as such served as a nexus to collect and unify many of the divergent strands. But in *The Manor* no character is given such centrality.[3] Nevertheless, an overriding control is present, except that it is exercised not by character but by structure. Because of its intensified historical burdens, *The Manor* is comprehensively contained by a series of character spectrums which like an ever-widening and contracting gyre pulsate from the center to the circumference and then back again to the center. Thus, whatever the fictional faults of *The Manor,* structurally Singer has sought to make his form his meaning.

II

The first spectrum is geographical and economic, the latter providing the impetus for the former. The manor of the title is the ancestral home of the aristocratic Jampolski family. After the unsuccessful uprising of 1863, the elder Count was imprisoned in Siberia; his older son Josef fled to England; his younger son Lucian to Warsaw. The town of Jampol, under the double jurisdiction of Jampolskis and the Church, prohibited any Jews from settling or setting up any businesses in Jampol itself. The Jews who lived in Jampol, including Calman Jacoby and his family, actually lived on the outskirts of town in an area called The Sands. If a Jew wished to enter the town itself, he had to pay a toll to the Church. But after the uprising and with business chaotic, Calman is put in charge of the Jampolski estates and manor house. Prospering, he and his family move into the town itself and thus open the door for other Jews to leave the ghetto of The Sands. As the Jews move out, poor Gentiles and peasants move in.

Singer does not restrict the geographical changes to rural areas. The same easing of ghetto lines was occurring in the cities. As Calman's business prospers, he journeys to Warsaw and there discovers that it "was so changed that Calman, who had not visited it since the rebellion, barely recognized it. Streets which formerly had been forbidden to Jews now had many Jewish residents" (12). Finally, when Calman remarries and moves into the manor house itself with Clara, the geographical pattern is complete. The economic dispossession of the nobility is followed by geographical dispossession.

The small house in The Sands has yielded to an elegant manor house. Calman's original simple lumber and lime business becomes such a complicated economic empire that he is no longer able to keep track of his own transactions but must employ accountants. His first wife, Zelda, who did her own laundry and cleaning and was often sickly and sexually unresponsive, is replaced by

Clara who has maids and footmen, is lustful, and has a child by another man. Calman who earlier is an observant Jew and regularly studies the commentaries, later worries about whether the food he eats at his own wedding and home is kosher. Clearly, the geographical base of the novel is symbolic and meant to give tangible expression to the eternal drama of loss in the face of gain. In The Sands Calman is recognizable to himself and to others as a Jew. In the manor, attired like a peacock for one of Clara's flirtatious parties, he is a freakish new thing. In short, Calman Jacoby acts out Singer's favorite biblical analogue of Jacob supplanting Esau; Lucian, in fact, says this of Calman and later of all Jews (104). But Calman's problem is that he does not so much replace as become Esau. Through his economic and geographical supplanting, he does not so much secure as nearly lose his birthright as a Jew.

The process of reduction through expansion all begins quite innocently. Having signed a contract to supply railroad ties for the czar, Calman finds it necessary to import Jews who speak Russian. But those who arrive are beardless, wear gentile clothes, smoke on the Sabbath, and flaunt Orthodox ritual. Thus, the process of bringing prosperity to the community also involves the possibility of undermining that community. Calman's increasing spiritual impoverishment finds its financial counterpart in the fact that as a poor man, he did not owe a cent; but now that he was rich he was deeply in debt: "The more Calman thought about it, the more he came to believe that he was the captive and not the master of his fortune" (52). But the final captivity occurs when he marries Clara and moves into the manor, the two acts serving as versions of his trespass.

Satan need not be present in fact for his favorite

temptation of mismatching couples to exist in practice. Clara Kaminer is young enough to be Calman's daughter, just as Clara's father, who marries a girl in her twenties, is old enough to be his new wife's father. Lest the Kaminer tendency toward mismatching appear coincidental and not pathological, Singer presents Clara as desiring to marry her own father and to make love to her own son. In other words, as in the short stories, mismatching is followed by the threat not only of incestuous coupling, but also of sexual blurring. For Singer presents Clara as another Risha—a mannish woman. Clara is always being praised because she has a "man's head" on her lovely shoulders (271). Although she is promiscuous, many men lose interest in her because of her "aggressive manner" (274). Finally, when she rides horseback, Singer describes her as an "Amazon in riding clothes" (298). Who is Clara ultimately? In Singer's lexicon, she is the Whore of Babylon—she is, as she appears in Calman's dreams, Lilith. Her lust coupled with her financial acumen and greed make her the living embodiment of the manor itself— that palace of aristocratic sexual indulgence and wealth. In marrying Clara, Calman, the Jewish Jacob, has wed the female Esau. Having no sons to carry on his name and to say *Kaddish* when he is dead, he marries a woman who does indeed give him a son, but one that is a throwback to idolatry and barbarism. The son is Sasha who lives up to his name by being a savage. He drowns chickens, dismembers his toys, and loves whips, swords, and guns. "The townspeople nicknamed him Ishmael" (261). Later in the novel, Sasha is compared to Ham, the son of Noah who discovered and called attention to his uncovered father in his tent. In the Bible, Ham is referred as as the Father of Canaan, and the commentaries further note that whoever betrays his father and his traditions is like Ham and as much a part of the barbaric enemies of Israel as if he were actually a Canaanite. Near the end of the novel, Calman, fearing the damnation of his soul, divorces Clara and moves back into the house he initially inhabited with his first wife. The rhythm of expansion finally is replaced by that of constriction. But before Calman frees himself from the wrong kind of slavery so that he may choose the right kind, his personal journey from piety to transgression is played out in the spectrum of both his immediate family and, subsequently, of his sons-in-law.

III

Calman and Zelda Jacoby have four daughters who range in age from eight to eighteen when the novel opens. One day Calman is about to journey to Warsaw on business. Each daughter bids him farewell and, in addition, makes a request. Like the questions asked by the four sons in the Passover service, what each daughter asks for shows what she is and what she will become in marriage.

The eldest is Jochebed, dutiful, shy, almost ascetic, like her mother. She wishes her father a safe journey with tears in her eyes but refuses to ask for any presents. Later, she marries the somewhat self-righteous Mayer Joel who similarily is respectful and obedient and who, by keeping to the traditional Jewish ways of his father, makes no contact with the wider, secular world.[4] Shaindel, next in age, is Jochebed's opposite. Dark like a gypsy, Shaindel is lively, sensual, and coquettish. She asks her father to bring her a necklace, shoes with buckles, ribbons, scented soap, etc. She later is to marry Ezriel Badad who as an intellectual and a scientist serves to bridge the spectrum of the Jewish family with that of assimilated Jews. Then, there is the romantic, Miriam Lieba, who is entranced with all that is fine and French in the world outside her home. She asks her father to bring her some novels. She is in the midst of reading one about a countess who elopes with a violinist to Paris. The book is prophetic, for Miriam Lieba elopes with Count Lucian Jampolski, goes to Paris, and converts to Christianity. Because Miriam is the only Jacoby girl to refuse an arranged marriage—Jochanan originally was proposed to her—Singer seems to be suggesting that romantic love was as damaging or inimical to traditional ways in secular learning, and that the reinforcement of both in Miriam Lieba serves as the threshold for conversion. Finally, Tsipele, the youngest, is pious and generous; she asks her father for a doll and a prayer book. She is to marry Rabbi Jochanan who is to become the spiritual leader of the Hasids of Marshinov.

In the four daughters of Calman and Zelda Jacoby, Singer has presented the essence of his novel. Moreover, because marriage in Singer's vision inevitably bears historical burdens, the Jacoby girls stake out the essential directions of the Jews in the transitional period of the Jewish Enlightenment; just as earlier Rechele in *Satan in Goray* was emblematic of the Jewish people during a time of messianic hysteria. Significantly, Singer strikes a balance; the directions are both conventional and radical. Jochebed and Tsipele, the eldest and the youngest, pair off to anchor the past in the future. Shaindel and Miriam Lieba, the middle girls, are linked by their temporalizing or violating of the old with the new. The symmetrical polarization and alternation of the daughters is mirrored by the rhythmic balance of opposites in the novel itself. Characteristically, Singer will conclude one chapter with assimilated Jews imitating gentile practices and begin the next with the Hasids chanting in the Marshinov house of prayer. In the former, worldly Jews will argue persuasively that where the Gentile goes the Jew follows and there is no point in resisting change and progress. In the next chapter, time stands still and God is still an available, permanent reality, removed from altering fashions: the Almighty is still "both the One who knows and the object of His knowledge" (173). By setting the relativistic and the absolutist side by side, Singer is able not only to present the full complexity of the Jewish historical spectrum, but also to resist, without intruding himself into the tale, the arguments of extremists. The Jewish secularists maintain there are no alternatives to assimilation, just as the traditionalists insist there is no other way but theirs. But through contrasts, Singer presents the other side of the coin to each and thus makes it clear that the exclusive claims are in reality partial. Above all, the range of Calman's daughters essentially describes the range of Calman's own journey.

The novel begins with Calman aligned with his eldest daughter Jochebed. Like her, and later her husband, Calman is initially a dutiful Jew. But then, with increasing wealth, he progresses to the increasing materialism and worldliness of Shaindel and her husband Ezriel Badad. When Calman marries Clara, the transitional pattern gives way to that of the apostate Miriam Lieba. Indeed, Calman comes to believe that he is no better than his daughter who in converting has forsaken both this world and the world to come. Finally, Calman, in divorcing Clara and in retiring to Marshinov, follows the model of his youngest daughter who, in fact, is married to the Rabbi of Marshinov. Thus, the children who are led astray are balanced by the children who serve as models for their own wayward parents. To be sure, it is not all that neat, for at the end of the novel, Calman's return to the center is counterpointed by the assimilation of

Ezriel Badad and the corruption of Count Lucian Jampolski.

IV

Like Asa Heshel, Yasha the Magician, and Jacob,
Ezriel Badad is a familiar Singer type, mostly because he,
too, is a fictional version of Singer himself. Indeed, Ezriel
is probably Singer's most transparent projection, for Ezriel's father is an unofficial rabbi on Krochmalna Street,
the same position held in the same place by Singer's own
father. Plagued by similar questions about existence that
troubled Singer's youth, Ezriel searches in vain for answers in secular books (35). Asa Heshel sought to relieve
his metaphysical frustrations through the new political
and economic messiahs of the twentieth century; Ezriel
Badad selects an equally powerful and attractive substitute—the psychoanalytical approach of Freud.

Throughout his life, Ezriel, again like Singer himself,
feared he was going mad. His endless doubts, his strange
dreams, made him tremble for the stability of his mind.
Even when he finally becomes a doctor specializing in
nervous disorders, he feels such an affinity for the deranged that his "brain was a little insane asylum of its
own" (393). Ezriel's mental dislocation is symptomatic
of historical dislocation, for Ezriel is caught between two
generations—between the God of his fathers and the new
God—Freud—of his generation and profession. While
studying analytical chemistry, surgery, and opthamology,
Ezriel unknowingly chants his lessons in the singsong of
the study house (281). Attending an elegant dinner party,
he is alternately at home and uncomfortable. He discusses
new psychoanalytical theories with other guests but does
so with all the backward shyness of the talmudic student

(393). The complex rules of etiquette at the dinner table remind him of the equally complex *Shulhan Aruk* which details the rules of Orthodox ritual. Aware of Weismann's arguments against acquired characteristics being inherited, he, nevertheless, resists choosing between Lamarck and Darwin but rather seeks to honor the flow of the past into the present by combining them; just as Asa Heshel seeks to fuse Spinoza and Malthus. Observing an autopsy in the morgue, Ezriel, unlike his fellow students, drifts off into metaphysical speculation:

> Why had the tall man hanged himself? Why had the redheaded girl jumped into the Vistula? How much did a person have to endure before he was driven to do such a thing? Were they now at peace? Was their sleep actually eternal? (285)

The historically inspired schizophrenia of Ezriel Badad is Singer's characteristic way of exploring normal forms of madness. None of his characters are normal in the conventional sense of the word. They either are normally mad or fanatically mad. In *The Manor*, Ezriel and Jochanan are normally mad. The Rabbi of Marshinov is no more free of temptation than Ezriel is of doubts. Calman Jacoby, in his prodigal journey, moves from normal to possessed madness, and in the process links Jochanan's morality to Ezriel's psychology: "Calman appreciated the words of the sages who claimed that all sinners were either partly or totally insane" (244). Characters like Lucian Jampolski in *The Manor,* Itche Mates in *Satan in Goray,* the Pilitskys of *The Slave,* Risha of "Blood," and Yoineh Meir of the recent "The Slaughterer," are totally mad and sinful. Indeed, such grotesques provide the extreme necessary to define the center of normal derangement. But because they begin at that center, their final religious and pathological distortions exist in embryonic form within each typically complex character. Indeed, toward the end of the novel when Ezriel contemplates having an adulterous affair with a convert, Singer describes him in the same terms as he does Lucian Jampolski (414).

The same strategy of tilting the present so as to become subject to the insights of the past appears in Singer's presentation of Ezriel's assimilated friends. At the apartment of Mirale, Ezriel's sister, a spectrum of Jewish intellectuals regularly gathers as a self-education group. Among them is Aaron Lipman who is a socialist and believes that the only hope for the Jews lies in discarding their Asiatic ways and supporting the peasants. Alexander Zipkin agrees, but goes further. An atheist, he endorses Voltaire's view that God did not create man but that man created God.[5] The point releases a heated discussion, but perhaps the most telling argument is advanced not by any member of the group but by Singer through his structure of contrasts.

Prior to this discussion, Singer presents Rabbi Jochanan tortured by a host of doubts, not the least of which is whether the Almighty exists. Jochanan finally recovers his faith and, curiously, does so through pretty much the same argument that Zipkin had used to deny the existence of God. How is this possible? For Singer, Zipkin's notion, far from settling the matter, really opens it up. For if man did create God, then God becomes whatever is the total identity of man. To free oneself from God, is to cut oneself off from one's otherness or moreness. Like Blake, Singer casts for contraries, and atheism is not a contrary but a negative. As the secret extension or metaphor of man, God, by virtue of his creation by man, exists as the fullness of man not yet realized. Ironically, by discarding what traditionally was God's, Zipkin becomes less of a man. He seduces Clara, makes her pregnant, and becomes a thief. He allows himself to be kept by Clara and then agrees to an arranged business marriage in which he functions as an obedient stud. Accustomed to using others and being used, Zipkin becomes a man of means, but one without a beginning or an end. If Ezriel is tortured by the past, Zipkin becomes tortured by the lack of both a past and a future. At the age of thirty, he decides that he has lived enough and contemplates suicide (339). Zipkin's independence from God has granted him the freedom to destroy himself. Forsaking morality, he becomes a political incendiary and pushes his socialism toward the extreme of nihilistic anarchy. Abandoning his full identity, he becomes a bewitched puppet, enslaved to the caprices of his fantasies and his lustful or materialistic keepers. Desiring to end his life, Zipkin is tortured by his inability to die. Clearly, Singer is not advocating that Zipkin become a Hasid. Singer himself did not. But what Singer does suggest is that what a man believes determines what he is and governs the possibilities of what he will become. Zipkin believes in little or nothing and thus reduces his life accordingly. In similar fashion, Singer answers the abstract ideals of Aaron Lipman with the terrible realities of history.

Toward the end of the novel, another discussion, which takes place in Mirale's apartment, centers on whether in the process of overthrowing the aristocrats one has the right to risk the lives of the innocent. Ezriel, who undoubtedly presents Singer's own view, says that this would be a crime. But all the others, especially Lipman and Mirale, oppose Ezriel and portray him as a precious innocent who " 'would like to have freedom brought

in on a silver tray with a lace doilie on it' " (329). The
discussion drags on and neither side budges. The next day
a bomb is thrown at Alexander II; and inevitably, at least
in Jewish history, the search for scapegoats begins. Pogroms break out in Poland and Russia. The father of
Mirale and Ezriel is beaten in the streets of Warsaw.
Twenty-two Jews, assaulted by an anti-Semitic gang, are
taken to the hospital. In Kiev the persecution is particu-
larly brutal and, suddenly, a number of Jewish intellectuals, who the day before had preached assimilation and
world Communism, become painfully conscious of their
Jewishness:

> It was the shaven ones, who emulated the Gentiles
> and spoke their language, who cried out in protest.
> In Kiev, as the Jews in the synagogue were mourning
> the victims of the pogroms, a group of Jewish uni-
> versity students entered. One of them, Alenikov, ran
> up to the reading desk and called out: "We are your
> brothers! We are Jews like you! We regret we tried
> to be Russians. The events of the past weeks—the
> pogroms in Elisavetgrad, in Balta, and here in Kiev—
> have opened our eyes. We've made a tragic mistake.
> We are still Jews!" (388)

Back in Warsaw, Aaron Lipman burns his collection of
socialist and assimilationist literature, breaks off with
Mirale, who remains loyal to the socialists, and cries out:
" 'How can Jews be connected with a party that incited
massacres in the name of social justice?' "

What is Singer's own position? It is hard to tell because he characteristically is both for and against his
characters; his own position is both continuous and dis-
continuous with theirs. Through Aaron Lipman, Singer
is involved in the modern world's utopian dreams, but

he also stands apart by his recognition that historical persecution inevitably follows in the wake of enlightenment and assimilation. Through Alexander Zipkin, Singer is responsive to Zipkin's religious doubts—perhaps, even to his nihilism—but Singer also values the necessity of moral restraint and the religious illusions of Gimpel the Fool. Through Ezriel Badad, Singer is inclined toward psychoanalytic theory, but he also stubbornly practices his own demonology and values a morality that reflects the traditional yoking of madness and sinfulness. Perhaps the scene that best reflects Singer's straddling occurs earlier in the novel when Mirale visits her father, Rabbi Menachem Mendel.[6] For a change, they fight. And in the arguments each one presents, Singer sums up his own dualistic stand through the confrontation of the generations.

Rabbi Menachem Mendel tells Mirale:

"The Talmud states that if we go into a spice shop, pleasant odors cling to us, but if we go into a tannery, we come out stinking. One is easily trapped by the words of heretics. Who are these contemporary philosophers? A pack of murderers and lechers!"

"Many of them are decent people."

"The body is everything to them. If, as you say, there is no God, then it does not matter what one does. At first we are tempted by some minor sin, but as soon as that is committed, the will lures us into more serious evil. Without law and a judge to administer the law, there is no reason why one should restrain oneself. Why not give in to evil completely?"

"Because one is a human being."

"A human being! If one does not serve the Almighty, one is even less than an animal. Animals kill only for food; murderers enjoy killing." (250)

If Rabbi Menachen Mendel provides the commentary, Singer provides, in the spectrum of the assimilated Jews, the cases in point. But perhaps the most radical incarnation of what assimilation can lead to appears in the character of Count Lucian Jampolski.

Like Lord and Lady Pilitsky, Lucian is a grostesque example of unbridled freedom. Indeed, in *The Manor* he is the supreme example of the manner in which minor sins lead to major ones. Lucian begins as an adulterer, moves on to embezzlement and thievery, and ultimately becomes a murderer. In the process, he seduces his stepdaughter, proposes to have relations with more than one woman at the same time, joins a secret Polish anti-Semitic society, needs increasing doses of outrage to give him a sense that he is alive, and finally requires that his lovemaking be accompanied by flagellation and violence: "Thoughts of love and murder never left him. He became incapable of dealing with everyday matters. It was almost as if he had been swallowed up by his grandiose dreams" (365). Lucian's brutality, sexual pathology, and anti-Semitism are all correlated manifestations of the philosophy of everything being permitted. That he is a Gentile and not a Jew does not invalidate but confirms the arguments of Rabbi Menachem Mendel for, as Singer's parallels make quite clear, many of the assimilated Jews and even Calman Jacoby are muted versions of Lucian and thus on their way toward bestiality and conversion, the two ends being satanic versions of each other.

To counteract such ends, Singer employs two strategies. First, Singer recommends normal madness as an antidote to total madness. To Singer man is neither perfect nor perfectible. The normally mad endlessly face problems of good and evil. A moral man is not one free of doubts or secret satanic urges but one who through faith, scepticism, or luck abstains from immorality. Above all, by portraying the destructive and reductive excesses of those who seek the peace and freedom of singular extremism, Singer negatively points to the wisdom of eternal tension. The same negative approach informs Singer's second strategy. Politically and religiously, his ultimate positions in *The Manor* tend, like the Ten Commandments, to be presented as a series of negatives. As such, his sceptical injunctions are meant to encumber the normally mad from becoming completely mad. Specifically, Singer's "thou salt nots" can be summarized by the following sceptical imperatives: reject any secular movement which claims to be messianic and incontestable; resist any idealogy which seeks to blur through propaganda or force the uniqueness of each people and self in order to legislate a nationalistic normalcy; oppose any political cause which preaches morality and seeks power to enforce that morality; suspect any system which fails to recognize man's destructiveness and imperfection and which, in its worship of progress, confuses evil with social ills and blinds itself to the regressive patterns of history; resist any permissive or heroic doctrine which glorifies the alienation of the individual from his communal roots and which is indiscriminate of the fate of the innocent; and above all, be suspicious of any cause which separates man from the necessary restraint and promise of his total identity, the Jew from his otherness in history and God.

V

The Talmud states that at first sin is a stranger, then a friend, and finally a master. That tripartite talmudic pattern describes the progression of nearly all the wayward Jews and Gentiles in *The Manor*. The pattern also provides the central organizational design of the entire novel as well as the means to pick up the thread of Calman Jacoby's story and his difference.

The Manor is divided into three main sections. Each one is tied to a particular Jewish festival and therefore to both the biblical and historical progress of the Household of Israel and the Jacoby family. Part One concludes on the festival of Purim which commemorates the saving of the Jewish people from the extermination planned by Haman. But as the novel indicates, the enemy is within as well as without. The Hamans and Hitlers of history have secret allies in Jews who decide not to be Jews. Near the end of Part One and just before Purim, Miriam Lieba elopes with Count Lucian and converts to Christianity. Calman Jacoby rends his clothes and recites the memorial service for the dead.

In Part Two, Calman Jacoby, although he does not become an apostate, nearly surrenders his Jewishness to Esau by marrying Clara Kaminer. However, toward the end of the second part, Calman divorces Clara, turns over all his business interests to Mayer Joel, and journeys to Marshinov. He arrives there in time for the celebration of Rosh Hashanah which marks the beginning of the Jewish New Year and the period of atonement.

At the end of the novel, Calman Jacoby returns to the beginning of the novel. He has moved out of the manor and now is living in the same house he had lived in with his first wife. In a separate room set aside for prayer, Calman has placed a Holy Ark, a Torah scroll, volumes of the Mishnah and the Talmud, and a Menorah. As the novel ends, Calman is meditating on a passage from the Mishnah dealing with the Day of Atonement. Chanting the passage in the traditional manner, Calman drifts back in time to the Bible and discovers there the same mixture of good and evil, freedom and persecution, belief and idolatry that he finds in himself, his family, and his times. But the difference is that there the contraries are presented together, not as mutually exclusive, and that the rabbinic sages eternally point "to what was right and what was wrong, what was pure and impure." Examining the arguments of the sages, Calman finds that they

> make him a kind of partner in sharing the Torah's treasures. Among these shelves of sacred books, Calman felt protected. Over each volume hovered the soul of its author. In this place, God watched over him. (442)

Following the arc created by the structure of the work, Calman spatially journeys from The Sands to the manor and back to The Sands; economically, from poverty to wealth and back to poverty; religiously, from slavery to false freedom and back to slavery; historically, from the patriachial Jacob to the sadistic Esau and back to the birthright of Jacob. To be sure, Calman Jacoby is not Singer's most sophisticated hero and his final faith and return are presented without his characteristic scepticism. Nevertheless, Calman Jacoby's journey of the prodigal son reaches out to complexity through the reverberating spectrums of his daughters and sons-in-law. Moreover, the tripartite form of the novel governs and informs Singer's equally complex structural journey to and through the modern world and concludes with a similar return to a concept of history that is as timeless as the Jewish festivals that serve as his eternal calendar and chronology.

Notes

1. *The Manor* was originally written between 1953 and 1955 and appeared in serial form in the *Forward*.
2. Building upon the basic study of this area by Montagu F. Modder, Edgar Rosenberg recently documented, especially in his third chapter, the emergence of portraits of saintly Jews in fiction (*From Shylock to Svengali: Jewish Stereotypes in English Fiction* [Stanford, 1960], pp. 39–72).
3. In the second volume, to be entitled *The Estate,* Ezriel Badad is to be given the same central role that Asa Heshel performed in *The Family Moskat.*
4. In "Pigeons," which appeared in *Esquire* in August, 1967, the leading character concludes that only the wicked make history. In *The Manor* only the divergent occupy fiction. Mayer Joel follows the traditional Orthodoxy of his father and thus is a minor character in a novel that stresses dislocation.
5. In "The Letter Writer," Singer sums up the common extremisms of fanatics and blasphemers:

> Herman Gombiner had long ago arrived at the conclusion that modern man was as fanatic in his non-belief as ancient man had been in his faith. The rationalism of the present generation was in itself an example of pre-conceived ideas. Communism, psychoanalysis, fascism and radicalism were the shibboleths of the twentieth century.

6. Recollections of his father's views in both interviews and *In My Father's Court* suggest that the words of Rabbi Menachem Mendel are really those of Singer's father, Rabbi Pinchos-Mendel.

MRS. ALVING: *I am half inclined to think we are all ghosts,*
Mr. Manders. It is not only what we have inherited from
our fathers and mothers that exists again in us, but all
sorts of dead beliefs. . . . we can never be rid of them.
. . . There must be ghosts all over the world.
—————Henrik Ibsen, *Ghosts*

"What an overwhelming lesson [God provides] to all artists!
Be not afraid of absurdity; do not shrink from the fantastic.
Within a dilemma, choose the most unheard-of, the most dan-
gerous solution. Be brave, be brave!"
—————Isak Dinesen, *Seven Gothic Tales*

9.

The Aesthetics of the Eternal Past

By all the standards of literature, Isaac Bashevis
Singer is a ghost and his work should not exist, let alone
be engaging. First, he is a living anachronism. He writes
in a language that is supposed to be dying if not already
dead. Singer sums up his own dislocation:

> The Yiddish writer not only belongs to a minority,
> but he is a minority within a minority. He is a para-
> dox to his own people. Theoretically, a Yiddish writer
> is dead; he moves around like one of my own phan-
> toms, a corpse who either ignores death, or is not yet
> aware of it.[1]

A sea serpent . . . does not think of itself as a mon-
ster. Nor does it worry that according to the zoologist,
it is nothing more than a legend. It is not easy to speak
a "freakish" language, to belong to an exceptional

people, and to be part of a literature that is openly suspect. I sometimes dread the professor who, after examining me to detect what specimen I am, will pronounce me a prehistoric animal or one of evolution's embarassing slips.[2]

Then, too, Singer is denied the consolation of keeping company with other Yiddish ghosts; his treatment of demonology precludes linking him with the generally more benevolent, earlier Yiddish tradition of Mendele Mocher Sforim, I. L. Peretz, and Sholem Aleichem.[3] Again he is aware of his apartness: "No other Yiddish writer writes about devils—or when they do, then only sceptically. . . . If I write about a devil, I treat him as though he exists; that's why I'm more a mystical than a symbolic writer." [4]

Above all, Singer seems to be equally out of place in modern or American times and terms. He is not familiar with the works of the so-called Jewish-American writers. Indeed, his own definition of what constitutes a Jewish writer would exclude nearly all of them from the group.[5] His isolation from even these contemporaries recently was confirmed by Irving Malin who in his book-length examination of Jewish-American writers did not deal with any of Singer's works.[6] Nor is Singer less of an anomaly when one turns from his situation to his substance as a writer. Most of his novels and stories are geographically removed from these shores by their eastern European settings and are chronologically distant by one to three centuries. Thus, although Singer arrived here in 1935, the bulk of his work evidences no sustained desire to portray the American experience or join the twentieth century (the two may be synonomous in his mind). But when *Short Friday and Other Stories* appeared in 1964, a change seemed to be in the offing. Two stories were set in America: one in Miami Beach, the other in the Brownsville section of Brooklyn. And on these two tales hangs a crucial distinction.

It would appear that these two American-based stories at last put Singer in American literature. The supposition is further supported by two earlier works, *Shadows on the Hudson* and *A Ship to America,* which deal with American characters and situations and which appeared serially in the *Forward* in 1957 and 1958, respectively; and by the recent collection of short stories, *The Séance and Other Stories,* many of which, including the title story, are set in this country and century. However, the real novelty of all these works is not their American settings and characters, but rather the fact that what takes place in Miami and Brooklyn is as nightmarish, demonical, and cosmic as what occurs in Lashnik, Frampol, and Tishevitz. Suddenly, we discover an old Polish crone weaving spells in eighteenth century Poland reappearing as a Cuban hag attempting to seduce and bedevil a man who has come to Miami to relieve his asthma. A noisy, *heimish* wedding in Brownsville provides the occasion for the same reunion of lovers separated by the Nazis as it does for those separated by seventeenth-century pogroms. The transmigrated sexuality of Reb Itche of "The Fast" is reproduced in an apartment on Central Park West; Dr. Gombiner of "The Séance" believes he sees the silhouette of his dead mistress in the bathroom. In "The Lecture," a Yiddish writer journeys to Montreal to deliver a talk and there meets an old cripple and her daughter who are the living incarnations of the author's Poland and of the worst crisis in his life. No, if Singer is here in America, he is here only in body, not in spirit.

Composing his first novel in the early thirties in Warsaw, Singer writes about the seventeenth century. Writing *The Manor* in the early sixties in New York, he hearkens back to the nineteenth century. No matter where Singer actually is, he is somewhere else in his fiction. No matter what the chronological setting of his stories, they ultimately give way to an earlier time. In Singer's vision, place is the plaything of his absolute tyrant, time. Setting is merely the stuff time needs for incarnation, just as a body is what a transmigrated soul requires to reenter space. The Proustian remembrance of things past is presented by Singer with a vengeance: his transmigration is a passport to remembrance of all things past.

To Singer nothing is old and nothing is new. The Torah is not dead because it is dated, any more than the twentieth century is alive because it is current. Nor are these mere poses. He is not engaged in a sentimental journey back to the past in order to instruct modern readers on the pieties of historical and biblical patriarchs. Characteristically, his rabbis are not saints and his favorite biblical story is that of Jacob supplanting Esau. Nor is Singer a quaint, designing exotic who situates himself in the past or juggles the present so that he may slyly and opportunistically move toward or adjust to the modern world or reader. His devils are real and terrifying, not symbols tricked out for easy allegorization or fashionable assimilation.

Clearly, to be heartened by Singer's shift to American settings and characters is to miss the tyrannical force of a vision which burns away the surface differences of Miami, Brownsville, New York, and Montreal to reveal the substance of seventeenth-century Poland. To rapidly modernize or universalize his dislocation [7] is to mute his obsessive, sometimes hysterical, preoccupation with a past that is so vital and durable that it not only brings the

dead back to life, but also makes them seem more alive
than those who really are. Indeed, Singer's entire strategy
is one of reversal. Far from moving toward or accommodating himself to the modern reader, he draws the reader
to him. Writers who cherish place are always aware of
surface differences and are adept at adjustments. Writers,
like Singer, who revere only time and are aware only of
what lasts after loss, stubbornly stand their ground. Ghosts
and sea serpents do not attract but repel; or, perhaps, they
attract because they repel. Singer's sorcery involves the
reader in a journey of progressive regression, nicely described by Arthur R. Gold in his review of *Short Friday*.
Commenting on the protagonist of "A Wedding in
Brownsville," Gold says,

> As his uncertainty becomes ours, we find ourselves
> sharing a mood in which these stories as a whole
> were probably conceived: we become unwilling to
> accept . . . the deadness of death; we choose to live
> in uncertainty if uncertainty holds the promise of a
> live encounter with beloved shades.[8]

In Singer's vision the past is never past. His fictional
world is so jammed with the dead that there does not
appear to be any room for the living. Ghosts and demons
so clutter the atmosphere with their epic machinery that
they obscure the heavens and, in mock-heroic fashion, be-
little the progress and pretensions of man. In one short
story, a man is called back from the grave by the shrewish
hysteria of his grieving wife; but he is so altered on his
unnatural return that the story concludes by affirming
the value of death. In another tale, two transmigrated
corpses are tempted into marriage by Satan and their
wedding night becomes a harrowing journey into a black

void; in the process, Singer uncharitably suggests this happens to the living as well. A pious woman who has died, but left a great deal of her good work undone, becomes a dybbuk and possesses, without resistance, the body of a young girl; and, indeed, through her adds to her saintly reputation. But to describe Singer's trafficking with the dead is not to explain its power or to distinguish its function from that of other authors who have served as receptacles of the past. What is special as well as justifiable about Singer's revival of the dead and Satan? Characteristically with Singer, the answers are both particular and Jewish as well as general and literary.

I

The two overriding biblical promises to the Jews were those of a homeland and of the Messiah. But even in biblical times essential Jewish history was that of exile; and subsequent history did not bring fulfillment. As a result, for nearly five thousand years there was nothing to arrest the intrusion of the past into the present. For centuries every newly born Jew was potentially a biblical Jew, for the original promise, still unrealized, was therefore still available. His hearkening back to biblical origins and promises became intertwined with the similar yearnings of all previous generations and served as the binder of collective identity. Then, too, because the Jewish Messiah had not yet come, the notion of final redemption became interlaced with that of a final homeland, and the confluence of both imparted to history the potential of biblical extension and revelation. And history, burdened with biblical promise and proximity, is Singer's recurrent source of the total past.

The ghosts of the past recover for Singer not just

chronological but Jewish continuity: "you cannot ignore history. The past is as alive as the present." Commenting on the experience of living in Bilgoray which was insulated from the modern world, Singer said, "In this world of old Jewishness I found a spiritual treasure trove. I had a chance to see our past as it really was. Time seemed to flow backward. I lived Jewish history" (290). To live Jewish history means to live with the reality of ghosts and to shackle personal identity to that of communal identity. It is the collective version of the psychological process of acknowledging parental involvement and determinism. In short, Singer's turning to the past is, from the Jewish point of view, not a form of retreat but a form of return.

And now for the general and literary justification. As already noted, the journey of the prodigal son or fool structures Singer's work. Indeed, the same pattern informs his own development and that of his biographical surrogates. Specifically, the journey follows the tripartite arc of the family chronicle. Raised in a traditional household, Singer in his youth yearned to break out of the tight circle of Orthodoxy and the ghetto. He eagerly read and was intoxicated by secular philosophy and literature, although he gradually discovered that the eternal questions still remain unanswered. He encountered a myriad of utopian movements, each claiming to have the key to heaven on earth. But as the heavens of Communism, Bundism, and Yiddishism, etc. turned out to be less than heavenly, and in a few instances hellish, Singer turned his awareness of Jewish messianic excesses to their modern substitutive counterparts. In the process, he discovered that the multiple messianic alternatives were so absolutist or relativistic that no morality or respectible terminus seemed possible: Spinozaism led to an affirmation of the Nazis; Communism preached world brotherhood and continued the pogroms; Yiddishism promised rebirth but hastened assimilation. Singer began to question whether the causes of modern freedom and liberality did not, in fact, represent a greater narrowness and slavery than what he had left behind. His scepticism, which originally had enabled him to free himself from the slavery of Orthodoxy, now served to free him from the freedom of the Jewish Enlightenment. Now free, he gradually began to experience the tug of the past and exercised his freedom by choosing to become a slave.

But the slavery is to totality. The prodigal son returns home but as a transmigrated soul. Singer does not confess his sins and embrace without reservation his father's Orthodoxy. He has seen too much of the modern world and probed too deeply the messianic overreaching of both Judaism and modern religions of humanity to forsake his insights. To be sure, in his memoirs and in his fiction, Singer acknowledges the wisdom of his father's traditionalism, but at the same time he is not blind to the excesses it also contains. In other words, Singer's scepticism works both ways. He looks at the past with a modern eye at the same time that he adopts traditional optics to scrutinize modernity. But he finally chooses the past as his basic setting because there, at least, totality is approximated. The past contains both the norm and the excess, both belief and divergence, both the ancient and the modern. To Singer truth is totality. And the sign of truth is tension—the intellectual tension born of converging duality—the artistic tension born of maximum form and time. Above all, the comprehensive tension he rediscovered in Bilgoray gave way to the ultimate past of the Torah and its classic duality of the Ten Commandments and the Golden Calf. If history is an extension of the Bible, then history for him becomes the stepping-stone to myth and the eternal drama of slavery and freedom.

Singer's choice of the past as his basic chronology represents his ultimate search for biblical and mystical proximity. Singer's strategy is that of compulsive compromise. He adjusts his search for the timeless by settling for periods and settings in which time exists, as it were, in slow motion. The *shtetl* is his pivot. Intact enough to serve as a faithful receptacle of the ancient, it, also, as a ghetto of exile, was peripherally edged and in touch with the modern. Krochmalna Street was in the Jewish ghetto, but a few blocks away flowed the plurality of modern Warsaw. To journey all the way back to the Bible would have transformed him into an historical novelist rather than a novelist of history. It would have made him a scholar of a dead past rather than an imaginative artist of one that by virtue of chronological proximity is not that past. Nor could he set his works in modern times and employ his traditional insights, in the manner of a rabbinic chorus, without running the risk of being labeled a fanatic or heavy-handed moralist. For the biblical and the timeless to emerge with any authenticity, they had to stand both the test of time and of this world, but in a world that was not too close or far from contemporary experience. Indeed, Singer's chronological positioning of the *shtetl* between the ancient and the modern finds its humanistic counterpart in man's locating himself properly on a vertical chain of being. Man finds his otherness reflected neither in angels who are inferior to God, nor in animals who are inferior to man, but in God who in his proximity to and difference from man provides the near and far of human nature. In short, Singer's past serves as his temporal version of the eternal point of view.

The characteristic arc of Singer's vision is thus not accommodating but separative—perhaps as a way of being accommodating. Like John Milton, he asserts an eternal past. Moreover, he does so in the same way, namely, by demonstrating that if a story is old enough, it partakes of what is both eternally old and new. Ted Hughes noted: "His work is not discursive, or even primarily documentary, but revelation. . . ." [9] And Dan Jacobson points to the power of transmigrated identification: "To our surprise, we find that we are more like these vanished people than we have ever guessed; and that their lost world, being so fully human, is, after all, contiguous with the one we already know." [10] Singer backs away from the modern world not so that he may leave it but so that he may have it encounter its shadow. He arranges a chronological compromise so that his fiction may serve as an historical crucible for the meeting of the living and the dead, the modern and the ancient. In the final analysis, he does not resurrect the dead or the Devil—readers do. By fleshing the word, readers give life to the dead and tap the enduring roots of legend. Alfred Kazin rightly finds in Singer's work the "power of literature to transform experience into myth, to give to the unrecoverable, the unbelievable past, its present status as legend." [11]

II

It is at this point that perhaps a final assessment of Singer's demonism as well as his artistic creed is both possible and meaningful. And, perhaps, the first matter to note is the relationship between Satan and the use of the past. Singer respects verisimilitude: his demons initially operate in superstitious times and villages and are sustained by characters who believe in the Evil Eye. But because in the process the Devil appears with a power and veracity that transcends the confines of verisimiltude, he acquires reality by granting it also to the past to which he was apparently restricted. In other words, the revival of Satan partakes of Singer's revival of the dead; as the Devil acquires power, so does the past. Satan has other than a chronological or historical role to play. Indeed, in his vision the Devil is forced to be an Atlas.

Singer is both a Devil's advocate and he is not; Satan is a necessary but partial means to totality. The Devil is never an end in himself, except to those whose presumption matches his. At best, he is means to a hidden end. Just as history serves as the backdoor to myth, so Satan serves to suggest his cosmic alternative. The Devil is the articulate, accessible, and tangible alter ego of a reticent, removed, and invisible God. Theologically and artistically, Satan is necessary to suggest the outline of the ultimate "unsculptured image" and to provide artistic concreteness for a vision that in part respects the injunction against graven images. Psychologically and artistically, the Devil also is necessary both to credit and to release another secret sharer—man's secret and unconscious desires. In other words, demonology provides the base not the end of Singer's quest for totality, as well as the means not the conclusion of Singer's theology and psychology. The unconscious and the cosmic are not alternatives but avenues to each other. The alignment of the interior life with that of the metaphysical prepares for the ultimate convergence of demonic and divine spheres.

In literary terms, Singer's use of Satan makes him a gothic writer. But to regard the gothic tale as merely a clumsy anticipation of Freud is to obscure the fact that the form continues to thrive after Freud. Even more important, he does not so much ignore or devalue modern psychology as parallel it with a demonology that insists on its own integrity and autonomy. That his gothic results may be comprehensible in psychological terms is to him not a sign that he has confirmed Freud but that his own way is equally valid and viable.[12] Above all, he employs Satan not to skirt but to revive moral choice. Satan is essentially man's shadow. Whatever substance he acquires is possible only with the consent of the original. In other words, the effectiveness of the Devil is contingent upon the agreement and the collusion of man's secret desires. Satan is a dream of wish fulfillment in the form of a temptation. As a result, far from serving as a scapegoat to exonerate man of responsibility, Satan is employed to bring renewed dread and urgency to moral dilemmas and to make personal choice a mode of self-creation or of self-destruction. Singer's Satan thus serves not only to vex man, but also to contribute to his continued vital existence.

Satan's temptations are legion: he is mortality dressed in the garb of immortality; he is license parading as freedom; his mission is to persuade the soul that it is the body.[13] But to Singer the essence of Satan's temptation— and, at this point, his psychology becomes theology—is to offer clarity. Both Singer and Satan realize that Judaism's dualistic center is so unrelieved and, as long as man lives, so unrelievable that many try to escape to the circumference. Satan always seeks to persuade man to get off the tightrope for the more solid footing of extremism. On that periphery, Satan spreads his wares and encourages man to take his pick of an infinite number of absolutist alternatives: Sabbatai Z'vi, Communism, Bundism, messiahship, etc—any will do as an antidote to endless duality and fearful symmetry. The clarity of extremism makes man singular and absolves him of the endless process of making and remaking the self. Satan argues that the past is dead and

Orthodoxy backward and, consequently, identity is an individual not a communal matter. Above all, Satan tries to persuade man either that he is self-sufficient and no longer needs God or that God is self-indulgent and no longer needs man. In other words, Satan is a straddler—he closes all the gaps Singer insists are necessary both for existence and art. Indeed, in his passion for explication, especially of the inexplicable, Satan is the eternal critic of God's artistry.

Singer gives life to the Devil in order to wrestle with him, for without tension there is no possibility of totality. His use of demonology for maximum ends also sets him apart from the work of most modern authors who applaud the demonic. The customary journey of the hero of alienation is from the center to the periphery. The heart of heroism is transcendence. Singer reverses the journey. His hero moves from the periphery to the center. The heart of Judaism is convergence. True alienation requires a hero to be both apart from and involved in what alienates him. To be sure, Satan glorifies the role of the lone wolf—a Steppenwolf perhaps—but, as Singer indicates in "Zeidlus the Pope," the temptation of such heroic singularity is a rehearsal for the temptation of conversion. And for Singer that results in irrecoverable and final alienation, for the convert is dead as a Jew.

Singer's theological answer to the Devil is not to deny his existence but, on the contrary, to support it as the necessary half of a total whole. Singer seeks to align God and the Devil, the study house and the brothel—indeed, all opposites—so that they become not enemies but allies, not alternatives but versions of each other. The result is a fusion of religion and psychology—a metapsychology—which informs all Singer's works and his biography as well. His father was a Hasid and a follower of wonderworking

rabbis. His mother was a rationalist. Singer takes after both. His heart inhabits the celestial and demonic realms of the Cabala; his mind is anchored to the earth and Maimonides. The result is a sceptical fidelity to everything freakish and miraculous and a guarded reverence for everything terrestrial and sensible. The excesses that have been attributed to Singer are not his but those of his characters. Violating his principle of convergence, those who exclusively ascend to heaven become inhuman; those who exclusively turn to the earth become bestial. Up and down turn out to be the same because the Devil occupies both extremes of the spectrum.

As half of a whole, Satan is a necessary evil. He thus compels choice and serves as a partner in sustaining a total cosmos. When Satan makes his half the whole, he is more evil than necessary. The cosmos then is contracted to the world, and time and space to the here or now. Extremists regard the world as nothing or everything, for evil is excess. Singer counters with the balance of Gimpel the Fool: "No doubt the world is entirely an imaginary world, but it is only once removed from the true world" (21). But perhaps his most powerful and unexpected reply to Satan as critic emerges in his notion of God as the supreme artist.

III

In many ways, *The Magician of Lublin* is Singer's *Künstlerroman* and contains the essence of his aesthetic position.[14] Tempted by Satan, Yasha the Magician steps off the tightrope of duality in order to pursue a life and art of singular self-satisfaction and assimilation. By the end of the novel, Yasha ends his life of personal and artistic promiscuity by entombing himself in a brick house as a form of penance. While in that prison, Yasha, reviewing

his life, broods on the value of restraint, both ethical and artistic, and in the process comes upon the following from the Cabala: "evil was merely God's diminishing of Himself to create the world, so that He might be called Creator and have mercy toward His creatures" (228).

Contemplating this passage, Yasha, for the first time, becomes aware that morality and aesthetics are one and for God the creative act is not solely an act of expression but also an act of inhibition. In creation, God willingly imprisons part of His being and willfully limits His immortal extent. Had He not, He would have created a world so crowded with His being that it would have been finished or perfected before it was born. If the world were a complete reflection of God, it would be a dead world as we know life to be; and there would be no room for man, let alone his art. But by withholding His fullness, God imparted to creation and especially to man the capacity to create and to fulfill himself and his world. In other words, God's initial act of creation was not a terminal act; His art is not a product but a process. God finds his eternal extension in man's history and art.

Although expression and inhibition are intended ideally to operate together in tension, and although God provides the supreme example for the convergence of contraries, more often than not, and especially in this world, that harmonious discord frequently appears as two opposing halves. Thus, the classic reticence of the Jewish God reflects the principle of inhibition whereas Satan's endorsement of the picaresque quest for Faustian self-realization mirrors the principle of expression. God, who is One, cherishes the constancy of the soul and jealously requires one wife, one Lord. The Devil, who is legion, applauds the variety of the body and urges the multiplicity of secularity and the secularity of multiplicity. Nevertheless, even the existence of a choice between the two is a gift of God's diminishing of Himself, for by restraining His omnipotence, He makes possible man's free will. Above all, by withholding His full identity, He makes necessary man's.

To Singer, God is the eternal artist; the Devil is the eternal critic. God's creative principles are built into creation because He means His art to last—through time. But He is a subtle artist. He does not intrude into His creation but hides His face in nature and history. God through Moses wrote the Torah; man composed the commentaries. There are, according to Singer, only "God seekers; no God finders." The mortal artist also should be unobtrusive; he should not tamper with his tale or explain his characters. Singer maintains "commentary is not too good for writing . . . facts never become obsolete, and commentary is always obsolete. This I consider an iron principle of literature which will remain forever." [15] In short, a writer must not serve food already chewed or digested; he must present experience not symbols of experience: "I feel symbolism should come out of the whole work; I don't approve of those people with whom on the first page there's already a symbol." [16]

To Singer a symbol cannot be stated but only generated; it cannot be fixed from without but must emanate from within. In addition, all genuine symbols are not specific but comprehensive; they are hidden binders that patiently gather their force and meaning behind a work and emerge, if they do, only coincidentally with its collective impact. Fictionists who see symbols before they see men and offer psychological explanations for irremedial dilemmas are to Singer opaque. They stand between the material and the reader, always tampering with and interpreting the former; and helping and thereby insulting and cheating the latter. But genuine storytellers are always transparent; in Singer's favorite phrase for the artist and God, they see but are not seen. The reverence an artist extends to his characters is the same that God extends to His creation—the dignity of a separate life. A character must stand by himself and not be propped by the commentary of his creator. As noted in *The Slave,* God speaks through deeds; the mortal artist through facts. The symbol, if it appears, must resemble God's face hiding behind creation, for a symbol is ultimately grounded in the eternal.

All this does not mean that Singer minimizes the conscious shaping of form. On the contrary, he laments the modern trend, represented by Pinter and others, to destroy all illusion and to present characters "with their insides spilling all over the stage." Again, Singer has recourse to God's example: "God gave everything a covering —rinds for oranges, skins for bananas, flesh for man. He did so to give us some peace from turmoil. Think of all that is going on in the human body! If it were not covered, we would be disturbed endlessly by all that activity. So it is with art." For Singer, to rend form in tatters in order to release the real truth results not in more reality, as it were, but in less; for covering does not merely contain but shapes content. To sever the mysterious bond between illusion and reality is to deny illusion a vital function in reality and to deny reality its body in illusion. Aggressive, outrageous art is to Singer essentially autopsy; and autopsies are performed only on dead men by artists who do not believe in ghosts or the afterlife.

Above all, Singer applies God's principles of creation to the artist with this difference: that in place of God's relationship with man, the mortal artist maintains a relationship with the reader. The writer who expresses all and witholds nothing dispossesses the reader. The result is a "dead" art in the sense that no room is left for the "life" of the reader. Indeed, Singer maintains that a corrupt partnership frequently exists between a lazy writer and a lazy reader. The lazy writer presents a character and rapidly tags him as malicious. The lazy reader thanks the author for being a commentator and doing the reader's work. A steady calvacade of pegged characters and explicit symbols pass before the reader's eye and he is able to rest content in his inertia. Such a writer, who is without wonder at creation and without reverence for its creatures, inevitably reveals the wisdom of the Second Commandment. As Singer noted, " 'Thou shalt not make unto thee a graven image' . . . is actually based on statistics. The odds are good that a poor sculptor will carve an idol." [17] Above all, the writer who fails to rely on the reader loses a valuable ally in facing the inevitable problem of artistic frustration.

Because no artist, not even God, can ever overcome the limits of language and material, and because no writer therefore can fully embody his vision with perfection, he faces, according to Singer, one of two choices. He either may be obsessed more by his failure to render fully his vision or be obsessed more by his vision than his failure to render it. In the former case, perfection and precision compel the artist to pursue alternatives. He knowingly or unknowingly may scale down the range and difficulty of his vision so as to bring it more in line with his ability to express it perfectly. Or he may bridge the gaps between his initial concept and its embodiment by controlling the interpretation of his characters and situations; he may write both story and commentary. The result is an art sealed in upon itself; it is both literature and criticism.[18] Its control is total, its complexity narcissistic or parasitic. On the other hand, the artist who cherishes his vision more than

his failure to render it fully and who sees in the resistance
of language and form the resistance of existence itself has
the opportunity to transform his obstacle into an opportunity. Specifically, he consciously inhibits and even mars
his work so that the reader can hopefully do what he cannot—perfect and redeem what is imperfect. To Singer the
test of talent is what it can withhold, just as the test of
God's power is what He decides not to do. Like the Ten
Commandments, Singer's works assert their meaning
through negatives. As an artist, he seeks to give maximum
expression to inhibition.

Singer's aesthetics thus yields and describes an art that
regards oddity as the true face of normalcy and pursues the
minimum as a way of gambling for the maximum. Part of
that gamble involves being an old-fashioned storyteller
and employing the strategy of protective distance. He approaches the world from afar—from the recesses of the
past and from beyond the grave. His supernatural world
seems insulated from modern apparatuses of analysis; his
characters are not buttressed by detailed motivations nor
are his devils tamed with psychological plausibility. His
entire approach and journey are so circuitous and incredi-
ble as to be initially unthreatening. But then the artistic
sorcery takes hold and the contraries begin to grip. The
distant and the exotic rapidly become the near and the
familiar; Satan appears to know us as well as a psychiatrist
knows his patients; the personality begins to recover its
hidden shadow or secret sharer; above all, the invitation
of inhibited art is taken up by the reader, and the minimum, incomplete vision is fleshed to fullness through response. By building into the structure of his art the Jewish
version of the prodigal son, Singer has encouraged his
readers—Jewish and not—to undertake a similar journey
of historical and biblical transmigration. In the process,

the prodigal, like Singer, discovers that his future is his past. Through his vision of the eternal past, Singer also has become typical of the modern writer to whom the longest way round is the shortest way home. Through his aesthetics of the eternal past, Singer is representative of the Jewish writer to whom the oblique and the sensational are the most powerful avenues to the center and to the true.

Notes

1. "A Phantom of Delight," *Herald Tribune Book Week* (July 4, 1965), Nevertheless, Singer remains hopeful about the future of Yiddish and, therefore, perhaps his Yiddish ghosts:

> In our history, between being sick and dying is always a long way. I admit that Yiddish is sick. It has many troubles. But I just don't believe that it will die. It may have the same lot as Hebrew. It will be for a time, perhaps, a language of the book rather than a spoken language. But it will revive, because nothing really dies in our history.

Quoted in "A Conversation with Isaac Bashevis Singer," *The Eternal Light*, 6. Finally, in this connection, a recent ironic note: In Singer's short story, "The Lecture" (1967), the leading character, who is an author, journeys to Montreal to deliver a talk on the promising future of Yiddish. Significantly, he loses the manuscript of his lecture.

2. *Ibid.*, p. 7.

3. This is a standard observation and yet it is not completely accurate. There are many folk and supernatural elements in Yiddish literature (see Sholem Aleichem's "The Clock," for example); and Singer, after all, did not invent the notion of the dybbuk. But even if it were possible to weave Singer into that earlier tradition, his inclusion would be resisted, as it already has been, by a number of Yiddishists. In particular, there is the strong and sometimes hysterical opposition of M. Z. Frank ("The Demon and the Earlock," *Conservative Judaism* [Fall, 1965], pp. 1–9); Jacob Glatstein ("The Fame of Bashevis Singer,"

Congress bi-Weekly [December 27, 1965], pp. 17–19); and
Charles Angoff ("Aspects of American Literature," *The Literary
Review*, X [Autumn, 1966], 5–17).

The reasons for questioning Singer as a Yiddish writer were
summed up by Milton Hindus in his review of the reissue of
The Family Moskat:

> It is said or implied that he concentrates his attention too
> much on repulsive Jewish types and practices, that the
> proportion of sensuality and superstition in his pages is
> offensive to the taste and that his attitude of detachment
> toward his material is utterly at variance with the warm-
> hearted humanitarinism characteristic of the fathers of Yid-
> dish literature, I. L. Peretz, Sholom Aleichem, and others.

Quoted from *New York Times Book Review* (March 14, 1965),
p. 4. Subsequently, Irving Howe added the following:

> It is hardly a secret that in the Yiddish literary world Singer
> is regarded with certain suspicion. . . . One reason is that
> "modernism"—which, as these people regard Singer, signi-
> fies a heavy stress upon sexuality, a concern for the irra-
> tional, expressionist distortions of character, and a seeming
> indifference to the humane ethic of Yiddishism. . . .

Quoted from "I. B. Singer, Storyteller," *Encounter*, XXVI
(March, 1966), 64–65. Finally, and elsewhere, Howe notes that
as a result of these practices Singer "seems to have cut himself
off from the mainstream of Yiddish literature" ("The Other
Singer," *Commentary*, 41 [March, 1966], 78).

Literary experience indicates that many crimes of critical ex-
clusion have been committed in the name of mainstream. One
need only recall the biases of Parrington in American literature,
the figurative deportation of Emily Bronte by F. R. Leavis because she did not fit into the great tradition of the novel, and
all the many authors who have been rediscovered after years of
being shunted to the side. As far as Jewish experience is concerned, there is the classic blindness of Graetz to mysticism,
which is matched by the subsequent resistence of Martin Buber
to rationalism. Above all, there is the matter of Jewish history.
The fact is there always has been diversity within Judaism, even
in biblical times. To be sure, the mutiplicity of forms and factions that followed the Jewish Enlightenment made the earlier
periods—Singer's favorite settings—appear relatively uniform

and even singular. But such, of course, was not the case, and Singer's renditions of divergence can be historically corroborated: God is One but His people are not. Besides, perhaps Singer even in negative fashion could not have written what he has without previous Yiddish writers, just as Joyce, for all his expiation and bitterness, could not have stayed with Ireland in his fiction without leaving it in fact.

4. Quoted from Brian Glanville, "An Interview with Isaac Bashevis Singer," *London Jewish Chronicle,* reprinted in *The Jewish News* (September 28, 1962), p. 28.

5. According to Singer, a Jewish writer must know both Yiddish and Hebrew, be saturated in Jewish history and traditions, and be familiar with both the Torah and the commentaries.

6. *Jews and Americans* (Carbondale, 1965). Malin is remedying that omission by serving as an editor for a collection of critical essays on Singer to appear soon.

7. So, it seems to me, Ted Hughes has done in "The Genius of Isaac Bashevis Singer," *New York Review of Books,* IV (April 22, 1965), 8–10.

8. "The Last of the Old-Time Demons," *Herald Tribune Book Week* (April 15, 1965), p. 2.

9. *Op. cit.,* p. 9.

10. "The Problem of Isaac Bashevis Singer," *Commentary,* 39 (February, 1965), 48–52.

11. "His Son, the Story-Teller," *Herald Tribune Book Week* (April 24, 1966), p. 10.

12. Michael Fixler neatly provides an example of the dovetailing:

> "The Black Wedding," for example, is obviously written with a fine understanding of sexual hysteria, but just as clearly the subjective hallucinations in the story of the girl read like a case of demonic possession. Here as in other instances in Singer's fiction, archaically primitive and sophisticated modern premises are presented as simultaneously plausible.

"The Redeemers: Themes in the Fiction of Isaac Bashevis Singer," *Kenyon Review,* XXVI (Spring, 1964), 374.

13. An excellent discussion of Satan's essential temptations appears in Charles Moeller's "Introduction" to a fascinating collection of essays, *Satan* (London, 1951); see especially, pp. xviii and xxiii. Singer, of course, is not alone in reviving the Devil. One could also mention Valéry (*Monsieur Teste*), Bernanos (*Soleil de Satan*), Charles du Bos (*Numquid et Tu*), C. S. Lewis (*The*

Screwtape Letters), Graham Greene (*Brighton Rock*), William Faulkner (*Sanctuary*), Flannery O'Connor (*Wise Blood*), and Nikos Kazantzakis (*The Greek Passion*). Indeed, it might not be farfetched to claim that, for all his Jewishness, Singer perhaps has more in common with the above authors than with the classical Yiddish trio.

14. The other main source of Singer's aesthetics is to be found in his essay, "Realism and Truth," *The Reconstructionist,* XXCIII (June 15, 1962), 5–9. Translated by Ada Auerbach Lappin.
15. "A Conversation with Isaac Bashevis Singer," p. 4.
16. Glanville, p. 28.
17. "Hagigah," [Festival of the Arts] *American Judaism* (Winter, 1966), p. 49.
18. Karl Shapiro, not incorrectly, charged T. S. Eliot with being a critic in disguise and for passing off *The Wasteland* as poetry ("T. S. Eliot: The Death of Literary Judgment," in *In Defense of Ignorance* [New York, 1960], p. 38).

Bibliography

I. Works

Because Singer writes in Yiddish, and because all his novels have appeared in serialized form, there are gaps in time—often considerable—between the date of original composition and the date of publication in either Yiddish or translation. As a result, the standard checkist of works in his case has had to be necessarily complicated by chronological annotations. Thus, although *Satan in Goray* appeared in translation five years after *The Family Moskat,* it was actually written seventeen years earlier and was first published in book form in 1935. To be sure, the chronological gaps of his other works are seldom so substantial, for the bulk of Singer's work to date was written in a twenty-five-year period from 1943 to 1968. Nevertheless, within that period a reasonably precise chronological order can be indicated, even for the short stories. For example, "Two Corpses Go Dancing," which appears in *The Séance and Other Stories* (1968), was first published in Yiddish in 1943 and in English, in *Commentary,* in 1965.

Where dates of original composition are indicated, they were provided or confirmed by Singer himself to the best of his ability. Often the dates of composition coincide with those of serialization for the simple reason that he had to write in that fashion. For access to unpublished or uncontracted material, especially revolving about the contents of *The Séance,* I am indebted to Singer and to Robert Giroux and Miss Lila Karpf of Farrar, Straus & Giroux.

THE NOVELS

Shoten an Goray [Satan in Goray]. Warsaw: Yiddish P.E.N Club, 1935. Composed in 1933 and serialized in *Globus* in 1934. Only novel not to be serialized in the *Jewish Daily Forward.*

Shoten an Goray un Anderer Dertailungen [Satan in Goray and Other Stories]. New York: Farlag Matones, 1943. First book published in the United States; also contains five stories listed and discussed under the section on *Short Stories.*

Shoten an Goray. Tel Aviv: Duir Co., Ltd., 1953. (In Hebrew.)

Satan in Goray. Jacob Sloan (trans.). New York: The Noonday Press, 1955.

Di Familie Mushkat [The Family Moskat]. New York: Morris S. Sklarsky, 1950. Vols. I and II. Composed and serialized in the *Forward* from 1945–1948.

The Family Moskat. Translated by A. H. Gross. New York: Alfred A. Knopf, 1950. One volume, slightly revised version, especially the ending, of the Yiddish edition published in the same year. First novel to appear in translation.

The Family Moskat. Translated by A. H. Gross. New York: Farrar, Straus & Giroux, 1965. A reissue of the 1950 English edition which was out of print.

Shadows on the Hudson. Written, according to Singer, in 1956 and serialized in the *Forward* in 1957. The novel is an interesting miscellany—a kind of transmigrated ship of fools. It deals with a group of people who come to the United States after the Second World War and settle in the Upper West Side of New York near the Hudson River (where Singer himself now lives). Singer presents their stories—mostly love stories— in the characteristic form of the past intruding into the present.

A Ship to America. Written, according to Singer, in 1957 and serialized in the *Forward* in 1958. Singer's most explicitly autobiographical novel, its hero is a writer who comes to New York from Poland, loses his passport, and is forced to live the underground life of an alien. On the eve of the Second World War, he returns to Poland to marry his beloved and to bring his son, by another woman, back to the United States.

The Magician of Lublin. Translated by Elaine Gottlieb and Joseph Singer. New York: The Noonday Press, 1960. Composed in 1958 and serialized in 1959 in the *Forward.* This is Singer's first novel to go from serialized to translated form without the intermediary of being published in Yiddish in book form, a pattern that characterizes the rest of his novels.

The Slave. Translated by I. B. Singer and Cecil Hemley. New York: Farrar, Straus & Giroux, 1962. Written in 1960 and serialized in the *Forward* in 1961.

The Manor. Translated by Elaine Gottlieb and Joseph Singer. New York: Farrar, Straus & Giroux, 1967. According to Singer, this work, totaling about two-thousand pages in manuscript, was begun in 1952 and completed in 1955. It appeared in serialized form from 1953 to 1955 in the *Forward.* Singer plans to amplify the present edition of *The Manor* and to reissue it along with the second volume, to be called *The Estate,* in the fall of 1969.

THE SHORT STORIES

Shoten an Goray un Anderer Dertailungen [Satan in Goray and Other Stories]. New York: Farlag Matones, 1943. Contains five stories: one, "The Jew from Babylon," Singer decided never to republish. The remaining four later appear in translated collections, as noted:

"Diary of One Not Born" in *Gimpel the Fool and Other Stories* (1957).

"The Destruction of Kreshev" in *The Spinoza of Market Street and Other Stories* (1961).

"Zeidlus the First," retitled "Zeidlus the Pope," in *Short Friday and Other Stories* (1964).

"Two Corpses Go Dancing" in *The Séance and Other Stories* (1968).

Gimpel the Fool and Other Stories. Translated by Saul Bellow, Martha Glicklich, Elaine Gottlieb, Nancy Gross, Norbert Guterman, Schlomo Katz, and Isaac Rosenfeld. New York: Noonday Press, 1957. First collection of short stories to appear in translation. Consists of twelve stories. With the exception of "The Old Man," which appeared in Yiddish in Warsaw in 1933, all were written in the United States over a fifteen-year period from 1942 to 1957. "The Diary of One Not Born" appeared in Yiddish in 1943. A number of the stories appeared in translation prior to their reissue in collected form. These include:

"Gimpel the Fool," *Partisan Review*, XX (May, 1953), 300–13.

"From the Diary of One Not Born," *Partisan Review*, XXI (March, 1954), 139–46.

"The Little Shoemakers," in *A Treasury of Yiddish Stories*. Eds. Irving Howe and Eliezer Greenberg. New York: The Viking Press, 1954.

"The Mirror" in *New World Writing*. New York: New American Library, 1955.

"Fire," *Commentary*, 24 (August, 1957), 135–38.

"The Gentleman from Cracow," *Commentary*, 24 (September, 1957) 231–39.

The Spinoza of Market Street. Translated by Joel Blocker, Shulamith Charney, June Ruth Flaum, Martha Glicklich, Mirra Ginsburg, Cecil Hemley, Gertrude Hirschler, and Elizabeth Pollet. New York: Farrar, Straus & Giroux, 1961. Consists of eleven stories. "The Destruction of Kreshev" appeared in Yiddish in 1943. The remaining stories range in date from 1958 to 1961 and include the following, which appeared in English prior to being reprinted:

"One Who Came Back," *Commentary*, 29 (February, 1960), 122–27.

"The Shadow of a Crib," *Mademoiselle*, 52 (March, 1961), 148–49.

"Shiddah and Kuziba," *Commentary*, 31 (March, 1961), 213–16.

"The Beggar Said So," *Esquire*, 55 (May, 1961), 79–81.

"The Spinoza of Market Street," *Esquire*, 56 (October, 1961), 144–48.

Gimpel Tam un Anderer Dertailungen [Gimpel the Fool and Other Stories]. New York: Central Yiddish Culture Organization ("CYCO"), 1963. This is Singer's last book published in Yiddish. It consists of twenty-four stories, but most of them were previously published either in Yiddish or translation. With the exception of "Kukeriku," which appears later in *The Séance* under the title "Cockadoodledoo," four of the stories appear later in the collection *Short Friday* (1964):

"The Faster" retitled "The Fast."

"The Last of the Demons" retitled "The Last Demon."

"On a Man I do Not Rely" retitled "I Place My Reliance on No Man."

"Big and Little."

Short Friday and Other Stories. Translated by Joel

Blocker, Chana Faerstein, Mirra Ginsburg, Martha
Glicklich, Cecil Hemley, Roger Klein, Marion Magid,
Elizabeth Pollet, Joseph Singer, and Ruth Whitman.
Consists of sixteen stories ranging in date, with the ex-
ceptions of "Zeidlus the Pope" (1943) and "Taibele and
Her Demon" (1953), from 1961 to 1964 and including
the following, which appeared in English prior to re-
publication:

"Taibele and Hurmizah," *Commentary*, 25 (February,
1953), 132–38. (Retitled "Taibele and Her Demon"
for collection.)

"Yentl the Yeshivah Boy," *Commentary*, 34 (September, 1962), 213–24.

"Alone," *Mademoiselle*, 55 (October, 1962), 118–19.

"A Wedding in Brownsville," *Commentary*, 38
(March, 1964), 43–49.

"Blood," *Harper's*, 229 (August, 1964), 87–94.

"Esther Kreindel the Second," *Saturday Evening
Post*, 237 (October 17, 1964), 50–52.

"Cunegunde," *Esquire* 62 (December, 1964), 135.

The Séance and Other Stories. Translated by Mirra Ginsburg, Elizabeth Pollet, Alizah Shevrin, Elizabeth Shub,
Alma Singer, Dorothea Straus, and Ruth Whitman.
Chronology is tightly established for this group because,
with the exception of "Two Corpses Go Dancing"
(1943), nearly all the stories appeared in translation
prior to being reissued. Ranging in date from 1964 to
1968, they include:

"Cockadoodledo," *Hadassah Magazine* (November,
1964), pp. 9, 27–28.

"Getzel the Monkey," *American Judaism* (Fall, 1964),
pp. 12–13, 53–56.

"The Séance," *Encounter*, XXV (July, 1965), pp. 14–
19.

"Two Corpses Go Dancing," *Commentary*, 40 (August, 1966), 45–49.

"The Warehouse," *Cavalier* (January, 1966), pp. 40, 88–90.

"The Boudoir," *Vogue* (April, 1966), pp. 148–49, 214.

"The Brooch," *Chicago Review*, XVIII (May, 1966), 7–17.

"The Parrot," *Harper's* (June, 1966), pp. 59–66.

"The Needle," *Cosmopolitan* (August, 1966), pp. 45–49.

"Pigeons," *Esquire* (August, 1967), pp. 76–79.

"Powers," *Harper's* (October, 1967), pp. 76–87.

"My Adventures as an Idealist," *Saturday Evening Post* (November 18, 1967), pp. 68–73. (Retitled "The Author" for the collection.)

"The Plagiarist," *Israel Magazine* (November, 1967), pp. 82–86.

"The Slaughterer," *New Yorker* (November 25, 1967), pp. 60–65.

"The Lecture," *Playboy* (December, 1967), pp. 184, 294–300.

"The Letter Writer," *New Yorker* (January, 13, 1968), pp. 26–54.

UNCOLLECTED SHORT STORIES ALREADY PUBLISHED

"Everlasting Joke," *Commentary*, 31 (May, 1961), 458–60.

"Sacrifice," *Harper's* (February, 1964), pp. 61–64.

"One Day of Happiness," *Cavalier* (September, 1965), pp. 19, 78–84.

"The Prodigal Fool," *Saturday Evening Post* (February 26, 1966), pp. 65–69.

"Dreamers," *The Reporter* (July 14, 1966), pp. 45–46.

"The Riddle," *Playboy* (January, 1967), pp. 164–66, 253–55.

"Match for a Princess," *Redbook,* 129 (August, 1967), 68–69.

MEMOIRS

Main Tatn's Bet-Din Shtub [My Father's Beth-Din Court]. New York: Kval Publishers, 1956.
In My Father's Court. Translated by Channah Kleinerman-Goldstein, Elaine Gottlieb, and Joseph Singer. New York: Farrar, Straus & Giroux, 1966.

CHILDREN'S BOOKS

Zlateh the Goat and Other Stories. New York: Harper & Row, 1966.
The Fearsome Inn. New York: Charles Scribner's Sons, 1967.
Mazel and Shlimazel or the Milk of the Lioness. New York: Farrar, Straus & Giroux, 1967.

ESSAYS

"Realism and Truth," *The Reconstructionist,* XXVIII (June 15, 1962), 5–9. Translated by Ada Auerbach Lappin.
"The Ten Commandments and the Modern Critics," *Cavalier* (June, 1965), p. 30.
"A Phantom of Delight," *Herald Tribune Book Week* (July 4, 1965), pp. 2, 7.
"What's in It for Me," *Harper's* (October, 1965), pp. 172–73.
"Introduction" to I. J. Singer. *Yoshe Kalb* [Yasha the Loon]. New York: Harper & Row, 1965.
"Peretz's Dream," *American Judaism* (Spring, 1966), pp. 20–21, 60–61.
"Once on Second Avenue There Lived a Yiddish Theater," *New York Times* (April 17, 1966), p. 3.

"Hagigah," [Festival of the Arts] *American Judaism* (Winter, 1966), pp. 19, 48–49.

"The Extreme Jews," *Harper's* (April, 1967), pp. 55–62.

"Introduction" to Knut Hamsun. *Hunger.* Translated by Robert Bly. New York: Farrar, Straus & Giroux, 1967.

TRANSLATIONS

Zweig, Stefan. *Roman Rolland.* Wilna: B. Kletzkin, 1927.

Hamsun, Knut. *Die Vogler.* Wilna: B. Kletzkin, 1928.

Hamsun, Knut. *Victoria.* Wilna: B. Kletzkin, 1929.

Remarque, Erich. *All Quiet on the Western Front.* Wilna: B. Kletzkin, 1930.

Hamsun, Knut. *Pan.* Wilna: B. Kletzkin, 1931.

Remarque, Erich. *The Way Back.* Wilna: B. Kletzkin, 1931.

Mann, Thomas. *The Magic Mountain.* Wilna: B. Kletzkin, 1932.

Glaser, Leon S. *From Moscow to Jerusalem.* New York: Max Jankowitz, 1938.

II General—Books and Articles

Alexandrova, Vera. *A History of Soviet Literature: 1917–1962.* Garden City: Doubleday & Co., Inc., 1963.

Alter, Robert. "Sentimentalizing the Jews," *Commentary,* 40 (September, 1965), 71–75.

Angoff, Charles. "Jewish Literature in England," *Judaism,* 3 (Fall, 1954), 408–17.

Bellow, Saul. "Cloister Culture," *New York Times Book Review* (July 10, 1966), pp. 2, 44.

——— (ed.). *Great Jewish Short Stories.* New York: Dell Publishing Co., 1963.

Boroff, David. "The College Intellectual, 1965 Model," *The New York Times Magazine* (December 6, 1964), pp. 36–37, 134–47.

Cohen, Boaz. "Art in Jewish Law," *Judaism,* 3 (Spring, 1964), 165–76.

Dawidowicz, Lucy S. (ed.). *The Golden Tradition: Jewish Life and Thought in Eastern Europe.* New York: Holt, Rinehart & Winston, 1967.

———. "Yiddish: Past, Present and Perfect," *Commentary,* V (May, 1962), 375–85.

Dubdow, Simon. *History of the Jews in Russia and Poland.* 3 vols. Philadelphia: The Jewish Publication Society, 1916–20.

Elbogen, Isman. *A Century of Jewish Life.* Philadelphia: The Jewish Publication Society, 1944.

Fackenheim, Emil. "Judaism and the Meaning of Life," *Commentary,* 39 (April, 1965), 49–55.

Faerstein, Chana. "Jacob Glatstein: The Literary Uses of Jewishness," *Judaism,* 14 (Fall, 1965), 414–31.

Frankel, Jonathan. " 'The Communist Rabbi': Moses Hess," *Commentary,* 41 (July, 1966), 77–81.

Glanville, Brian. "Anglo-Jewish Writers," *New York Times Book Review* (April 17, 1966), pp. 2, 40.

Goldin, Judah. "The Contemporary Jew and His Judaism" in *Spiritual Problems in Contemporary Literature.* Ed. Stanley Romaine Hopper. New York: Harper & Bros., 1952.

Graetz, Heinrich. *History of the Jews.* Philadelphia: The Jewish Publication Society, 1895.

Heilman, Robert. "Variations on Picaresque (*Felix Krull*)," *Sewanee Review* (Autumn, 1958), pp. 547–77.

Heschel, Abraham. *Between God and Man.* New York: Harper & Bros., 1959.

Howe, Irving, and Greenberg, Eliezer (eds.). *A Treasury of Yiddish Stories.* New York: The Viking Press, 1954.

Jaspers, Karl. "Freedom and Authority," *Diogenes,* I (1950), 25–42.

Kazin, Alfred. "The Jew as Modern Writer," *Commentary,* 41 (April, 1966), 37–41.

Kronenberger, Louis. "The Jewish Writer and the English

Literary Tradition: A Symposium," *Commentary*, 8 (1949).

Le Carré, John. "The Undercover Man," *New York Times Book Review* (June 27, 1965), pp. 2, 24.

Leftwich, Joseph (ed.). *Yisroel: The First Jewish Omnibus*. New York: Thomas Yoseloff, 1963 (rev. ed.).

Malin, Irving, and Stark, Irwin (eds.). *Breakthrough: A Treasury of Contemporary American-Jewish Literature*. New York: McGraw-Hill, 1964.

Malin, Irving. *Jews and Americans*. Carbondale: Southern Illinois University Press, 1965.

Mirsky, D. S. *A History of Russian Literature*. New York: Alfred A. Knopf, 1960.

Moeller, Charles (ed.). *Satan*. London: Sheed and Ward, 1951.

Partridge, Eric. "Degraded Language," *New York Times Book Review* (September, 18, 1966), pp. 2, 20.

Podhoretz, Norman. "Jewish Culture and the Intellectuals," in *Doings and Undoings: The Fifties and After in American Writing*. New York: The Noonday Press, 1964.

Poggioli, Renato. *The Poets of Russia: 1890–1930*. Cambridge: Harvard University Press, 1960.

Ribalow, Howard V. "American Jewish Writers and Their Judaism," *Judaism*, 3 (Fall, 1954), 418–26.

Rosenberg, Edgar. *From Shylock to Svengali: Jewish Stereotypes in English Fiction*. Stanford: Stanford University Press, 1960.

Rosenberg, Harold. "Is There Jewish Art?" *Commentary*, 41 (July, 1966), 57–60.

Scholem, Gershon G. *Major Trends in Jewish Mysticism*. New York: Schocken Books, 1941.

———. *On the Kabbalah and Its Symbolism*. New York: Schocken Books, 1960.

Schwarz, Leo W. *Mutations of Jewish Values in Contemporary Fiction*. (The B. G. Rudolph Lectures in Judaic Studies.) Syracuse: Syracuse University, 1966.

————. *The Jewish Caravan.* New York: Farrar and Rinehart, 1935.

Simon, Ernst. "The Jews as God's Witnesses to the World," *Judaism,* 15 (Summer, 1966), 306–18.

III Articles on Singer and Selected Reviews (Significant studies indicated by a *)

Angoff, Charles. "Aspects of American Literature," *The Literary Review,* X (Autumn, 1966), 5–17.

Ash, L. "Portrait," *Wilson Library Bulletin,* XXXVII (December, 1962), 356.

Baumbach, Jonathan. "Short Friday," *Saturday Review* (November 21, 1964), pp. 49.

*Blocker, Joel, and Elman, Richard. "Interview with I. B. Singer," *Commentary,* XXXVI (November, 1963), 364–72.

Chayefsky, Paddy. "Of Dybbuks and Devilkins," *The Reporter* (April 22, 1965), pp. 40–43.

Elman, Richard. "*In My Father's Court,*" *New York Times Book Review* (May 8, 1966), pp. 1, 34–36.

————. "The Spinoza of Canal Street," *Holiday,* 38 (August, 1965), 83–87.

*Fixler, Michael. "The Redeemers: Themes in the Fiction of Isaac Bashevis Singer," *Kenyon Review,* XXVI (Spring, 1964), 371–86.

Frank, M. Z. "The Demon and the Earlock," *Conservative Judaism* (Fall, 1965), 1–9.

Glatstein, Jacob. "The Fame of Bashevis Singer," *Congress bi-Weekly,* 32 (December 27, 1965), 17–19.

Girson, Rochelle. "Interview with I. B. Singer," *Saturday Review* (July 16, 1962), p. 19.

Gold, Authur R. "The Last of the Old-Time Demons," *Book Week* (April 16, 1965), p. 2.

Goodheart, Eugene. *"The Spinoza of Market Street,"* *Saturday Review* (November 25, 1961), p. 28.

Hemley, Cecil. "Isaac Bashevis Singer" in *Dimensions of Midnight: Poetry and Prose.* Athens: Ohio University Press, 1966.

*Hindus, Milton. "Isaac Bashevis Singer" in *Jewish Heritage Reader.* Ed. Morris Adler. New York: Taplinger Publishing Company, 1965.

*Hindus, Milton. *"The Family Moskat,"* *New York Times Book Review* (March 14, 1965), pp. 4, 44–45.

*Howe, Irving. "Demonic Fiction of a Yiddish Modernist," *Commentary,* 30 (October, 1960), 350–53.

*————. "I. B. Singer, Storyteller," *Encounter,* XXVI (March, 1966), 60–70.

————. "Stories: New, Old and Sometimes Good," *New Republic,* 145 (November 13, 1961), 18–19.

————. "The Other Singer," *Commentary,* 41 (March, 1966), 78–82.

*Hughes, Ted. "The Genius of Isaac Bashevis Singer," *New York Review of Books,* IV (April 22, 1965), 8–10.

Hyman, Stanley Edgar. "Isaac Singer's Marvels," *New Leader* (December 21, 1964), pp. 17–18.

*Jacobson, Dan. "The Problem of Isaac Bashevis Singer," *Commentary,* 39 (February, 1965), 48–52.

Kahn, Lothar. "Isaac Bashevis Singer," *Commonweal,* LXXXI (January 22, 1965), 538–40.

Kazin, Alfred. "His Son, the Storyteller," *Herald Tribune Book Week* (April 24, 1966), pp. 1, 10.

Lauter, P. "Jewish Hero: Two Views," *New Republic,* 139 (November 24, 1958), 18.

Miller, Warren. "Last of the Line," *Nation,* 200 (January 4, 1965), 15–16.

Schott, Webster. *"Short Friday,"* *New York Times Book Review* (November 15, 1964), pp. 5, 64.

*Schulz, Max F. "Isaac Bashevis Singer, Radical Sophistication and the Jewish-American Novel." Paper read at the MLA Convention, (December, 1967); scheduled for publication in *Southern Humanities Review*.

Wolkenfeld, J. S. "Isaac Bashevis Singer: The Faith of His Devils and Magicians," *Criticism*, V (1962), 349–59.

Index